A QUESTION of DEATH

An illustrated
Phryne Fisher Treasury

KERRY GREENWOOD

*Poisoned
Pen
Press*

To all my faithful friends and colleagues at Sunshine Legal Aid, who have endured my extravagant irruptions into their ordered world with enviable patience.

With thanks to my forgiving friends, David and Dennis, Jeannie and Alan, Belladonna and Monsieur, and to three cafes, Alfamie, Delizia and the Gravy Train, without whom we might all have starved ...

© Copyright 2007 by Kerry Greenwood

First published in Australia by Allen & Unwin in 2007

U.S. Edition 2008, 2014

10 9 8 7 6 5 4 3 2 1

Library of Congress Catalog Card Number: 2008923148

ISBN: 9781464203626   Trade Paperback

Poisoned Pen Press
6962 E. First Ave., Ste. 103
Scottsdale, AZ 85251
www.poisonedpenpress.com
info@poisonedpenpress.com

Illustrations by Beth Norling
Design and layout by Lisa White

Printed in the United States of America

APOLOGIA

Dear reader,

Thank you very much for buying this book (and if you haven't bought it yet, please do so—I have cats to feed. It would make an ideal present for anyone who likes history, clothes, fashion, food or beautiful young men...have I left anyone out?).

No one was more surprised than me when Phryne was adopted into so many homes. She was a little taken aback as well. I trust that these stories will amuse you. They certainly amused me.

As you will see, sometimes I try out some of the cast of a novel in a short story to see if they like me enough to stay for a whole book, there being a great difference between 3000 and 85,000 words, and an author needs to pick her company if she has to give house room to them for so long. If you like the 'Carnival' people, you will meet them again in *Blood and Circuses*.

Oh, and by the way, please do not write to me and complain that the plot from 'Hotel Splendide' is stolen from a Hitchcock film, or a horror movie, or any other recent source. It is an urban myth, first written down by Alexander Woollcott in the 1920s, which is why I thought Phryne would like it. I had a really good idea for the Vanishing Hitchhiker, too, but there was such a fuss about 'Hotel Splendide' that I ditched the idea.

And go easy on the cocktails, is my advice. A green chartreuse hangover is as impossible to describe as it is to endure.

Why not e-mail me on kgreenwood@netspace.net.au if you enjoyed this book? And if you didn't, give it to an op shop at your earliest convenience.

Kerry Greenwood

CONTENTS

On PHRYNE FISHER

I began to write mysteries because I was trying to get published—trying very hard, a soul destroying, painful process which I wish never to repeat. The novel I had to sell was not a mystery but an historical novel, and I had been hawking it around the publishers for four years. The only reason I did not give up is that I am myself a very obstinate person. I submitted it to the Australian Vogel Literary Award, a competition for unpublished manuscripts. They did not give me the prize, but one of the Vogel judges asked me to come and see her, and told me that she didn't want the historical novel but could do with a couple of mysteries. I agreed so fast that the words echoed off the wall, and then sat on the tram going down Brunswick Street wondering what I had gotten myself into. I had never written a mystery before. I had been reading them since I learned to read, but I had never written one and didn't have the faintest idea how to begin.

So I began with a character. If I had the protagonist, I reasoned, she could tell me what to do next. I had decided to place these mysteries in the 1920s—in 1928 in fact, because I had written a legal history essay on the 1928 wharf strike, my father being a wharf labourer, and had done extensive work on 1928 from newspapers and interviews. I knew what she looked like. My sister Janet has a perfect 1920s face and figure: small, thin, elegant, with black hair and pale skin and green eyes. At that time Janet had a bobby-cut, too. She looked just like a flapper. Then I needed a name. I had been looking at 1900 birth notices for some reason and a lot of them were Ancient Greek names—Psyche, Irene, Iris. These ladies (the naïve Psyche, Irene the Goddess of Peace and Iris the nymph of the rainbow) were far too respectable to be the sort of person I wanted my heroine to be, but then I remembered Phryne, a courtesan in Ancient Greece, so beautiful that Apelles used her for his Aphrodite, and so rich and notorious that she offered to rebuild the walls of Thebes as long as she could put a sign on them, 'The Walls of Thebes; Ruined by Time, Rebuilt by Phryne the Courtesan'. My kind of woman. Her last name is derived elaborately as a scholastic joke. She is a Fisher of Men, as all detectives are. Her name also reflects the Grail Cycle *Le Roi Pêcheur*, the Sinner or Fisher King. I have always liked that absurd pun on Sin and Fish. And there was a street in Paris called rue du Chat qui Pêche which was a good place to find a gigolo—all of the information had come to me piecemeal from various sources. It was coagulating in my head as I sat on the tram, and when I got off the tram in Melbourne I had the name of my heroine, Phryne Fisher, I knew what she looked like, and I was working on where she came from. I gave her a poor background to make her appreciate being rich and a title so that she could not be overawed by Society.

Because I wanted her to be a female wish-fulfilment figure, I wanted her to be like James Bond, with better clothes and fewer gadgets. There was no female hero in the same vein as Leslie Charteris' Simon Templar, the Saint. In fact, as the Saint books were published in the same period of the 1920s, I wanted to make her Simon Templar's younger, more level-headed sister. All I really did was take a male hero of the time and allow her to be female. No one thinks it odd that James Bond has blondes and no regrets. I only ever thought I would have two books published, so I tried to pack everything I wanted to say about female heroes into them. The modern women detectives are afflicted with self-doubt, neglect their diets, worry about exercise, think they may be growing fat (as if fat was a disfigurement), and are generally burdened with low self-esteem and guilt. I wanted a character without guilt, with boundless self-esteem—as a role model, perhaps. She was no challenge to invent. All I really felt that I actually invented was the name and the background. She blossomed from the moment I wrote the first line of *Cocaine Blues*, and after the first five chapters I had no further control over her. I feel like I discovered Phryne, rather than invented her.

She's a bold creature for the 1920s but not an impossible one. None of the things she does are out of the question for that brittle, revolutionary period. And, yes, Kerry Greenwood can fly a small plane (though I've only flown once in a Tiger Moth) and Kerry Greenwood can—or rather, has for the purposes of research—fired a handgun such as Phryne carries. The research is essential to make the books convincing, and besides, I love original research. Historical novels walk a fine line. Too much detail and the reader is bored. Too little and it fails to convince. The ideal state for the reader is one where she trusts the writer to tell her everything she needs to know. Consider Maigret's Paris or Ellis Peters' Shrewsbury. And I find it essential for me to know what streets Phryne walks down. Fortunately, a lot of Melbourne is still much the same as it was in the 1920s. I use all the bits that are extant.

My favourite detective writer, Dorothy Sayers, always included a slab of solid research in her books and I decided, in homage, to do that too. In each of my novels you will find out something different about Melbourne in 1928, as well as the detective story. It is not so much a mission as a gift to the readers.

The process of writing one of these novels is odd. I choose a new aspect of Melbourne which I would like to research—the theatre, the circus, jazz, flying, the docks—and then spend six months finding out all I can about it. About one hundredth of what I actually know about the subject ends up in the novel, but I need to know it to write the book. In fact, I worked out that for each novel I do as much work as a PhD student would for a thesis (but the novels are more fun to read than a thesis). After a while the story starts to build up pressure, and finally it wakes me up at three in the morning and insists on being written. Other writers have a young and beautiful muse who descends in fire to inspire them. If I ever saw my muse she would be an old woman with a tight bun and spectacles poking me in the middle of the back and growling, 'Wake up and write the book!' and I always do. Because if I don't, the book gets vague and fades away. I do not plan the Phryne books at all. Once I have done the research, I just have to write fast enough to keep up. The actual writing takes about three weeks.

I have written many other novels with other heroines, but Phryne is my favourite, and I am delighted every time she drops in with a new book.

HOTEL *Splendide*

Desperate diseases demand desperate remedies
Proverb

'But please! You must know me! Oh, why won't you help me?'

Phryne Fisher, sitting in the lobby of her Paris hotel, laid down *The Times* (Fog on Channel: Continent Isolated. Snow on Points at Haslemere. Plague in Bombay, Thousands Stricken. Test Team Defeated in Australia) and turned at the sound of the plaintive, flat, Australian vowels. Born in Richmond to a cleaning lady and a drunken remittance man, christened Phryne the courtesan instead of Psyche the nymph, so poor that she had challenged the big boys for the old tomatoes from the pig bins of Victoria Market before being whisked to England, an Hon to her name and wealth. She had no reason to remember Australia with any favour. But the voice brought back hot sun, eucalyptus leaves, ice cream made of real cream. She folded the paper and listened.

'Phryne! We'll miss the first act of the *Nibelungs*!' urged Alain Descourt. He was soigné, fascinating and rich. The only flaw in his character that Phryne had so far discovered was a devotion to Wagner. He made the mistake of laying a hand on Phryne's arm. One did not try to compel Miss Fisher. She stood, quite deliberately, and went over to the desk.

'*Mais, Madame...je ne sais pas!*' protested the *patron* in the most arrogant, fast, slurred French at his disposal. Phryne knew that he prided himself on his perfect English. She had no time for Parisian games with what was evidently a distressed Australian.

'*Alors*, Jean-Paul?' she asked acidly. Phryne's French was very quick and accurate, and she was well known to the Hotel Splendide as an English milady with limitless wealth and nice taste in young men. Jean-Paul threw out his arms in a wide gesture which almost, but not quite, toppled his coffee cup.

'This is Madame Johnson. Twice she has been here tonight! The lady is as mad as birds,' he said. '*Folle comme des oiseaux!* She says that she and her husband came here, but there is no signature in the register, and we do not have the passports, which is the law, as you know, milady. She never came here.'

He showed Phryne the red-leather register in which there was no entry for Johnson. Phryne shoved the register over to Mrs Johnson.

'Hello,' she said, giving the woman her scented black-gloved hand. 'My name is Phryne Fisher. Can I help you?'

'Thank God!' exclaimed Mrs Johnson. 'They won't believe me. They've stolen my husband!' she said, and burst into tears. Again, by the look of her.

'Jean-Paul,' said Phryne quietly, 'if a large pot of coffee and a bottle of the good cognac is not placed in the blue withdrawing room within the next minute, I will be quite cross.'

Jean-Paul heaved a martyred sigh, snapped his fingers, gave the order to an underling, and exchanged a glance with Alain Descourt. Women, the glance said. Nothing to be done about them.

Phryne manoeuvred her charge to the small room, supplied her with a handkerchief, a soft chair, a glass of cognac and a cup of coffee, and sat down to await coherence. Husbands, regrettably, did go astray in Paris. It was a very good city for going astray in. Usually they came back penniless from Montmartre, reeking of cheap perfume and guilt.

Mrs Johnson was young and would have been pretty before she had wept her face into sodden misery. She wore a good but colonial travelling costume, evidently purchased in Melbourne. Her favourite colour was pink. She had walked a long way in shoes not meant for distance. At some point she had fallen and landed heavily on both knees. She was certainly distraught, but she had spoken in sentences. Phryne reserved her decision as to her charge's actual mental state. And while Phryne dealt with this Distressed British Subject, the *Ring of the Nibelungs* would be bellowing along and perhaps she might only have to endure the last act.

Finally Mrs Johnson sniffed, gulped, gasped, and sipped some coffee.

'Can you tell me about it?' asked Phryne.

Mrs Johnson found that she was talking to a dazzling woman dressed in an evening dress of scarlet brocade with black gloves and a diamond clip. There was a band of diamonds around one upper arm and around her throat. She had black hair cut in a cap and the most piercing green eyes. A young man hovered discontentedly in the background.

'I came here from the station,' she said. 'With my husband. Arthur. We came off the *Orient* and took the train to Paris.'

'Yes,' said Phryne. 'The Gare du Nord.'

'Then we took a taxi to this hotel. We registered—I'm sure I saw Arthur sign! They took our passports and showed us to Room 311A. We put down our things and had a bath—you get so filthy travelling on the train. Then Arthur said he felt sick. He was running a temperature. I asked that manager—that little rat who pretends he doesn't know me!—to get a doctor. The doctor came, a young man. He told me to go out and get some medicine from a pharmacy, so I went, and when I got to the pharmacy they didn't have it, and I didn't have any more money for any more taxis, so I walked to another pharmacy and they didn't have it either, so I came back here. It was a long way. I must have been gone two hours.'

'Do you still have the prescription?' asked Phryne.

'No, the second chemist kept it. He said he'd send it

on. Then I got lost. I've never been to Paris before. I got scared and…a man… spoke to me and I ran and fell. But I found my way back here and then…all this has happened.'

'Are you sure that this is the right Hotel Splendide? It's a common hotel name in Paris.'

'Yes, of course! I know the clerk. And the furnishings.'

'Interesting,' murmured Phryne. She was full of admiration. This young woman, a total stranger in one of the most confusing cities in the world, had accomplished a fine feat of backtracking to get to her destination again. Even now, under the influence of cognac, coffee and a sympathetic listener, she was beginning to recover. They bred 'em tough in Australia. She deserved support.

'And when you returned, the clerk said…?' Phryne prompted, raising her voice over the sounds of a discontented young man making 'we're missing the opera' noises at a side table.

'He said he never saw me before and there was no room 311A. He showed me. There isn't, either. Just a blank wall. No space for the key in the key board behind the clerk. No name in the register. This trip was our honeymoon,' said Mrs Johnson. 'It was wonderful—Egypt, India and Ceylon, and all that. I never knew people could be so happy. I've never been apart from Arthur from the day we were married. And now he's gone. Like he's never been.'

She started to cry again. The rodent which Phryne had detected had grown into a Sumatran beast which

Sherlock Holmes might have had to deal with.

'You will stay here,' she said gently. 'Alain will divert you with stories from the opera. I will go and interview the clerk. I will be back soon,' she said. She rose gracefully and withdrew.

'Talk to me, Jean-Paul,' she murmured to the *patron*, leaning confidingly on the desk. 'The lady's story is very collected for a madwoman.'

'I will show you myself,' said the *patron*. 'Jacques! Mind the desk.'

While he was turned away Phryne quickly flicked the register open at another page. 'Why, how curious,' she commented. 'This is a new register. And I could have sworn, when I came in, that there were pages and pages left in the old one. What a busy hotel this is, to be sure.'

'Indeed,' murmured Jean-Paul, giving her an uneasy glance. Still, she was only a woman, though a clever one. 'This way, milady.'

The third floor was reached by a hydraulic elevator and Jean-Paul opened the two sets of doors with a flourish. 'There is no room 311A,' he said. 'As milady can see.'

The Hotel Splendide ran to red plush wallpaper and Empire furnishings, picked out in gilt. Phryne paced the corridor until she came to the last room on the left, 310. Opposite it was 311. After that there was just an expanse of vermilion to the corner. Phryne, one hand against the wall, leaned down to adjust a stocking and rewarded Jean-Paul with a flash of pearly knee.

'I see,' she murmured. 'Yes. Well, let us go down by the stairs.'

Jean-Paul offered the distinguished lady his arm and she

accepted. He glanced down at the composed face under the diamond headdress and saw her lips moving. She might have been counting. There was, he reflected, no understanding the nobility. When she smiled at him in the lobby, however, he was certain that he had convinced her. She had the innocent smile of a happy baby. He went back to his desk, whistling 'Auprès de ma Blonde'.

Phryne returned to the withdrawing room. Alain was just concluding the plot of *Tristan und Isolde*. Mrs Johnson was looking rather glazed. Wagner had the same effect on Phryne. She sympathised.

'Then she sings her last song and dies,' he concluded.

'And not before time,' said Phryne. 'Now, Mrs Johnson—'

'Call me Beth?' asked Mrs Johnson. She was much recovered, red-eyed but not likely to have hysterics. Phryne thanked providence for the healing gift of brandy.

'Beth, then. And I am Phryne. Did you catch the name of the doctor?'

'Dupont,' said Beth, biting her lower lip to aid concentration.

'The Paris equivalent of Smith. I thought so. And...what can you smell?'

She held the palm of her left glove to Beth's face. She sniffed.

'Jicky. Rice powder. And wallpaper paste.'

'Precisely. I have two more questions. Do you trust me? And will you do as I ask you?'

'I have a question, too,' said Beth Johnson. 'Do you believe me?'

'Every word,' said Phryne. The nail-bitten hand clutched the black glove in a firm grip.

'Then the answer is yes and yes.'

'Good. Alain, we need you.'

'We're already late,' fretted Alain.

'There are other nights,' said Phryne, in such a meaningful voice that Beth Johnson blushed and Alain rocked a little on his heels. 'I promise I will sit through the whole Ring Cycle with you in future. I am asking for your assistance as a true son of France with the aim of preventing a catastrophe to Paris. Will you help us?'

Alain, veteran of Verdun, patriotic to his cynical core, stood up straight and saluted. 'Your orders, my colonel?'

'You need to find the nearest doctor and bring him here. Don't waste time looking for this Dupont. The woods are full of them. Just the nearest.'

'That would be my old comrade, the army doctor Lestrange. He lives just off the Place l'Opera. Where a fine production of Wagner is even now ending its first act,' he added with emphasis. Phryne ignored this.

'Go get him, and speedily. Meanwhile I am going to tell Jean-Paul that madame has admitted the error of her ways, and I am taking her to rest in my suite before we set out to find the real Hotel Splendide where her husband is doubtless waiting for her.'

'Hey!' objected Beth. She received a forty-watt glare and subsided. 'Very well, Phryne.'

'Come along,' said Phryne, and swept them away.

———

Beth Johnson had had such a strange evening that the rest of it could not have been odder. She was, however, sure that this elegant lady had the matter in hand and that, however confusing things might yet become, somewhere at the end of it she would find Arthur. So she obediently ate a small but delicious supper, allowed her feet to be bathed by a deferential maid, and snuggled into a sofa in Miss Fisher's palatial rooms. She was wrapped in a fleecy gown and was a little muzzy with cognac. But she did not feel like crying anymore, even though she had been provided with a new perfumed handkerchief.

In an hour, the tall young man was back with a scowling, black-bearded doctor. Mrs Johnson opined that she would not like to meet him down a dark alley. But he bowed politely over her hand and bowed even more deeply over Phryne's.

'Milady,' said Dr Lestrange. 'Had my addle-pated friend told me that the summons came from you, I should not have demurred. I have never forgotten that ambulance rocketing into our hospital under shellfire, and the shock I got when I saw that the driver was not only a lady, but a beautiful one.'

'Very pretty speech,' approved Phryne. 'Thank you for coming. Now, I am about to do something thoroughly unlawful, and if you do not want to watch I should stay here with madame until I have done it.'

'What is this act of illegality?' asked Alain.

'I am going to set fire to the hotel,' said Phryne. 'Come when you smell smoke.'

The door closed. The two men eyed each other uneasily.

'Does she mean what she says?' asked Lestrange.

'Invariably,' sighed Alain.

'And we are going to wait until we smell smoke?'

'Of course,' said Alain. 'Me, I am not clever. But milady— she is. She knew who was stealing from my father's vineyard seconds after I told her about it and constructed a trap which caught the thief and freed an old servant of the estate from suspicion. So if she says she is going to burn the hotel down, then she will do as she says, and I will do as I am told.'

'Your lamb-like faith does you credit,' said Lestrange. 'And certainly she has no fear. She drove Toupie's ambulances through hell and around shell holes as cool as some cucumbers...ah,' he added, as shouts of 'Fire!' and the clanging of a big bell offended the quiet precincts of the Hotel Splendide. 'And now?'

'We go out,' said Alain. 'And up.'

Beth Johnson had not understood one word in ten of the

fast, idiomatic French. She leapt to her feet and shucked her woolly gown. Alain offered his arm and they went out into smoke-filled corridors, threading their way up through the frightened throng to the third floor.

There they saw, in the thinning reek, Phryne Fisher in her scarlet brocade wielding a poker. She was attacking the blank wall beyond room 311.

'Come and help,' she yelled. 'We haven't got much time.'

Galvanised, both men came to her side and found that she had peeled a swathe of wallpaper away from what was palpably a door. Beth Johnson attacked it with her fingernails.

'They did a remarkably good job in such a short time,' said Phryne dispassionately. 'New register, bit of coloured wax in the key board, fast work with the red plush. But it was still wet when I touched it.'

'Can you get the door open or shall I find a jemmy?' asked Lestrange.

'No need,' said Phryne, producing a key from her bosom. 'I pinched it out of Jean-Paul's drawer when his back was turned. Beth, perhaps you should stay here. We don't know what we are going to find—'

'We're going to find Arthur,' said Beth Johnson. 'And dead or alive, he is my husband.'

The door creaked open. A gust of stale air puffed out. Trunks were stacked against the far wall. The bed was occupied.

Beth screamed and flung herself on her husband's body. Lestrange pushed her gently aside and leaned down close to listen at the cracked lips.

'He's alive,' he said. 'Just. I need water, cold water.'

'Why did they do all this? What's wrong with him?' said Alain from the doorway.

'Ask your friend,' said Phryne. 'Beth, can you get that window open?'

'He's got a high fever,' said Lestrange.

'Check the armpits and groin for swelling,' instructed Phryne.

'You suspect...' began Alain. 'That is why you said it would be a catastrophe for Paris? You think it's....'

'There is plague in India,' replied Phryne. 'It was in the paper I was reading. The *Orient* calls at Bombay.'

'But we didn't land there.' Beth Johnson lost patience with the window latch and broke the pane with the heel of her mistreated shoe. 'We went on. We never stopped at Bombay.'

'Jean-Paul leapt to the wrong conclusion. Doctor Lestrange? What's wrong with your patient?'

'Why, malaria, of course,' said Lestrange gruffly. 'Thousands of thunders! Is someone going to get me some water, or shall I go myself? And, please, Miss Fisher, is this hotel going to burn down around us?'

'No. I lit a wastepaper basket full of

rags at each landing. They will be out by now. Any moment Jean-Paul will pound up the stairs and demand—'

'What is going on here?' came the *patron's* voice from the corridor.

Phryne smiled seraphically, diamonds glittering as she moved. 'Such timing. Ah, Jean-Paul. This is going to be a very expensive evening's work for you.'

'Milady? What are you doing? Mad, like all the English.'

'Almost convincing, *patron*. This man has malaria, not the plague. His wife has almost been driven out of her mind, and how long were you going to leave Arthur Johnson in that sealed room?'

Phryne could see various options flit across Jean-Paul's face. Stout denial? Not plausible. Outraged hotel owner? He could already hear the tone of milady's contemptuous laugh. Complete and utter submission and explanation? Nasty but feasible. His hotel, which he had striven all his life to expand and guard, was already lost. No travellers would ever come here again after milady told her tale.

'*Vae victis,*' he said, raising both hands. 'Woe to the conquered. Command me.'

'Move Mr Johnson into a suite and

bring whatever Dr Lestrange orders, and do it with amazing speed.'

Phryne waited while a covey of attendants carried Arthur Johnson downstairs to the Royal Suite and scurried off in search of the potions Dr Lestrange required. Beth Johnson walked beside the stretcher, holding the slack hot hand in her own. She had forgotten everyone else in the world. For the first time in her life, Beth Johnson was beautiful. Phryne beckoned to the *patron*.

'Come with me, Jean-Paul.'

He sighed and followed with Alain. When Phryne had regained her own suite, she discarded her gloves, marred with paste and smoke. She sat down, poured a glass of cognac for all three of them and asked, 'Well?'

Jean-Paul gulped and filled his glass again. His voice was rough with remembered terror. The suave hotelier was gone. Here was a man frightened out of his wits.

'I was in India. When the plague struck last time. My brother caught it. He died. It starts with a high fever. The buboes come later. I knew that the Australian had it. I had to save Paris.'

'And your hotel?'

'Yes, and my hotel. If anyone thought that a plague victim was here....'

'So you called a doctor?'

'No doctor, just my cousin. He sent madame off to find a mare's nest, and we....'

'And you were going to remove Arthur Johnson? Or were you just doing an Edgar Allan Poe on him and walling him up alive?'

'He was nearly dead,' said Jean-Paul. 'If you saw how they died in India, in heaps, too great for the living to bury.... I was going to bring in a doctor in the morning. If he was still alive.'

Phryne examined Jean-Paul. He was shivering. His fear of the plague was real enough. He was as white as a swarthy man could get and still be conscious. His five o'clock shadow looked like an ink-stain. His hands kneaded each other ceaselessly.

Phryne made up her mind. Justice, she had always thought, ought to be about compensation rather than retribution. Despite the delicious temptations of revenge.

'All right. I have a solution. I like your hotel and do not want to see it closed and you jailed. You do not have plague in the hotel, just malaria. That is not even notifiable. We will say nothing about it. Provided that you will allow the Johnsons to stay here free of charge until he is perfectly well. You will purchase suitable medical care and send a cousin or two to show Beth Johnson around the sights of Paris, including a complete spring costume from a suitable fashion house. And listen closely, Jean-Paul. You will play no such tricks again or by God you will be sorry. I shall see to it personally. Also, you owe me a pair of gloves. Is it agreed?'

Jean-Paul, reprieved, fell on his knees and kissed milady's dainty feet.

'Now, is this all over?' asked Alain Descourt, helping Phryne up after Jean-Paul had gone and Dr Lestrange had reported his patient would recover.

'Yes, but it has been diverting, hasn't it?' She smiled her innocent smile again.

'Not as diverting as the *Ring*,' said Alain from the door.

'Come along. You promised. And we still have time to catch the last act. My favourite.'

Phryne Fisher swung her opera cloak around her shoulders and followed. Wagner was regrettably Wagner, but a promise was a promise.

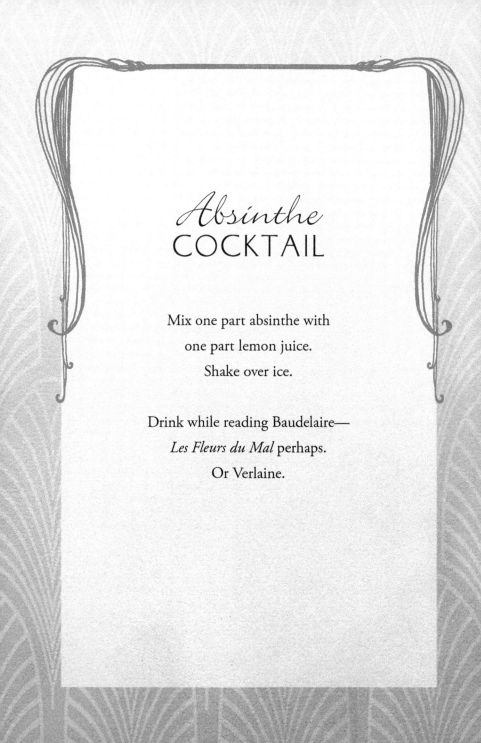

Absinthe
COCKTAIL

Mix one part absinthe with
one part lemon juice.
Shake over ice.

Drink while reading Baudelaire—
Les Fleurs du Mal perhaps.
Or Verlaine.

The Voice *is*
JACOB'S VOICE

The voice is Jacob's voice, but the hands are the hands of Esau.
Genesis, 27:22

'Do come in,' invited Death, and bowed.

Dr Elizabeth MacMillan, who had wrestled many a fall with this august personage, returned the bow and entered the Hon. Miss Phryne Fisher's house. There were lights, a buzz of conversation, and a tinkle suggesting filled glasses. Miss Fisher's Winter Solstice party, to which all of her friends and everyone to whom she owed a favour had been invited, was evidently going well.

Death pushed his mask back onto

his forehead, rumpling his fine blond hair, and revealed the ingenuous face of Lindsay Herbert.

'Mr Herbert,' Dr MacMillan exclaimed in her precise Edinburgh accent, 'you have chosen an unchancy disguise!'

'Always wanted to be macabre,' confessed Lindsay, smoothing down his robe and propping his sickle against the door. 'Dashed hot, these draperies! Ever since I read that thing of Poe's...what was it called?'

'"The Masque of the Red Death", I believe. I hope that you are not a bad omen.'

'I don't think so—party's going swimmingly as far as I can see, though it's a crush. Who are you masqueradin' as, Doctor? You look forbiddin' in that sheet.'

'This is not a sheet, young man, it is a *toga virilis*, and I am Julius Caesar—observe my laurel crown.'

'Oh.' Lindsay could never remember who had won between Caesar and Pompey, even though he had been forced to study the Civil War. He was about to offer *'Gallia in tres partes divisa est'*, which was all he could remember of the work in question, when Phryne swept into the hall, drew closer to Dr MacMillan and whispered in her ear, 'You are mortal.'

'Correct,' said the doctor. 'And well guessed. Now who are you, I wonder? Magnificent, Phryne!'

Phryne stood back a little to allow the older woman to admire her. The black hair was drawn back under a red wig, and she had a crown bright with emeralds, a gold dress, and ropes of pearls.

Dr MacMillan made an Elizabethan bow. 'Your Majesty Queen Elizabeth, I am honoured.'

'I've even got the petticoat,' said Phryne, displaying it, a fine silk one with gold edging. 'Put me down in any part of my realm in my petticoat and I would be what I am. Lindsay, you can come in now and have a drink. Mr Butler has finished making his next batch of cocktails. Come along.' She laid a jewelled hand on each arm, and Julius Caesar and Death escorted her into the drawing room.

It was full of people. Dr MacMillan was provided with a glass of good Scotch, and Lindsay collared two cocktails made to Mr Butler's own jealously guarded recipe. Jazz, provided by gramophone records, rose above the chatter of thirty guests.

'Who,' demanded the singer tinnily, 'stole my heart away? Who?' He seemed destined to remain unanswered.

Dr MacMillan found herself next to a young woman whom she had previously had as a patient.

'Well, Miss Gately—' she peered beneath a layer of make-up to confirm that this Columbine was indeed Miss Gately—'how are you?'

'Hellish, thank you,' muttered Miss Gately. 'What a press of people! I wonder that Phryne invited half of them.'

'Oh?' Dr MacMillan surveyed the room. 'Why?'

'Well, there's that policeman she's so fond of,' snapped Miss Gately, as a pirate in seaboots passed. 'Detective Inspector Robinson, isn't he? And I'm sure those three don't belong.'

She indicated a group of people dancing very close together: a cat in a skin-tight theatrical suit, head covered by a full mask; a carnival baby, plumped out with cushions, in lacy drawers; and a sleek and scarlet devil. They were all managing to eat somehow, and by the way they were giggling, had got at the cocktails fairly early. Dr MacMillan recognised in the devil a certain Klara, whom she had treated for venereal disease, and assumed that her companions were also ladies (or indeed gentlemen) of the night. She shrugged.

'They seem to be enjoying themselves.'

'Oh, I expect they are! They wouldn't often get into society like ours.' Miss Gately was generously including Dr MacMillan in this term, and Julius Caesar suppressed a grin. 'And I'm sure that she can't have known about Jacob and Esau Tipping, or she wouldn't have invited both of them.'

'What is wrong with them?' asked the doctor, who had tired of Miss Gately's company some time before she met her.

Two gentlemen were standing at the buffet, which was laden with expensive treats, like champagne ices and smoked salmon sandwiches. One was dressed as a Doge, with the Phrygian cap in red leather and the scarlet robes. His hands were burdened with rings. The other, who resembled him closely, was clad in full Renaissance gear, jewelled chain and rings, flowing heavy, embossed velvet. Both had dark eyes and short black beards. Miss Gately was incandescent with scandal.

'They are brothers, you see, and they hate one another. Their father made a most peculiar will—all the Tippings have been odd, though they are so rich. The grandfather made a killing on the goldfields, I believe, selling grog to the miners, or something, and he only had one son, and that son only had two sons, twins, and they hate each other.'

'Oh, yes?'

'Yes. Jacob is the Doge and Esau is Lorenzo de Medici. So overdone, but they never did have any taste. Their grandmother—' her voice sank—'was a gypsy, see? It's in the blood.'

Dr MacMillan, who had seen enough blood to fill a lake and had deep doubts about heredity, snorted.

'So their father, he was a friend of my mother's, horrible man, all tea and temperance, he died about two years ago and left this ridiculous will....'

Across the room, Jilly Henderson, attired as a Supreme Court judge, which she knew that she would never be, was telling Queen Elizabeth the same story.

'It was a mistake to invite them together, Phryne. Their father left all his property to the one who, by the time he was twenty-five, had never been drunk. They've had it in for each other since they were babies.'

'Oh? And when do they turn twenty-five?'

'Tomorrow—rather, tonight, at midnight. I only know about it because my firm represents the estate, and we had to get counsel's opinion as to whether Esau, who is the elder by one hour, would come into his inheritance before Jacob.'

'And does he?' Phryne settled her brocade skirts, a little taken aback. There were still things that she didn't know in the Melbourne social scene, and she did think that someone might have warned her about the Tipping brothers. She did not want a quarrel to mar her party, which was going particularly well.

'No,' Jilly grinned. 'Counsel found it impossible to give an opinion based on precedent, but gave it as his view that the court would take judicial notice of the fact that each new day begins at one second past midnight. So tonight's their last chance. They have both been very good or very careful,' added Jilly, who was, after all, a lawyer. 'And the trustee hasn't managed to catch either of them tippling.'

'Who is the trustee?'

'Severe old gentleman in the Puritan garb. Just about suits him. And he's nicely named, too. Mr Crabbe. Temperance lecturer. Can't stand the man. Tried to stop us keeping port in the office. Said that Mr Latham's best crusty '86 was an alcoholic poison. You should have heard what old Latham said after Crabbe was gone! "My best port, alcohol!" he sputtered. "Alcohol is what they put in compasses!" Oh dear, he was wild, but we just close the door of the inner office when Crabbe inflicts his instruction on us and warn all the clerks not to offer him a drop, or breathe on him if they've been imbibing at lunch. He's been dogging the Tipping brothers' footsteps ever since the will was read.'

'What, is he paid to do this?'

'No, he's got a monomania about alcohol. In fact talking about him makes me dry. Let's have another of those delicious cocktails.'

'Who are the women hovering around the brothers? The tall lady in that pre-Raphaelite thing and the short one in tights?'

'Viola, that's Viola Tipping. She always comes to costume parties as the Shakespeare heroine, though I think that Viola in the play must have been more...well, boyish. You'd never take Viola for a boy, would you?'

'God's teeth,' said Phryne in character, 'Never! Is she Jacob's wife?'

'Yes, and the beggar maid, as in "King Cophetua and the Beggar Maid", that's Tamar Tipping, Esau's wife. I can't say that I take to either of them, Phryne dear. Viola gushes and is as hard as nails, and Tamar is cool and distant and as hard as nails. Never mind. Why, by the way, did you invite them?'

'I owed them both an invitation. This party was to clear all my social debts before the beginning of spring, and of course I invited all my friends so that I should not be distracted with tedium.'

'Well, I do think that someone could have told you,' said Jilly, summoning a server with a judicial wave.

Despite the Tipping brothers, the party was going well. Phryne drifted from conversation to conversation, smiling on social enemies and providing drinks for friends. She had edged quite close to the Tipping brothers and their guardian and listened as she danced a foxtrot with the delectable Lindsay. He was wondering how difficult it was going to be to remove Miss Fisher from her armoury of clothes, if she allowed him to stay after the guests went home.

Lindsay looked for Dot, Phryne's companion, and sighted her, a Sèvres shepherdess, blushing like a poppy under the avalanche of compliments which a tall young Grenadier Guard was pouring

into her ear. Dot would be able to help. She, presumably, had got Phryne into this mountain of a garment, and she would know how to get her out again.

Lindsay sighed. 'Can I stay tonight?'

The red wig and crown inclined, the green eyes, matching the emeralds on her head, cut through his mask.

'Perhaps, if you merit it,' she said. Lindsay attempted to hold her closer, and was foiled by the density of the brocade gown, and painfully spiked by the stomacher.

'Perhaps?' he whispered.

Phryne smiled. 'Perhaps. Now hush, I'm eavesdropping.'

Esau Tipping as Lorenzo the Magnificent jutted a defiant beard at his brother and said, just above a whisper, 'You're contemptible.'

Jacob Tipping, as the Doge of Venice, swallowed an ice and snapped, 'So are you.'

'And no returns,' whispered Lindsay in Phryne's ear.

'You will never inherit!' said Jacob. 'My father meant the property to go to me!'

'You are wrong, brother,' snarled Esau. 'He loved me best and he meant it to go to me!'

'Loved you best!' sneered Jacob, forgetting to speak softly. 'Who was it looked after the old man? Who visited him every day? You never went near him! You and that wife of yours, you didn't care two straws for him!'

'What about that wife of yours, then?' Esau was also forgetting to keep his voice down. 'You set her on the old man, to flatter him and pat him and mother him, and it didn't work, did it, brother? He wasn't convinced by all that coaxing and petting. "Oh, Daddy dear, do leave your Viola something to remember you by".' The voice rose in a scathing imitation of his sister-in-law's gushing manner, and Jacob bristled.

'He didn't get taken in. He left her nothing but his pocket watch, and a few jewels that anyway would have gone to the eldest son's wife. No, my father was no easy touch,' added Esau admiringly.

Phryne, unashamedly listening, thought that the elder Mr Tipping sounded as if he had had a hard life between these brothers. Still, he had made them what they were. Both wives, Phryne noticed, were mortally offended. Viola was attempting to summon suitable tears for a wounded heart, and Tamar had frozen into a pillar of ice. Phryne wondered if, like an iceberg, she was about to sink a few ships.

'How dare you!' demanded Jacob. 'How dare you speak about my wife in that tone! At least I married a real woman, not an armful of granite.'

Phryne was about to intervene before the personalities became more general, but a dry voice cut in. 'You are quarrelling,' it observed. Mr Crabbe in Puritan collar, looking like he was about to order a witch to be burned, was not Phryne's ideal man, but he was effective.

'Yes, so we are. And tomorrow is our birthday,' said Jacob. 'A toast, brother! To our birthday!'

'Now, now,' said Mr Crabbe, in a voice that was probably meant to be soothing but sounded as though he had been told some time ago about the term and had never got around to practising. 'You are brothers and you should be friends.'

'I'd be friends if he would,' smiled Jacob, putting down his glass.

'Withdraw what you said about my wife,' said Esau, and Jacob smiled more widely, showing all his teeth.

'If you withdraw what you said about mine.'

'I withdraw.'

'I withdraw.'

There was an indrawn breath behind both men as their wives realised that the insults were going to go unavenged. Phryne hushed Lindsay, who had been about to suggest that they move away from this uninteresting family quarrel. Both twins' glasses were on the table in Phryne's line of sight. Mr Crabbe picked them up, turned to the punchbowl to refill them, and handed one to each brother. They stared at each other.

'Change glasses,' said Esau, fumbling with his long sleeve. 'It's not that I don't trust you, brother, but I've known snakes with more integrity.'

Jacob grinned and handed over his glass.

'To our birthday!' they chorused, and drank.

Phryne was about to move away when Lorenzo suddenly clutched at his throat and choked. He fell towards the Doge, who was also giving at the knees, and then there was nothing of the Tipping brothers but a blur of scarlet and ermine as they collapsed onto the floor.

Odd things often happened at Phryne's parties. No particular notice was taken, except by Dr MacMillan and a pirate who in private life was a Detective Inspector of Police. The pirate and Julius Caesar inspected the fallen.

'Dead,' said Dr MacMillan.

'As doornails,' agreed Detective Inspector Jack Robinson.

'Poison?'

'Yes.'

'In the alcohol.' The doctor sniffed at each glass. 'Very neat alcohol, at that.'

'Thus fall the unbelievers,' exclaimed Mr Crabbe, lifting his hands and his eyes to heaven. 'Look at the time!'

It was ten minutes to midnight.

Phryne detached Lindsay and said, 'Come along, now. We'll send all these people into the other room and close this door.'

She ushered her guests out of the room, gently shoving those who appeared to be incapacitated from surprise or gin. Lindsay shut the door and leaned on it, his robes swishing around his ankles, his mask over his face, rendering him both antic and alarming. Behind him, the music began again, and a flood of talk. This was one of Miss Fisher's most interesting parties.

'Well?' she asked.

'Both dead, and both had taken alcohol, though that is not what killed them,' said Jack Robinson. 'Both as dead as the dodo; something very quick. Curare, perhaps?' The rising inflection was directed towards Dr MacMillan, who shook her head.

'I won't know until there is an autopsy.'

The Tipping wives, who appeared to have suffered the fate of Lot's spouse, began to speak.

'Do you mean that Jacob is dead?' exclaimed Viola, clasping her hands. 'My Jacob?'

'Esau, get up,' implored Tamar, descending to cradle his head in a flowing mass of draperies. 'Oh, Esau, just like you, to die before the time! Now what will become of me?'

Phryne, who was not very shockable, was shocked. She hoped that better obsequies would be spoken over her own corpse.

'Sit down, ladies, there, on the sofa. Mr Crabbe, could you sit down? I recommend this armchair.'

Mr Crabbe paid no attention. Tall and stiff, reminding Phryne of a statue of John Knox, he was denouncing the brothers.

'I told their father,' he said funereally, 'I told him! Bad seed, I said they have gypsy blood in them, they are unreliable, and they will take to drink! Now look at the harvest of this wicked substance! Two brothers dead in their prime and their wives are widows. The hand of the Lord is upon them!'

'Yes, yes, I'm sure that it is,' agreed Phryne. 'Now you will sit down, please.'

Cold grey eyes glared into hers, alight with the red flare of fanaticism. Phryne stood up straight, set her crown in place, and glared haughtily back, in a manner befitting her disguise. Mr Crabbe, lowering his gaze, sat down as requested.

'Despite what Mr Crabbe says,' Jack Robinson had taken up the gentleman's dominant position in front of the fireplace, 'they didn't die of drink.'

'But they took drink,' observed the doctor. 'Polish spirit, perhaps, or vodka. Pure alcohol, perhaps.'

'Where would one find pure alcohol?'

'A hospital, a pharmacy, even a perfumery. They use it to make scent,' said the doctor. 'Had we not better call the police?'

Jack Robinson grinned at her. 'I am the police,' he reminded the company and stripped off his eye patch and scarf. In the pirate's breeches, loose shirt, and thigh-length seaboots, he was dramatically effective and oddly at home.

He searched in both brothers' pockets and placed his spoils in his scarf.

'Handkerchiefs, keys, cigarette case and lighter, nothing unusual.'

'What's that?' asked Phryne. 'Keep everyone out, Lindsay.'

Lindsay had a brief conversation, and said over his shoulder, 'Miss Henderson wants to come in.'

'All right.'

Jilly Henderson was admitted and Lindsay shut the door again.

'What's up?'

Phryne answered, 'It looks like the two brothers should have been renamed.'

'Renamed?'

'Not Jacob and Esau, but Cain and Abel.'

This biblical reference woke Mr Crabbe from his trance. He had been sitting as ordered, but on the very edge of the chair, and

now he half rose, his denouncing finger boring a hole in the air.

'I told their father!'

'Yes, yes, doubtless,' said Phryne crossly.

'Did they poison each other?'

'So it seems, Jilly. What can you remember about the estate of their father? What was it? Land?'

'No, not that I recall. Shares, mostly, and quite a lot of money. It's in trust, of course.'

'I see.'

Both wives began to stir. The shock was wearing off.

'Oh, Jacob!' wailed Viola. 'I told you it was dangerous, and I said that we should just wait!'

'Esau, I knew it wouldn't work,' cried Tamar.

Both women stopped and stared at each other. Phryne held her breath. They were about to give her some useful information.

'What?' asked Tamar. 'Did your husband intend to make my husband drunk and get the money?'

'Did your snake of a husband intend to get my angel drunk and get the money?' echoed Viola.

'Well! I never heard of such a thing!'

'Well! I never heard of such a thing either. How?'

'How?' asked Tamar.

Viola sobbed aloud. 'How did that brute intend to cheat my poor Jacob?'

'The same way that dear Jacob intended to cheat poor silly Esau, I expect.' Tamar was recovering. It was possible that Esau would not be sorely missed.

'Well?'

Tamar, shaken, raised her glass to her lips. Phryne dived across the room and snatched it out of her hand.

'I don't think that the punch would agree with you, Mrs Tipping,' she said, sniffing at the glass. 'Bitter almond—now, I don't recall putting that in the punch. Catch him, Lindsay!' she cried, as the black-clad figure broke for the door. There was a brief struggle, then the Puritan was down on his face, and Death was perched jauntily between his shoulder blades.

'Mrs Tipping, tell me how Jacob was going to spike Esau's drink.'

'Simple, I knew it wouldn't work. It was too simple,' wailed Viola, still not following the course of events and wondering why the pirate had removed her glass gently from her hand and stood it on the mantelpiece. 'He was going to supply the stuff—him!' She pointed to the fallen Puritan. 'He has pure alcohol, for his temperance lectures, to demonstrate what happens when you dip an earthworm in it.'

'What does happen?' asked Lindsay, who was floating with events, as he always did, and had no idea why he had been asked to fell the elderly gentleman who was presently serving as his cushion.

'It shrivels up,' said Phryne. 'Do belt up, Lindsay! Mrs Tipping,' she said to Tamar, 'how did Esau mean to get Jacob drunk?'

'The same way. That man came to my husband with an offer... to make the old man's will more fair, and Esau agreed. They were to change glasses and the glass which was given to Jacob would be the one with the alcohol in it. Then Jacob was to drink and Mr Crabbe would certify him drunk and the money would go to—'

'I see.' Phryne would have found the situation amusing if it was not for the presence of two dead men on her parlour floor.

'So both brothers meant to do down the other and inherit under this ridiculous will. But Jacob did not mean to kill Esau, did he?' she asked Viola, who shook her head.

'And Esau did not mean to kill Jacob, did he?' she asked Tamar, who snapped, 'Of course not.'

'And John Knox here was to supply the booze.' Phryne was thinking aloud. 'He made the same offer to both brothers, and they both accepted, and if they were both found drunk they would not have inherited. What's the reversion of the estate, Jilly? Do you remember?'

'Oh, yes, the wives get five hundred pounds apiece and the rest goes to some temperance organisation. I forget the name... Sons of Water-Drinkers, something like that.'

'So you decided to kill them, Mr Crabbe. I wonder why? It was a risky thing to do, but you would have got the money, all of the estate, because I'll bet that you are the founder and sole member of the Sons of Wowsers.'

The black figure under Death squirmed.

'Oh, but wait a moment.' A thought had struck Phryne. She went to the buffet and found a bottle of Scotch, examined the cork and seal, then stripped it and poured herself a drink to assist cogitation.

'I see,' she said softly.

She strode over to the recumbent Puritan and hauled him to his feet. Glittering in the electric light, the shimmer of her gold dress was hard to look at, but Mr Crabbe seemed to have more difficulty with the furious green eyes.

'You don't have the money, do you?' she said with icy clarity. 'You spent it, didn't you? It wasn't enough to just disinherit the brothers, because then you would have had to pay the wives their husbands' share. You had to kill them.' Phryne had backed Mr Crabbe up against the mantelpiece. 'You monster; you nasty wicked hymn-singing hypocrite!'

'It was the Lord's work,' he faltered. 'The Lord told me to take the infidels' gold and spend it on a temple for the glory of his name and the cause of temperance!'

Mr Crabbe turned from her eyes, grabbed the glass standing on the mantelpiece and gulped it down. Phryne could not stop him. Dr MacMillan watched as the tall man swayed and crumpled.

'Dead?' demanded Phryne, as pirate and Roman bent over the fallen murderer.

'He'll live to hang,' she commented, taking off her laurel wreath and chuckling.

'Wasn't that glass poisoned?'

'Only with alcohol,' she said. 'He's drunk good Scotch whisky for the first time in his life. That was my glass.'

———

Stretcher bearers came and went. The wives of the dead brothers were taken home by policemen. Lindsay, who had been told that he could stay, was attempting a joyful Charleston and was finding that Death should confine himself to the waltz. Jack Robinson farewelled Phryne at the door.

'Thank you, Phryne, it has been a very nice evening,' he said soberly. 'And a nice solution. Do ask me again when you haven't scheduled a double murder, won't you?'

He bowed, kissed Miss Fisher's hand, and turned to leave.

There was someone at the door. Masked and cowled, Death bowed the Detective Inspector out of Miss Fisher's house.

Nursery FIZZ

A temperance drink,
'nursery fizz' is comprised
of equal parts dry ginger ale
and sparkling grape juice.

An interview with
Phryne Fisher

FAVOURITE FOOD?
White peaches. I could bathe in them.

FAVOURITE COLOUR?
Expensive.

FAVOURITE SCENT?
Jicky or Cinq-à-Sept by Guerlain.

FAVOURITE DESIGNER?
Erté, Dior, Worth.

READING RECENTLY?
Miss Dorothy Sayers' Lord Peter Wimsey books, and Beverley
Nichols, such a clever young man and very sound on cats. Also
Geoffrey Chaucer and Herodotus, quite the best guide to the
ancient world.

WHAT INSPIRES YOU?
Green chartreuse.

WHAT DEPRESSES YOU?

The obstinate failure of the revolution to arrive.

BEST PIECE OF LIFE ADVICE?

Don't die. While there's life, there's Château Mouton Rothschild.

FAVOURITE CASE?

The Spanish Ambassador's son's kitten. It was a very charming, if grave, kitten. Come to think of it, so was the Ambassador.

WORD OR PHRASE FOR WHICH BEST KNOWN?

'Mr Butler, could we have another cocktail?'

GREATEST REGRET?

The hobble skirt.

GREATEST PLEASURE?

I could say, while wearing a new dress, drinking Veuve Clicquot and eating truffled quails' eggs and Beluga caviar with lemon and rye-bread toast in excellent company with dancing to follow, but that sounds trite. Everything is a pleasure, except politicians.

ADVICE FOR TRAVELLERS?

A smile, a song, and a wad of the local currency will get you most of the things you may require abroad, except English tea.

Marrying
THE BOOKIE'S DAUGHTER

Rendering good for ill,
Smiling at ev'ry frown,
Yielding your own self-will,
Laughing your teardrops down;
Never a selfish whim,
Trouble, or pain to stir;
Everything for him,
Nothing at all for her!
Love that will aye endure,
Though the rewards be few,
That is the love that's pure,
That is the love that's true!
WS Gilbert, *Patience,* or *Bunthorne's Bride*

'Phryne,' said Lindsay Herbert. 'Will you marry me?'
Phryne Fisher had been drowsing, lying naked

on her moss-green sheets with the young man's head on her shoulder. Now she was shocked awake. She released Lindsay and slid down so that she could look into his face, and a highly inappropriate laugh was smothered at birth.

A golden boy, slim and beautiful, rising on one elbow to look earnestly into her green eyes, light hair curling away from a high forehead, round blue eyes, a sweet red mouth now drawn tight over white teeth. Her gaze left the face and slid down over the body. Lightly tanned skin lay smoothly over the slender musculature of a runner. Squared chest, flat belly, long legs.

'Why, Lindsay, I...I don't know what to say...' Phryne groped for a response, mightily puzzled. What had brought this on? 'I...I am very honoured, of course...'

'Well, what do you say?' he demanded roughly. 'Yes or no?' She did not reply.

He sat up abruptly. 'It's time we got married,' he stated.

'Why?' asked Phryne, reaching for her long dressing gown and pulling it on. It was patterned with green and scarlet macaws and suddenly seemed gaudy.

'Well, because...because we get on so well. I know I'm not very clever at law and things, but I've got excellent prospects. ...Father will give me a job in the firm....We could be very happy, Phryne.'

'I thought that we were very happy.' Phryne was finding it hard to keep her countenance. 'Get up, Lindsay, and we shall discuss it and have some tea. Look, it's five o'clock—perhaps a cocktail as well.'

'Yes or no?' demanded Lindsay, not moving.

'You can't expect an instant answer to such an important

question, Mr Herbert,' Phryne said coldly. 'I have said that we will talk about it.'

And she vanished into her dressing room to assume the usual habiliment of a lady going down to tea in her own house in 1928.

Lindsay was left alone. He swore explosively and scrabbled for his clothes.

Half an hour later Phryne found herself entangled in an argument which even Mr Butler's cocktails did not mitigate or unravel.

'But why, Lindsay dear? We are perfectly all right as we are,' she protested.

'Damnation, old thing. We don't need a reason for getting married! Everyone does it!' the young man spluttered into his ginger beer. 'I don't know why you won't say yes!'

'I don't know either,' said Phryne slowly.

'It's because I'm not clever, isn't it?' he demanded suddenly, with a broad, generous gesture which distributed his drink over a considerable portion of the room. 'You only like clever chaps. That's what it is.'

'No, no, Lindsay dear, that isn't it,' objected Phryne. 'Not at all. I think you're lovely just as you are. And you are quite bright, sometimes, though not at the moment.'

'It can't be my prospects,' he mused as Mr Butler refilled his glass and began unobtrusively to mop ginger beer off the couch. 'It must be... it must be...' He stared piteously up into Phryne's eyes and whispered, 'another man.'

'Lindsay, dear—'

'No, that's it, I see it all now,' he said feverishly. 'Another man, of course, a clever chap with lots of money—he's the one you want.'

Phryne leaned over and took the glass firmly out of his hand. She was unable to account for this strange fervour and was beginning to apprehend a scene. And she liked Lindsay, who was usually delightful, a good lover, and an excellent and socially acceptable escort, who was rapidly rendering himself unfit for female company.

'Now listen,' Phryne planted herself on his knees to keep the young man still and took a fistful of the soft, light hair. 'You listen to me, Lindsay. I am what I am and I behave as I wish and I will not be dictated to by anyone. If I want lovers, I take them. If I do not want to be married, I will not be married and there's nothing you can do to make me! Do you hear?'

There were tears in the eyes of the flushed face turned up to hers. She did not release her grip.

'Then the answer's no?'

'If it is?'

'Then I'll go away, Phryne, I'll walk out that door and you'll never see me again. I can't go on like this. I'm never sure of you.'

'And you'd be sure of me if I was married to you?' She could not stop her eyebrows from rising.

The young man drew a long breath and said earnestly, 'Yes, if we were married, then...'

Phryne judged him calm enough for her to resume her seat. She did so, loosing a few flax-pale strands of hair from between her fingers as she listened.

'Then?'

'If we were married, then you'd belong to me. I'd belong to you.'

'And?'

'Then we'd be happy.'

'Because I belonged to you?'

'Yes. You could sell this house and come and live with me. We could buy a big house in Toorak and have a country estate and a place near the sea and we'd have such larks, Phryne, just you and me, without a lot of people bothering us. I could finish law and go into Father's office. In the winter we could go skiing, and sailing in the summer and—'

'And we could have a little cottage with roses around the door and Old Mister Moon peeping in through the window?'

'Yes. You don't have to say it in that tone of voice. It could be fun. Please, Phryne. I don't want to lose you. You could give up all this detective work and go to parties with me, and the opera, and all sorts of jolly things. And we could have...children? Two, perhaps, eh? Lindsay Junior and a pretty little girl like you must have been. Please say yes, Phryne. It came into my head because the pater is going on about being settled and the mater keeps introducing me to nice girls and...'

'Well, what's wrong with the nice girls?'

Phryne lit a cigarette. She didn't want to break Lindsay's ingenuous heart, so she was listening. Lindsay reached out and ran a skilled hand down her breast and heard her gasp.

'That's what wrong with the nice girls,' he said simply. 'They're nice.'

'Of course they are. That's how they are trained to appear. You may be agreeably surprised at what they are really like. Lindsay, I can't decide something as important as this immediately. I have to think about it. Can you wait for an answer?'

'If I have to.'

'You have to.'

'Then I can wait,' he said miserably. He was not, however, altogether cast down. Phryne had not rejected his honourable proposal out of hand. There might still be a chance of securing her for his own.

'And in the meantime,' she said, taking another cocktail and returning his glass to the young man, 'I am going to a wedding on Saturday. The Sackville girl. Will you be my escort?'

'Of course. The Sackville wedding, eh? I didn't know you moved in those circles, Phryne.'

'Which circles?'

'Racing ones.'

'I don't, but the wretched girl is one of that pest Celia's protégés, so I really haven't a choice. You know how she takes up the petite bourgeoisie's ghastly daughters and launches them on what she fondly thinks is Society. Well, she launched Amelia Sackville, doubtless on the strength of her papa's fortune. All got from doing down the working punter, Bert says.'

'Stout fellow, Bert,' commented Lindsay.

'I see, so you propose to allow me to continue my friendship with the working class if we are married?' Phryne asked teasingly.

Lindsay took her seriously and pondered his reply. He said solemnly, 'Well, no, Phryne, you won't need them if you aren't detecting anymore.'

'Of course.' Lindsay wondered what he had said to bring that metallic ring into her voice. 'Yes. So, poor Amelia is to be sacrificed at the altar.'

'Who is she marrying?'

'You know him, Lindsay dear. Fletcher. Tom Fletcher.'

'Good Lord, yes old Fletch getting shackled for life. How the mighty are fallen. He was my House Prefect at Grammar, you know, a fiend at rowing. Captain of the football team. But not just a rowdy; bit of a ladies' man. Nothing in skirts was safe from him. Cost his father a packet in breach of promise payments, buying them off, I gather. Imagine him marrying the bookie's daughter.' Lindsay laughed. 'Well, and that's what one would expect, too.'

'Why?'

'Terrible gambling bug he had, old Fletch. Used to run a book himself, at school. On the Melbourne Cup, you know, not as a business or anything.'

'And what's he like?'

'Good chap, you know. Still plays for the OM's football team, does a bit of coaching of the fours.'

'Yes, but what is he like?'

Lindsay gaped. 'I've told you,' he said lamely.

Phryne gave it up. 'Never mind, dear boy. I'll pick you up at two; full soup and fish, we have to go to a very swish reception afterwards.'

'St Peter's, Eastern Hill, I assume?' he asked, accepting his coat from Mr Butler.

'St Peter's, Eastern Hill,' Phryne agreed.

———

'Marriage,' said Phryne, unaware that she had spoken aloud.

'Marriage, Miss Phryne?' echoed Dot. 'Are you thinking of getting married, Miss?'

Phryne looped a long necklace of amber beads around her neck, and said to Dot's reflection in the mirror, 'I've been asked.'

'Oh, Miss, how exciting! Who is it?'

'Lindsay Herbert. What do you think?'

'Oh, Miss, they say he's ever so rich, and he's very well connected.'

'So you believe I should marry him?'

Dot was Phryne's maid and companion. She had always disapproved of detection as an occupation for a lady. Mirrored Dot clasped her hands.

'Well, Miss, you like him,' she said slowly, 'you...er...know him.'

Phryne grinned, and Dot blushed. 'And, well, Miss, getting married, you'd have to give up all this dangerous detective work. You know how I worry about you.'

'Why would I?'

Dot stared. Some things, she felt, were self-evident.

'Mr Herbert wouldn't like his wife to be doing something so... so...'

'Unladylike?' Phryne's smile now showed quite an array of teeth. 'What else would Mr Herbert not like his wife to do?'

'Well, Miss, it's to be expected. Gentlemen will have their house ordered the way they want, after all. Perhaps you could do some charity work. But married ladies don't work. Everyone knows that.'

'No? What about you, Dot? Aren't you a lady?'

'That's different. I'm not married, and I've got myself to keep. But my husband won't like me to work. He'll keep me.'

'How sweet,' said Phryne without any inflection. 'The straw coloured dress, please, Dot.'

––––––––

A caller was announced at three the next afternoon. Mr Butler came into the drawing room where Phryne and Dot were examining the library catalogue.

'No, I don't think so, Dot dear, I really can't bear romances. One more heaving bosom, thunderstorm, and frilly white nightgown and I'll scream. Get me some thrillers. That new one, Charteris, he sounds good. Yes, Mr Butler?'

'Mr Aloysius Fletcher to see you, Miss.'

'Never heard of him. What does he want?'

Mr Butler came a little closer and said quietly, 'It's the racing gentleman, Miss Phryne, the one whose son is marrying the bookmaker's daughter.'

'Oh, yes. Well, I've finished with the catalogue, Dot dear. Send it off, and you might stay, if you don't mind. I don't know how racing gentlemen behave. Wheel him in, Mr Butler.'

Mr Aloysius Fletcher was not alone. He strode into the room, large and magnificent, if a trifle past his prime, a big, stout, fleshy man in a quiet charcoal suit evidently chosen by his wife. His own taste announced itself in the shape of a violently patterned cravat and a horse-shaped gold stickpin with a diamond glaring from the middle. He had another diamond on his left hand, big enough to choke a parrot.

Scurrying behind him was a small, thin, plain woman of perhaps thirty. She was so self-effacing that she was hard to see. Her long blonde hair was scraped back into a migraine-inducing bun. She looked modestly down at the carpet. She was clutching a large black-bound diary in her arms, and had a pencil behind her ear.

'Miss Fisher?' he bellowed.

Phryne offered him her hand and he shook it hard, then let it go as though he had found himself holding a fish. Phryne judged him to be a severe man on china and invited him to sit down, hoping that he was reliable with chairs.

'I'm Aloysius Fletcher,' he said. 'Perhaps you have heard of me.'

'Yes,' said Phryne. 'I've heard of you.'

'You know my son's marrying the bookie's daughter on Saturday?'

'Yes, I'm coming to the wedding. And who is your companion?'

'Companion?' He started and looked around. 'Oh, that's just Smithy, my secretary. Sit down, Smithy. She's a fool,' he confided in a ponderous undertone. 'But

she'll do if I watch her like a hawk. Yes, well, Tom's managed to snare the bookie's daughter. Stout fellow, Tom. The family might get back the money the scoundrels have taken off me all these years!'

He laughed. Phryne watched politely. Mr Butler offered a drink and was sent for whisky and soda— 'And don't drown the whisky!'

Phryne waited until Miss Smith had found a perch on the extreme edge of the sofa, and then said, 'To what do I owe the honour of your acquaintance, Mr Fletcher?'

'Meaning, what do I want, eh?' He laughed again. 'Well, I want you to do something for me. Smithy! Show Miss Fisher the drawings!'

Smithy jumped, dropped the diary, and scrabbled for three spilt sheets of paper. She handed them to Phryne. They were watercolour drawings of jewellery done by an expert hand, showing a bridal set comprising High Victorian brooch, zone, necklace, earrings, and tiara. They were heavy, solid, and respectably opulent.

'Yes?'

'They're the family heirlooms. The gift of the bridegroom, you know. Not that I expect a girl with pots of money like the bookie's daughter will care for them. But it's a tradition, y'know.'

'Yes?' Phryne was beginning to dislike her unwanted guest so much that she was hoping he would choke on his whisky, even though it was not the good whisky. Mr Butler had his own system of class determination.

'They're missing.'

'I see.'

'I went to the safe this morning—it's in Smithy's room, so that there is always someone in the way if burglars break in. The safe was open and the room had been torn apart, eh, Smithy?'

Miss Smith nodded.

'And the jewels were gone.'

'Have you called the police?'

'Of course, but they won't get quick results. I told my son about it and his friend Herbert—you know him, apparently—said that you could find things faster than Sherlock Holmes. So here I am, Miss Fisher, asking you to help.'

'I'm afraid that I'm rather busy, Mr Fletcher.'

'Come along, girl!' barked Mr Fletcher. 'I came to get you, and get you I shall. M'wife's upset. And Herbert said you were a genius. Should have known better than to trust the little twerp.'

Phryne considered this. She detested Mr Fletcher, but Lindsay's good opinion of her was flattering and should be supported. She nodded, got up, and found her handbag.

'Very well. My fees, Mr Fletcher, are high. Can you pay them?'

'Fees?'

'Yes. This is my profession, you know.'

Mr Fletcher appeared to have been struck dumb. Smithy said in a soft, deep voice, 'There won't be any trouble with the fees, Miss Fisher. Can you come now?'

'Yes.'

Mr Fletcher was assisted to his feet and they left the house.

————

Phryne examined the room. It was a small, crowded bedchamber, where all the things in the house which were not immediately needed were stored. Smith's bed stood in front of a collection of walking sticks, golf clubs, and tennis rackets. Her clothes hung in a cupboard which also contained a vacuum cleaner and several boxes of illustrated racing papers. The only signs of her occupancy were hundreds of exquisite pen drawings pinned up all over the walls. Phryne exclaimed, 'They're beautiful! Who did them?'

'Smithy. She's always scribbling,' grunted Mr Fletcher. 'See, there's the safe, and it was open. They must have got in through the window.'

Smithy's only window was small but unbarred, and a smashed pane announced that the lock had been rendered useless.

'Hmm, yes. What was in the safe?'

'Nothing else of value. Papers, mainly deeds and so on.'

'Was the jewellery in a box?'

'Yes, about ten inches by ten inches square. Why?'

'Just wondered.' Phryne noticed that a tin trunk had also been forced open. From the female underclothes and drawing materials, she judged it to be Smithy's. A bottle of green ink had been smashed, and the trunk's contents appeared to have been tipped out and then roughly piled back inside.

'Hmm.'

'Well? Can you find them?' demanded Mr Fletcher.

Phryne smiled up into the beefy face. 'I'll try.'

'Good. Come up and see m'wife, will you? She's upset.'

It was possible to gauge the degree of upset from the sobbing and wailing which was apparent in the hall. Mr Fletcher muttered something about an appointment in the stables and fled. Smithy, unexpectedly, gave Phryne a sympathetic look, revealing that she had beautiful, large, expressive eyes the colour of forget-me-nots. She led Phryne into a sizeable room which contained a tall young man, a well-dressed young woman, and an older woman in the throes of what appeared to be inconsolable grief.

'Mama, please!' the young man begged. 'Smithy, can't you do something with her? Oh, I beg your pardon,' he added when he caught sight of Phryne. 'Hello! Are you Miss Fisher? Herbert's told me all about you. I'm delighted to meet you.'

He was a very good-looking young man, Phryne thought, with chestnut hair and brown eyes and a full red mouth. He held her hand a little longer than was necessary, and the quality of the contact suggested that Lindsay had indeed told him all about Phryne. She smiled wickedly and released herself.

'This is Miss Sackville, my fiancée. Amelia, this is Miss Fisher. She's going to find the family jewels.' He grinned down at her and she shook her neat head.

'I told you, Tommy, I don't care about the family jewels. I've got jewels enough of my own.' The girl was taller than Phryne, offhandedly elegant, in a lapis-lazuli suit with sapphires in her ears. Her dark hair was bobbed, her cosmetics reticent, and her manner unaffected. She was holding Tom Fletcher's hand to her breast as though she was cradling it. 'I just want you, old thing,' she said.

Tom Fletcher smiled and replied, 'And on Saturday you will be mine.'

Phryne caught her breath. This was the exclusive love which she had been thinking about; one creature claiming another, in complete indifference to the rest of humanity. For a moment, her heart ached. She wondered how it would feel to love like that, or trust like that, so perfectly and forever. Phryne had never before considered that there might be someone so close to her always, in whom she could have such single-minded faith.

Mrs Fletcher stopped sobbing. Smithy was fussing around her with salts and brandy, and a large gulp of spirit had temporarily taken her mistress' breath away.

Smithy introduced Phryne. There was little that she could say.

'I'll do my best, but the wedding is on Saturday, Mrs Fletcher. I think you'd be better leaving it to the police. It is their business, you know.'

'That's what I say,' agreed Tom vehemently. 'Leave it to the cops. That's what we pay taxes for, isn't it?'

But Mrs Fletcher looked like she was about to start wailing again, and Phryne, to keep the peace, agreed to continue her investigation.

Another inspection of Smithy's room revealed nothing positive, although Phryne did notice that folios of drawings had been emptied and rifled, and the contents replaced carelessly. She sat on the floor with Smithy to smooth the paper and stack it again.

'These are very fine,' said Phryne admiringly, leafing through life drawings of a nude young man, executed with loving care. The muscles were shaded with red chalk. The face was turned away.

Smithy snatched them from Phryne's hand and crumpled them into a ball. 'I'm not good on the figure,' she said hastily.

'I'm better at still life.'

Phryne admired flowers and fruit and asked, as she was leaving, 'Did you go to art school? You're very good.'

A painful blush burned Miss Smith's face. 'No. I couldn't afford it. I've been working here since my mother died, when I was sixteen. She was Mr Fletcher's cousin. He gave me a job and a place to live. It was...very kind of him.'

'Was it?' asked Phryne dryly.

One gleam of passionate emotion was allowed to escape from Smithy's blue eyes, and then it was veiled. 'Of course,' she muttered.

———

By the afternoon of the next day—which was Friday, the day before the wedding—Phryne had the solution to the mystery of the missing jewels and was at a loss as to what to do. She took a long walk, returning out of breath and with the problem still unresolved. She was also considering Lindsay's proposal. After all, Phryne was twenty-eight. She might never get another proposal so fitting. Yesterday's glimpse of the lovers, perfectly and passionately devoted to each other, had planted a splinter in her bosom. Tom and Amelia, smiling at each other with the kind of embracing, exclusive smile that forced all of the world out past the boundaries of their magic circle, and declared 'mine'. But Phryne and Lindsay, the sweet boy with the soft mouth, forsaking all others, alone with each other for the foreseeable future? She had never experienced perfect love; was it possible that it had never come because she had never tried hard enough?

It could probably be accomplished, she thought, if she put her mind to it. She reached her own door still wondering and found the front hall full of flowers.

'What are these?' she asked, looking for a florist's label. Australian flowers, strange and spiky: waratahs, banksias, and sheaves of gum leaves. She inhaled the bush scent with delight.

'They're from Mr Herbert, Miss,' said Dot from behind a shrubbery of everlastings. 'He wants you to marry him.'

'Yes, I know.'

'Have you decided, Miss? 'cos Mrs Butler was asking.'

'Mrs Butler? Why?'

'Because of the arrangements, Miss, they'll have to find another place.'

'Oh, Lord!' Phryne dragged herself out of the scented haze. 'Tell Mrs B that I haven't made up my mind, but in any case I shall be keeping them on and this house, too. A fig for all this perfect love,' she snarled. 'I don't think I'm strong enough for marriage, Dot.'

Suppressing a private delight in muslin and wedding veils and orange blossom, Dot handed Phryne an armload of wax flowers and went off to the kitchen, leaving her mistress in possession of a magnificent fit of bad temper.

———

Phryne dressed for the wedding in a state of bemusement. She did not know what to do for the best, or even what to avoid for the worst. The state of the window, the folios, the reputation of Tom Fletcher and Miss Smith's position in the house seemed to point to one conclusion, but the research which Dot had undertaken had not confirmed it. Phryne got out of the bath, scented with Jicky, and allowed herself to be dressed in champagne coloured stockings and underwear, and then sat in front of the mirror while Dot brushed her hair.

'Glass on the outside,' she said aloud.

'Miss?'

'Glass on the outside of the window,' she said, 'means that the window was broken from the inside. And no one would search flat cardboard folios for a box ten inches by ten inches. The burglar wasn't looking for jewels. There's only one solution, Dot, and I don't know what to do. Tom Fletcher and his Amelia, they really seem to love each other, Dot. At least, she loves him. Whatever that means. Oh, these society scandals are too, too enervating. One will have nothing to talk about for months and months but the disruption of the Fletcher boy's wedding. And it will not aid the lady. I have it. Stop brushing, Dot, run down and get Lindsay on the telephone. He'll be at the Fletchers' if he's not at home—Tom Fletcher is an old friend of his.'

Phryne allowed Dot to drop her apricot and silver dress over her head and then found her bag and her cloche as Dot ran for the telephone.

'Lindsay dear, it's Phryne. Can you give Tom Fletcher a message? It's important.'

'Yes, I'm going there now to see the poor fish into his garments and help old Jack to keep custody of the ring. What's the message? Don't tell me you've fallen for Tom, like all those other swooning females?'

'Lindsay, have you ever known me to swoon?... Well, then.

Tell him to bring the jewels to the ceremony with him. You can carry them. They're in a box, ten by ten.'

'But I thought that they were stolen!'

'They were. But Tom has them now, or my name's not Phryne Fisher. Then scurry home again and I'll pick you up in an hour. Will you do it?'

'Oh, of course, Phryne. If you say so,' he replied stiffly.

'It is offended—see, it stalks away,' quoted Phryne, hanging up the phone. 'Mr Butler! A cocktail, if you please. I am in need of strengthening. And I wonder,' she added to herself, 'now that Tom Fletcher knows that I know his secret, what he will do. This should be an interesting afternoon.'

Mr Butler supplied the cocktail, made with special care and to a secret recipe, and forbore from comment.

————

St Peter's, Eastern Hill was crowded, and Phryne had some difficulty manoeuvring herself through the press of Melbourne's shrillest and most fashionable in order to sit next to Smithy outside the church. The secretary was unbecomingly attired in a charcoal suit evidently cut out with some agricultural implement, and a dark cloche was dragged brutally down over her high forehead.

Tom Fletcher was hopping from foot to foot, smoking like a chimney and, when he thought himself unobserved, taking little nips from a flask kept by his best man. Lindsay Herbert, in full elegant evening dress, sat next to Phryne nursing a box on his knee and looking bewildered.

'What did Tom say when he gave you the jewels, Lindsay?'

'He said he had to go through with it, whatever happened. He said he was sorry, to tell you that he was very sorry.'

'I see.'

'What is going to happen, Phryne?' begged Lindsay.

She kissed him on the cheek. 'I haven't the faintest. Hark, here comes the bride.'

There was a stir at the door. The groom threw away his cigarette, paled, and was escorted into the church. A carriage drew up and out of it the bride stepped, supported by a rubicund father bursting with pride. Amelia was draped in a Valenciennes veil so generous that it flowed over her and in careless folds to the ground. Her gown was of ice-pale silk, dipping down towards her heels, embroidered in silver with lilies and garlands. She carried a trailing bouquet of gardenias, and their sweet indecent scent reached Phryne and Smithy in their pew, stirring both of them in different ways. Smithy clutched her hands together and shut her mouth hard. Phryne breathed in the scent and remembered a certain hot night and the taste of salt on a young man's skin....

The organ pealed, a voluntary which slid into the full triumphal wedding march, and the bride was led towards the altar, leaning on her father's arm, to be given away to her husband.

Smithy began to shiver. Phryne took her arm.

'Are you feeling faint?' she asked. 'Why don't we go out? Very close in here.'

Smithy turned on Phryne eyes, which reminded her of a mortally injured dog, and nodded.

They reached the church wall, which was low, and sat down. Phryne lit a gasper and said quietly, 'It wasn't like that at the registry office, was it?'

'No.'

'But Dot couldn't find anything in the records.'

Smithy groped in her bag and thrust a folded piece of paper into Phryne's hand. She read it.

'That's why,' she commented. 'I didn't ask her to go back far enough. How old were you, for God's sake?'

'Sixteen,' muttered Smithy. Phryne realised that she was a lot younger than she looked. Life could not have been easy in Mr Fletcher's house, in possession of such a secret and despised by her employers, used like a domestic animal and mercilessly overworked.

'That's what Tom was looking for, when he staged that break-in and searched your room.'

'Yes. I loved him,' she said through clenched teeth. 'I loved him so much! There I was, small and insignificant and plain and worthless, and he paid attention to me. He liked me—no one liked me—and ...and...'

'And you slept with him?'

'Not until we were married. I held out for that. I was brought up well. If I'd wanted to be a whore I wouldn't have put up with old Fletcher all these years. Then he got tired of me. Years ago he got tired of me. And I stayed because.... I still love him, I suppose. And I had nowhere else to go.'

'And what are you going to do?' asked Phryne gently.

'There's a bit in the service—I looked it up. Where they ask if anyone has just cause or impediment...I was going to...'

'Stand up and object? Well, you have just cause, all right, just cause indeed! You have been treated monstrously, Smithy. Smithy, what's your name?'

Smithy shook her head as though she could hardly remember. 'Chlöe. My mother...liked...novels.'

She started to cry helplessly. Phryne cupped a hand under the small chin and forced Chlöe to look at her.

'Listen, Chlöe, I think I can deal more advantageously for you than just disrupting the wedding. I know that it will make you feel better for the moment but what are you going to do after that? You can hardly expect to stay with the Fletchers. And I doubt if they'll give you a good character reference. And Tom...Tom is not likely to be much use to you, is he?'

The bowed shoulders shuddered, and Chlöe Smith whispered, 'No.'

'Right. Give me that marriage certificate. Have you got old Fletcher's diary with you, as always? Has it got a cheque book in it? Good. Ah, Lindsay,' she added as the young man came up to them. 'Miss Smith is a bit overcome. Can you stay with her? Give her some brandy if you've got some. I'll be back in a moment, Chlöe.'

Chlöe stared at Phryne as she stalked back into the church. Lindsay sat down beside her and patted her gently. Emotional women did not worry or embarrass Lindsay.

'Mr Herbert—can I trust her?'

'Who, Miss Fisher? Of course. Have a little taste of this, now, just a sip. You can trust Phryne. If she says she'll fix it, then it will be fixed. I would trust her with my life,' said Lindsay, and Chlöe Smith leaned against his tailored shoulder and sipped brandy and closed her eyes.

By the exercise of barefaced intimidation, Phryne managed to smuggle herself into the seat next to old Mr Fletcher as he opened a hymn book with which he was evidently unfamiliar. Phryne laid the fatal certificate over the words of 'O Perfect Love' and watched his eyes bulge as he read it. He turned on her, about to demand an explanation, and she put a finger to his lips.

'Calm, Mr Fletcher,' she said. 'We don't want to cause a fuss, do we?'

'What do you want?' he choked. 'Where is Smithy? I'll tear her limb from—'

'No you won't. If you want this marriage to go ahead, then you'll have to pay up. Your son abandoned the poor little thing and you don't value her. She needs an independence or...'

'Or?'

Phryne was interested in the colour of his face—a glowing purple—but reflected that it clashed lamentably with her gown. She opened the order of service and laid a finger on one line. He read it. There was a smothered silence.

'Dearly beloved, we are gathered together here...' began the Bishop in a high, nasal, parsonical tone. Mrs Fletcher took out a lace handkerchief and began to cry decorously.

'Well? How much?'

'Five thousand. Invested, that should be enough.'

'Five thou—!' he began, then hushed as several people turned to look at him.

'It is a state which should be entered into reverently, discreetly, advisedly, soberly and in fear of God, duly considering the causes for which matrimony was ordained,' said the Bishop, with a reproving glance at the groom's father.

'All right. Later.'

'Now,' said Phryne, laying his own cheque book on the marriage service, and unscrewing his own fountain pen which she had somehow abstracted from his top pocket. For a moment she was worried that he would die of apoplexy before he could sign, but he filled in the cheque, and she took the book out of his grasp, waving it a little to dry the ink.

'I'll keep the certificate in case you try to stop the cheque,' she said coolly. Then she stood up as though her movement was part of the service and walked down the aisle and out of the church.

Smithy had cried out years of suppressed humiliation and pain onto Lindsay's shoulder, and was feeling a little better. Lindsay's closeness was comforting, and his perfect faith in Miss Fisher's effectiveness was infectious. She had also told him the whole story, and he had been considerably and gratifyingly shocked.

'I never would have thought it of old Fletch. How did it go, Phryne?' he asked.

'I've stung Papa Fletcher for five thousand of the best and brightest,' she said. 'Do you want to come back inside, Chlöe?'

Chlöe clung to Lindsay's arm in a way which he found touching, and Phryne led them inside, along the side aisle to where Tom Fletcher could see them. He stood straighter when he saw Chlöe Smith. Ever since Phryne's message about the jewels had arrived he had been waiting for this.

'Therefore if any man can show any just cause or impediment why they may not lawfully be joined together, let him now speak, or else hereafter forever hold his peace.'

Tom Fletcher stiffened, his gaze on Smithy—the familiar and ill-used Smithy, who was in a position to ruin his life. Tom did not beg for mercy. He blinked once and Amelia's hand stole out to take his, divining that something was wrong. There was a silence thick enough to slash with a sabre.

Leaning on Lindsay, Chlöe Smith smiled slightly, and in that smile released herself from Tom Fletcher. She nodded to him.

'I require and charge you both,' the Bishop continued, wondering what these three were doing standing in the side aisle and hoping that something socially unfortunate was not going to happen, 'as ye will answer at the dreadful day of judgment, when the secrets of all hearts shall be disclosed, that if either of you know any impediment why ye may not be lawfully joined together in matrimony, ye do now confess it.'

Amelia looked up at her soon-to-be husband. He looked at Chlöe, who nodded again. Tom Fletcher gusted out a sigh of relief which caused the altar candles to flicker, and said nothing.

———

Phryne saw Chlöe Smith into and out of Mr Fletcher's house and into the car, with the trunk full of drawings. She drove her to a suitable boarding house, paying the first week's rent and seeing the young woman settled.

'I really couldn't do anything else, could I?' she asked, sitting down on the bed and bouncing. 'This is a nice bed. It's got springs.'

'My dear girl, revenge is always sweet but it is not generally profitable. Now make sure that you bank that cheque first thing

Monday morning. You can post the certificate to Mr Fletcher as soon as you have the money.'

'I've got nothing to do. I've worked for them all my life. I kept the household accounts and minded the dog and looked after Ma Fletcher when she had conniptions and dealt with the servants and paid the bills and they never appreciated me or noticed me and now I've got nothing to do.' Miss Smith seemed to have grown younger. She tore off the ugly hat and pulled her hair out of its bonds. Hairpins flew like fireflies. A cascade of corn coloured hair tumbled down over the charcoal suit. 'What shall I do? What shall I do now?'

'Why, anything you like. Why not go to art school? Buy some nice clothes. And you may find another young man,' suggested Phryne.

Chlöe thought about it, running her ink-stained fingers through the silky strands. 'No. I don't know any young men. And I'm not a virgin. No one will marry me now. Oh, but what about Tom? What if he has...children? Won't they be...'

'No, that was not a legal marriage, Chlöe. Both of you were underage. Neither had you parental permission. You could have caused a massive scandal, though. So you can marry again, if you want to. You're in the same position as a widow.'

'I'll never forget him—Tom, I mean. Yes, I am a widow. It's like he's dead.' She wept for a few minutes, then tossed back her hair and wiped her red eyes. 'I think I'll have a cat. A house first, then a cat. I can afford a house, can't I? Oh dear, I'm going to cry again. Don't stay with me. I like being alone. I have to think. I haven't been able to think, not since Tom brought Miss Amelia home. But you must go back to the wedding, Miss Fisher. Tell Tom to be happy. And don't worry about me. I'm free,' said Chlöe Smith, and laughed a little as she realised that it was true. 'I'm free of them all. At last.'

Phryne drove away, humming. After a while she found that she was singing *Patience's* song: 'Rendering good for ill/Smiling at ev'ry frown.' Mr Gilbert had a satirical sense of humour, but it was hard to tell from the song whether he was exercising it or not. 'Everything for him, nothing at all for her!' Phryne bit her tongue and found that she was unable to avoid the conclusion which had been forming in her mind since she had seen the lovers. Lindsay and Phryne were not like that. They could never be. Striving to place Lindsay in the position of Tom had forced her into the position of Amelia, and Phryne would not fit into the frame. She could not do it. She could not marry Lindsay Herbert.

She pulled the big car over and stopped to press both hands to her breast, sick with sudden loss. Beautiful Lindsay, so smooth and deft and loving. A hallucinogenic flash showed her the long body lying on her green sheets, the red mouth which would never again open under hers. Never. If she did not marry Lindsay, he would go away to find his own Amelia, and she would never touch him again, never see that turn of the head when the hair fell just so over his eyes, never kiss the nape of his neck again.

Even so, she thought, putting the Hispano-Suiza into gear and resuming her journey. Even so, she could not marry Lindsay Herbert.

———

Phryne found a chair after dancing with a succession of rowers who had no use for tempo and no regard for her feet, and Lindsay brought her a glass of champagne and a water-ice. The moment could not be delayed any longer. She drew a deep breath. 'Thank you, Lindsay dear, and I won't marry you,' she said, gulping down the drink and beginning thirstily on the ice. Lindsay gasped.

'I'm sorry, my dear, and I love you very much, Lindsay, but I have thought about it and I can't do it.'

'But...' protested Lindsay. Phryne put down the dish and took his hand.

'You are lovely,' she said softly. 'Don't think that I don't love you.'

'I love you too, Phryne, old girl, listen—'

'I'll miss you,' she added, with tears springing to her eyes as she realised how much she would indeed miss him. 'But I can't, Lindsay dear, I really can't.'

'Phryne, please ...'

'This has been a hard decision to make, Lindsay, so don't argue with me. Please don't make this more difficult than it is.' He had come closer and now kissed her cheek. The caress, so familiar and delightful, went through Phryne like a knife. He was saying something which she did not hear. Then he pulled away from her and dashed across the room to the wedding presents. Returning, he solemnly handed her a silver fish slice.

'What's this for?' she asked, wondering if he had taken leave of his senses. He sat down next to her, seeming rather jaunty for a man whose matrimonial plans had just been dashed.

'I had to get a word in edgewise somehow. I know you won't marry me. That's all right, Phryne, if we can go on as we have been. Seeing that poor Smith girl has rather turned me off matrimony, don't you know.'

'Oh? Get me another glass of champagne, will you?' Phryne felt rather faint with relief.

'Yes.' He collected two glasses from a passing waiter. 'Anyway, I told the pater that if I married I could only marry you, because I loved you like billy-o, and he turned red and choked and went off the idea completely. Not such a good idea, marriage, eh? What do you think?'

Phryne looked at the bride and groom, enthroned at the high table. Amelia, glittering in Victorian garnets, was laughing as her spouse kissed her hand. Whatever explanation Tom had produced about that strange pause in the ceremony, he had clearly been believed, accepted, and forgiven. The lace was thrown back to reveal the pure line of the bride's head and the groom's profile, dark against the white wall behind. They were engrossed in each other, elevated with relief and wine, and as beautiful as they would ever be.

'Not for me, thank you,' said Phryne, and kissed Lindsay Herbert hard on the mouth.

Champagne
PUNCH

4 ripe pineapples
2 cups sugar
1 bottle white rum
2 cups lemon juice
1 cup grenadine
1 bottle brandy
1 cup cherry liqueur
8 bottles champagne

Marinate the peeled and cut-up fruit
with sugar and rum overnight. Add all the
ingredients, except the champagne,
and mix well. At the last moment,
pour in the champagne. Fizz!

Phryne's
FAVOURITE SHOES

The Vanishing of
JOCK McHALE'S HAT

God defend me from my friends
Proverb

Miss! Miss Phryne!' screamed Dot, belting up the stairs as though bears were after her. It was a measure of her social progress that six months had allowed her to call the Hon Miss Phryne Fisher 'Miss Phryne'. She rounded the corner to Phryne's boudoir and hurtled through the open door. Beyond, in the leaf-green bedroom, she knew that her mistress was at least partially awake, for she had ordered Greek coffee half an hour before.

Phryne rubbed both hands through her short black hair and yawned, dragged on a silk dressing gown, and hauled herself upright. Her current beautiful young man was sound asleep and she drew a corner of the quilt over his delectably smooth shoulder after kissing it lightly, and went out to see what the matter was.

Her maid Dot was usually a model of decorum and order.

'I almost hope that the house is afire, Dot, or you have some fairly devastating news, because otherwise I shall be miffed. What's up? What time is it?'

'Miss, the Archbishop's secretary is on the telephone. He wants to see you!'

'What, the secretary? And is that a reason to wake me?'

'No, Miss,' puffed Dot indignantly. 'The Archbishop! A professional matter, he says!'

'Well, it would hardly be a religious one,' murmured Phryne. 'I feel absolutely foul. I must have a bath and some breakfast. Say, ten o'clock?'

'Miss, it's eleven now!'

'Oh dear, I have overslept.' Phryne smiled reminiscently. 'Well, say twelve thirty, and ask him if he would like to stay to lunch. Then tell Mrs Butler if he is, and come back and find me some clothes. And aspirin.'

Dot sped off, and Phryne called after her, 'Which Archbishop?'

'Mine,' replied Dot and ran down the stairs.

Phryne mixed herself a fizzy powder, supposed to be sovereign for an overindulgence in alcohol, and made a mental note that cocktails concocted of gin, Cointreau and vermouth should be crossed off her list of potables. She ran a sumptuous bath, liberally laced with *Nuit d'Amour* salts, and soaked herself comprehensively, trying to remember how one addressed an archbishop. Was it my Lord Mannix? His Excellency Mannix? Dot would know.

———

It appeared that an archbishop was 'Your Grace'. Phryne, clothed in neat and modest dark blue against her wishes for a bright scarlet wool dress that Dot considered was much too short and tight, was sitting by the fire in her sea-green parlour, sipping coffee. The young man had gone, much to Phryne's regret, though she was sure that he would be back. The tea table was set and decorated, as His Grace could not stay for lunch. Dot, in a clean uniform, was fussing about the room until Phryne lost patience.

'Sit down, Dot, do! You shall stay while he is here, if you please. I can't imagine what a Prince of the Church wants with me! Did the secretary give you a clue?'

'No, Miss.' Under direct orders, Dot was constrained to sit down on the very edge of a chair. 'But it must be important.'

'Important to him, I suppose, or he would not be consulting me. I'd have thought an archbishop would have better methods of finding things out and enforcing his will than by employing a heathen like me! It must be a task, Dot, there must be something he wants found, or someone, that he can't do by respectable channels. Have you seen him before, Dot?'

'Me, Miss? When would I see an archbishop? But he's well thought of, Miss. The priest at St Mary's thinks he's wonderful.'

'And who am I to argue with the priest at St Mary's? That will be him, Dot. Take a deep breath and don't be so nervous. He's only a man, you know.'

Dot's protest at this blasphemy was stifled as Mr Butler showed two men into the parlour. One was tall and distinguished, not as old as Phryne expected, with sharp eyes and a bony, intelligent face. The other was middle-sized, dressed in threadbare best, with a ruined Celtic complexion and the pale blue eyes of a hero or fanatic. He raised those eyes to take in the parlour and Phryne herself with extreme dislike, then lowered them again. The Archbishop allowed Dot to kiss his ring without any haste or embarrassment, and blessed her. Phryne stood up to greet him and held out her hand, which he took and released with no discernible pressure.

'Your Grace,' said Phryne. 'Do sit down.'

'May I introduce my companion? This is Mr McHale, who is the coach of the Collingwood football team.'

Mr McHale muttered something and sat down gingerly. His hands seemed to grope for each other in a wringing gesture, as though he was used to holding something that was no longer there. He looked down in surprise and locked both hands together lest he betray himself. The Archbishop accepted tea. Mr McHale wanted nothing.

'Well, Your Grace, to what do I owe the honour of your company?'

'You undertake discreet enquiries, do you not, Miss Fisher?'

'I do.'

'I am faced with a problem which could be crucial to the success of Mr McHale's team, in which I am of course interested, but more importantly involves the credit of my church,' said the Archbishop, taking a sip and putting down his cup. 'And I cannot invoke any of the people who usually help me, because they may be involved. Will you help?'

'What can a sheila do?' snarled Jock McHale suddenly and with frightening hostility. 'What use is she?'

Phryne was filled with fury, but not a flicker showed on her face.

'Mr McHale, if you please!' said the Archbishop sternly. 'Please overlook this outburst, Miss Fisher, he is a rough fellow. It's like this. McHale, a devout man, came to the service in my cathedral on Sunday. After mass, he was kind enough to talk to some of my young men about football. At some juncture, while he was in my church, someone stole his hat.'

Both men looked at Phryne solemnly. She repressed a laugh. The Archbishop continued.

'I gather that you do not follow football? Obviously not, or you would have known about it. That hat has been Mr McHale's companion, I might say talisman, for many years. He feels lost without it, and there is an important game this week, against Richmond. Collingwood must win to make sure of being in the finals and their coach has lost his principal lucky token. It is vital that it be returned. Vital for Mr McHale and his team; vital also for me, because it was stolen in my church. You have less than a week, Miss Fisher, but I will double your usual fee, and I will give you all the help I can. I feel very strongly about this,' said the Archbishop,

and Phryne could see that he did and respected him for it. She also had something to prove to Jock McHale. Sheila, eh! Phryne poured herself some tea.

'I will try,' she said. 'Describe the hat.'

'Grey felt, though now it is a little greenish, battered, because of Mr McHale's habit of twisting it between his hands.'

Phryne stood up. 'I will come to early mass tomorrow, Your Grace, and have a look at the scene of the crime.'

The Archbishop winced a little, took his leave affably, and swept Jock McHale along in his wake. Phryne sat down to think, reached for the telephone, and called up her minions.

———

Bert and Cec were more at home in Phryne's parlour than her earlier visitors had been and knew a lot about football.

'Me, I don't follow the VFL, my team is Port—,' said Bert. He was short and stout, and Cec, his mate, was tall and thin; together there were very few things they could not do. Cec smiled his spaniel smile and accepted tea—black and syrupy, as he liked it.

'Well, you see, Miss,' said Cec, who did follow the VFL, it seemed, 'Collingwood won the last premiership—that is, '27— and there's every chance they'll win again this year. They've got a lot of money and some hard men supporting them, and they can buy players, and rough! Street fighting's nothing compared to a match against the Magpies. But everyone knows about Jock McHale's hat. You see him at every game, wringing it, bashing it—even wearing it, sometimes. It's an old battered grey thing, like a pot, with the brim turned up at the front. And someone's pinched it! The poor old bloke must be having heart failure.'

'He seemed to be very upset,' agreed Phryne. 'Why would anyone take it?'

'To put the mozz on the 'pies,' stated Bert, taking a cake. 'Good cakes these. No one could want the old relic.'

'Why take it in church?'

Bert and Cec looked at her. 'Why, Miss, I don't reckon he ever takes it off if he's not holding it. They say he sleeps in it. And seein' it, I could believe it. But every man takes his hat off—'

'In a church. Of course, how silly of me. Put the word out, Bert. I want that hat, and I'll pay for it. I don't want to know who took it. The Archbishop's probably excommunicating him now, divine vengeance should be enough for him.'

'All right, Miss. But a man with a real down on Collingwood might think it was worth it,' said Bert and took his leave.

———

The next morning Phryne, up and dressed at what she considered to be daybreak, sat at the back of St Patrick's and observed. It was a beautiful building, though a touch overdecorated for Phryne's taste, and the statue of the Sacred Heart near which she was seated gave her cold shudders. The pew which Jock McHale inhabited was in the middle, near the nave, and Phryne had already searched around it. Her veil scratched her face, the Latin service was incomprehensible, and she dared not yawn. There were no corners in this church for a hat-stealer to hide; he would have had to be in the congregation.

The service ended. '*Ite, missa est,*' announced the priest, and the people started to shuffle out. Phryne put back her veil and walked boldly up to the priest, who was emerging from his robing room.

'Good morning, Father. I'm Phryne Fisher, and the Archbishop has given me leave to speak to you.'

'Ah yes,' said the young man, blushing. 'Miss Fisher. Nice to meet you.' He pumped her hand with vigour; a strong young man.

'You were celebrating mass last Sunday, were you not?'

'Yes. A terrible thing. The Archbishop is furious.'

'Did you notice anything that might help? I gather that you know what has happened.'

'Oh yes, His Grace told us.'

'Us?'

'Me and the altar boys, and the seminarians. Mr McHale was talking to them about football.'

'Where?'

'In the forecourt.'

'You were there?'

'Yes, Miss Fisher.'

'Did Mr McHale have his hat then?'

The young man thought deeply, scratching his head. Then he blushed again.

'No! He didn't! It's such a horrible old hat, Miss Fisher, so battered, that he often folds it up and shoves it in his pocket. No, he didn't have it in the forecourt. Oh, I am glad!'

'Why should that make you glad?'

'It means that it went missing in the church. The boys and the students couldn't have taken it.'

'But that means the thief was in the church itself, and the theft took place during the service!'

The fresh face blanched. This was a transparent young man. 'Oh, Lord, so it does.'

'Never mind. Now, come and show me how your service works. What's your name, by the way?'

'Father Kelly. The Archbishop told me to help you all I could, Miss Fisher.'

'Now, you are a member of the congregation, coming in from outside. Where do you take off your hat?'

'At the door, Miss Fisher.'

Father Kelly wondered that so much intelligence and drive were contained in this small, fashionable, Dutch-doll woman. Her green eyes were as bright as pins.

'You sit down.'

Father Kelly murmured his way through the mass, sitting down, kneeling, and rising in the right places. It had by now dawned upon him that Miss Fisher was not a daughter of the Holy Church.

'Does anyone pass along the aisle while the service is going on?'

'Yes, of course. I mean, yes. The communicants go up to the altar and come back, and the collection is taken.'

'By whom?'

'Members of the congregation, usually. Last Sunday there were four, all respectable men—Mr Davis, Mr McLaren, Mr O'Reilly, and Mr Flynn.'

'What's this?' asked Phryne, and dived for a scrap of paper poking out from under the hassock. It was torn from a larger sheet, and in stern script bore the words 'Thou shalt have no other Gods before me'. Father Kelly examined it.

'Out of one of the schoolbooks,' he said dismissively. Phryne folded the paper and obtained the address of the respectable member of the congregation who had borne the plate to Mr McHale.

———

Mr Flynn was not at home. The bedraggled maid who answered the door said he was at his work and directed her to the office of John Playford and Sons, Religious Publishers, where her master worked as a clerk. It was still too early in the morning for the man to have lunch, so Phryne telephoned her own house to see if there were any messages.

'Two, Miss Fisher,' said Mr Butler's magisterial voice. 'One from Mr Bert, who was calling from the Royal Melbourne Hospital. He said that neither he nor Mr Cec was much hurt, and he would call on you at two this afternoon. The other from an unknown person, who attempted to be threatening. I informed him that his conversation would be reported to Detective Inspector Robinson and he rang off. I gather that the person was concerned for his football team and seemed to think that you were a threat to it.'

'What has happened to Bert and Cec?'

'A small contretemps, Mr Bert says, Miss Fisher.'

'I knew I shouldn't have got involved with religion,' muttered Phryne darkly. 'Call the Archbishop's secretary, Mr Butler, and tell him of the threat. I think I know who made it, and I will be surprised if I get another. And disappointed. I'll be back by two. If I'm held up, ask Bert and Cec to wait.'

She rang off, seething. It was known that organised crime had something to do with this football game—thousands of pounds were wagered on it every week down every back lane in Melbourne. Phryne was fairly sure that she knew where the hat was, if it was still in existence, and had half a mind to retrieve it and burn it herself. The adulation that men gave to football was quite beyond Phryne. It seemed to equal and surpass the delight she herself took in food, sleep, intellectual puzzles, clothes, and beautiful young men. Odd. But she had Jock McHale to astound, and that was not a revenge to be passed up lightly.

She drank real coffee in a bohemian haunt in Russell Street until it was time to go and beard Mr Flynn.

The boy at the reception desk of John Playford and Sons gave her a fast and impudent once-over before he freed his mouth from a corned beef sandwich and called into an inner office, 'Mr Flynn! Someone to see you!'

A gaunt and elderly man stalked out to the desk.

He took in Phryne's figure, hat, silk stockings and smile, and stepped back half a pace.

'Why, Uncle, don't you recognise me?' she cried, taking him by the arm. 'I have come to take you to lunch because I'm only up in the city for the day. Come along, we'll be late.'

Mr Flynn, utterly astounded, allowed himself to be led to the front door. The office boy ran after him with his hat, which he took and put on, still staring.

'There's a tea shop not far from here,' said Phryne brightly. 'Come along, and there won't be a fuss.'

Mr Flynn was seated and supplied with tea before he found his voice.

'Young woman, who are you, and what do you want with me?'

'I'm Phryne Fisher, and I want Jock McHale's hat. I know you pinched it. I know how, too, and when. Do you think it was fair to the Church to commit such an offence during the service? But I don't want to get you into trouble. I just want the hat, then it can all be forgotten.'

Pale blue fanatic's eyes stared into hers.

'No.'

'What do you mean, no?'

'I will not give it to you.'

'Aha. So you stole it?'

'I took it, yes.'

'While the poor man was rummaging for a penny to put in the plate, and you were leaning over him?'

'Yes. You are very astute,' he said with distaste. 'Very clever, Miss—Fisher, was it?'

'Miss Fisher is me. Why did you take it?'

'Because that man has created in that miserable scrap of felt one of the false idols, like the Golden Calf. He could have a holy medal of a saint's image, with all of a saint's power, but he chooses to invest his faith in a hat! Such a thing is blasphemous. It was an affront to the altar to bring it into the church. I have watched him for years, at matches, wringing that hat, fondling it, even crying into it. It was indecent.'

'Granted that it was indecent, have you the right to judge other men's sins? Has Jock McHale no free will? Can he not be allowed for his salvation to turn away from the hat, and have you not, by stealing it, removed every chance of such renunciation from him? Is that just?'

Mr Flynn gulped some tea. Phryne tasted hers; it was as hot as molten metal. It seemed Mr Flynn had a mouth of pure leather, to go with his heart and his religious convictions.

'I...do not know.'

'And another thing. Your own Archbishop has asked me to find this...this artifact. Don't you believe in the Prince of your own Church? If the Archbishop doesn't see anything wrong with it, how should you?'

'The Archbishop!' gasped Mr Flynn, greying around the mouth. 'Lord help me! How shall I amend my sin?'

'Simple. You give me the hat and I'll return it. Then you go to confession and purge your soul.'

Mr Flynn reached into his coat pocket and laid on the tea-table a flattened bundle of greyish felt. The brim was bent out of shape. They both stared at it.

'Thank you, Mr Flynn,' said Phryne, stuffing the relic into her handbag. 'Don't worry. I'll fix it.'

She rose, paid the bill and left. Mr Flynn stared into his tea and began to cry.

———

Phryne arrived home in a high state of excitement to find her parlour inhabited by Bert, Cec, and Dot. Bert had a black eye and Cec a bandaged hand.

'What happened to you two?' demanded Phryne, tossing her handbag aside and shedding her coat.

Bert grinned. 'We went out to put the word about, and met a few of the Collingwood men. We had a few words and there was a bit of a barney, but you shoulda seen them. There's no sign of the hat, though, Miss. They was searchin' for it too, and we had a word about it once we stopped belting each other. They ain't found a trace of it, and neither have we.'

'Ah,' said Phryne with deep satisfaction. 'But I have. I can't say it suits me, though,' and she straightened out and donned Jock McHale's hat, grinning up at them from under the sad, drooping brim.

———

'But who took it?' asked the Archbishop, marvelling as Jock McHale turned the hat around in his hands suspiciously, as if it might have been an impostor.

'Ah well, one of your congregation who will shortly be confessing to one of your priests. His motives were odd, and

I'm not going to discuss them. But I think that you are satisfied with the outcome?'

The Archbishop smiled. 'Most impressive, Miss Fisher. Name your fee.'

'Twenty pounds,' said Phryne promptly. 'Damages for two of my men, who were a little battered in your service.'

'I trust that you suffered no more...er...harassment, Miss Fisher? I was very concerned to hear of the telephone call.'

'No, I haven't heard a peep out of whoever it was. Football produces strange passions.'

'I trust that your agents were not seriously hurt?'

'Nothing that ten quid apiece won't cure.'

'But your fee, Miss Fisher?'

'I would not think of taking one, Your Grace. I look on it as sixpences tinkling into my heavenly money box.'

Phryne got up to leave. Jock McHale jammed the defeated grey hat onto his bullet head and shook her hand.

'Thanks,' he muttered. 'You're a very clever sheila.'

Phryne took the compliment as it was meant. After all, she *was* a very clever sheila.

KERRY GREENWOOD

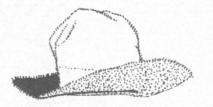

Tea CAKE

2 tbsp butter
½ cup caster sugar
1 egg
1½ cups self-raising flour
4 tbsp milk
A pinch of salt

Topping

2 tbsp melted butter
1 tbsp cinnamon
1 tbsp caster sugar

Cream the butter and sugar. Gradually add
the egg to the creamed mixture, then add
the flour and milk alternately, half at a time,
and beat well. Place mixture in a greased
sandwich tin and bake for 20–25 minutes.
Turn cake out onto a cake cooler while warm
and brush with topping.

Puttin' On
THE RITZ

Or where the gorgeous east with richest hand
Showers on her Kings barbaric pearl and gold
John Milton, *Paradise Lost,* Book 2.1

Phryne Fisher removed herself with difficulty from the Austin's front seat. The makers had obviously decided that cars were to be worn tight about the hips that year. The road was quite busy, so she allowed her escort, William Barlow, to take her hand. Fully three cars passed while they waited on the curb. Light rain drifted down, rendering the streets slick and shiny.

Situated next to the Princess Margaret Club, the Ritz was an unobtrusive two storey building entered through a wine cellar. Phryne negotiated the steps without difficulty and listened with interest to the barrels gurgling. An ambrosial scent overwhelmed them as they came up into the restaurant to be greeted by Antoine, the *maître d'hôtel.*

KERRY GREENWOOD

Antoine was as perfect, Phryne thought, as the icing sugar groom on a wedding cake. He was, unusually for Melbourne, genuinely French, from Lorraine.

'M'sieur Barlow, 'ow delightful. I 'ave your reservation. Madame,' he added, his eyes widening a flattering half-inch at the sight of Phryne.

Phryne took this as her due. She was arrayed in a claret coloured evening dress by Poitou, tunic-cut, loose and gorgeous. It had golden and black grapes embroidered around the hem and it had cost her, if not a king's, at least a crown prince's ransom. With it she wore gold slippers and a very fetching cap of the same purple as the dress, decorated with a bunch of golden grapes. She was pleasantly conscious of being quite, quite stunning.

'If you will be seated,' suggested Antoine. 'Here we 'ave a nice table. The menu I shall bring directly.' He snapped his fingers and another dinner-jacketed worthy floated towards him. ''ere is the wine steward.'

William and Phryne sat down at a table by the wall, where the lights were subdued and it was possible to converse. The wine steward approached with what looked like Volume I of the wine list and William said hurriedly, 'You order the wine, Phryne, there's a good fellow. I don't know anything about it and this chap always makes me feel like a squib.'

Phryne smiled at the wine steward, waving away his list. 'I want a bottle of burgundy, the '08 if you still have some. Then a bottle of Veuve Cliquot, the '23, with dessert. We will discuss liqueurs later.'

The wine steward, crushed, wrote this on his little pad and went away.

'Splendid.' William leaned back in his chair. 'Thank you so much.'

He was a tall and rather rumpled young man, with thick curly chestnut hair which would not stay back despite liberal applications of Floris tonic. He had earnest brown eyes like a Jersey cow. (Phryne had once spent a week on Jersey and eaten herself sick on cream. They were, however, quite her favourite cows.)

William Barlow was also a lawyer, working with the small firm which employed her friend Jilly. The Barlow family, Phryne recalled, included two brothers, both lawyers—William and his brother John. William was affable and generous. Phryne had only met John once and had been unfavourably impressed by his only topic of conversation, which was money. Phryne did not find money, per se, at all interesting.

With Herbert, the father of the Barlows, she was all too familiar. He had been pursuing her relentlessly since her arrival in Australia. The spectacle of a red-faced, overfed and arrogant industrialist going down on one knee had not amused her at all, and she had instructed her staff that she was never to be at home to Mr Barlow Senior.

'For entrée?' asked Antoine's voice, snapping her out of her reverie. 'Madame would like *hors d'oeuvres variés*? Quiche Lorraine? Perhaps a terrine?'

'Quiche Lorraine,' said William. 'That's that sort of egg and bacon pie thing? Yes. I'll have that.'

Antoine was a professional *maître d'hôtel*, so he did not respond visibly to this graceless description of the chef's masterpiece, but he blinked and under his breath said something actionable in French. Phryne intervened before he combusted.

'I would like the terrine, please,' she said sweetly. 'Is it *de maison*?'

'No, Madame, it is *canard à l'orange*.'

'*Bon*,' said Phryne. She was hungry and wanted something solid to eat while William told her whatever it was that he had brought her here to learn.

She sipped her glass of burgundy and said, 'Will, old thing, I am enjoying myself and all that, but what do you want to tell me? Can we get it over with, so that we can devote all of our attention to the food?'

'Oh well, yes, of course. But it's not a nice tale, Phryne. It's like this. You know that my mama died ten years ago.'

'Yes. I'm sorry.'

'She wasn't,' said Will frankly. 'She was sick of being in pain, poor old girl, and it came as a relief to all of us. But since then my papa has been...er... misbehaving himself.'

'Yes,' agreed Phryne gently.

'And—the thing is—I don't know—'

'Have some more wine, draw a deep breath and tell me from the beginning.'

The young man did as instructed and said clearly, 'He's lost Mama's pearls.'

At this inauspicious moment, their waiter arrived with their entrées.

Phryne watched her companion tuck into the quiche as though he was starving while she daintily but thoroughly demolished the terrine, which was remarkable.

'The pearls were left to me,' William continued,

dusting crumbs off his ear. 'I was going to sell them to set up a Poor Persons' Defence Fund with Jilly. You know how the defendants *in forma pauperis* just get a court appointed barrister, sometimes not the best or the most experienced. Jilly feels that this bears particularly heavily on women. They seldom have any money behind them and no support, because they've usually killed their husband or their kids. I agree with her—in fact, we were thinking of setting up a partnership. She's a cracking good solicitor, Jilly is, and she's right when she says that the firm isn't giving her a chance at the big cases. She says the closest she came to a murder trial was foiled when you went and found the real murderer, Phryne.'

Phryne laughed. 'That is true, she was very cross with me. Will, this sounds like a good idea. Do you want me to supply some funds? A loan, perhaps?'

'No, no, Phryne, not at all.' The young man made a sweeping negative gesture, and Phryne removed his glass of wine from its path. 'No, I didn't ask you here for that, not at all.'

'All right, Will, you have adequately demonstrated that you don't want money from me. Here, take your glass back and tell me what you do want in words, preferably, of one syllable, there's a dear!'

Will gulped some wine and spluttered, 'I want you to find the pearls and get them back.'

'Find?' Phryne scented an unusual use of the word. 'Don't you know where they are?'

'Well...yes. I mean, I think I do. My papa is—well, you know what Papa is like. He'll be dining here tonight, I think. He usually does on a Wednesday. With Mrs Priscilla Veale.'

'Priscilla Veale?' Phryne coughed on a laugh.

'Yes, his...er...friend.'

'English really is an amazing language,' commented Phryne. 'What sort of friend, Will? Do you mean a lover?'

The young man blushed. 'Yes, I think so. He wants to marry her. She's a seamstress, so all the family is up in arms. They say she's a designing hussy. But Papa is not precisely a catch, either. Look, here they come. That's Mrs Veale.'

A gaudy woman fluttered in, accompanied by the red-faced Mr Barlow. Antoine seated them considerately out of the public eye, near the wall, three tables away from Phryne and her companion.

'Well,' said Phryne, considering Mrs Veale. She wore an extravagant gown of blue and green veined like a butterfly's wings, and was suspiciously blonde for her years, with an appliquéd chocolate box prettiness. If not mutton dressed as lamb she was definitely shin of ox dressed as Veale. Nonetheless, she was expensive. Her corset alone must have required ten yards of industrial quality elastic, and pearls gleamed at her neck. The face that Phryne caught sight of as Mrs Veale responded to Antoine's flattery was overly made-up and powdered to the pallor of death.

'Gosh, Phryne, she's wearing them!' said Will despondently. 'If my papa has actually given her the pearls, there isn't a chance that she'll hand them over.'

'Can't you ask your father for the money instead?' Phryne suggested.

'I have but he just temporises. John's all right. He snaffled the ruby and diamond set which Mama left for him as soon as she died—took it out of the safe. I don't think Papa has much remaining money these days. He has been flinging it about rather.'

'That is not so good. Have you tried explaining to the lady that they were your mother's pearls and asking her whether she'll give them back to you?'

'No, of course I haven't!' The young man seemed shocked. 'And I really can't sue her for them. That would be washing the dirty family linen in public with a vengeance. I'm afraid that it's all up with our scheme for the Poor Persons, Phryne, unless you can think of something.'

'I still consider there's no harm in asking,' Phryne cautioned, and the young man went purple with embarassment.

'I couldn't,' he confessed.

'Well then, we'll work out some sort of plan. Here comes Antoine. What do you want for a main course?'

'I don't know,' said William glumly. 'You order.'

'Madame?' Antoine had overheard the last comment. 'What would please you? The *boeuf à la bourguignonne* is excellent and *le chef* 'as made a truly delicious *filet en cochonailles*. Or perhaps you would prefer *tournedos*? We 'ave zem *à la Béarnaise*, *à Rossini*, or *à la Beauharnais*.'

'*Le filet*,' decided Phryne. '*Avec pommes de terre à la lyonnaise et salade verte*—vinaigrette. *Merci*, Antoine. There, my dear, this will be delicious, I promise. What is your papa ordering?'

A loud voice could be heard demanding a decent plate of brown Windsor soup and a cut off the joint. Antoine winced.

'Oh dear,' murmured Phryne. 'A cut off the joint, when he could be ordering *filet en cochonailles*. I'm afraid that your papa is a truly wicked man.'

When their main courses had arrived Phryne bit into the delicate flesh of the *filet* and listened to Mr Barlow make an idiot of himself. She was profoundly glad that she was not his companion. It seemed to be getting to Mrs Priscilla Veale, too.

'Do sit down,' she said shrilly, pulling at his coat-tails. 'Herbie! Everyone's looking.'

'I want roast beef,' demanded Mr Barlow. 'And I can pay for it too.'

'A chic boulevardier the old pater isn't, is he?' murmured his son. 'By Jove, Phryne, I think that this is the best beef I've ever tasted.'

'Indeed it is.'

They ate in silence, while Mr Barlow was placated with the offer of *roti de boeuf* and Mrs Veale ordered *boeuf en daube*. Phryne remembered idly that this dish was made with red wine. It gave her an idea.

'Antoine, that was absolutely superb,' William Barlow was enthusing to the *maître d'hôtel*. 'I never tasted anything like it.'

'I will convey your compliments to ze chef, m'sieur. Some dessert, perhaps?'

'In a moment. I must go over and say hello to my father.'

Antoine expressed, verbally

and through his stance and his raised eyebrow, how very surprised he was to find that such an appreciative young man— accompanied moreover by such a *soignée* woman—was related in any way to the *cochon noir* (or black pig) currently occupying the nearby table. He murmured, 'As you wish,' and left William to finish his lyonnaise potatoes.

Phryne rose as Mrs Priscilla Veale passed her on the way to the ladies', while William pushed his plate aside and went to exchange hearty inconsequentialities with his father.

'You're looking well, Father.'

'Feeling well, too, my boy. Amazing what a good effect a woman's company has on a man.'

William winced. He endured a powerful handshake and then saw with relief that Phryne had returned, after a brief discussion with Antoine. He retreated to his own table, where Miss Fisher appeared to be elated.

'I think that it is time for the champagne,' said Phryne. 'Yes, here it comes—my favourite vintage. Apart from that, Antoine, *mon brave*, just some cheese, camembert perhaps, with fruit. And coffee of course—*café noir*, if you please.'

At that moment, a shriek came from the other table. Antoine muttered, 'Zis is too much!' and all the diners turned to attend to the fuss.

Mrs Veale was holding in her hand a string, hook and clasp. 'My pearls! They must have fallen off into the stew!' she cried.

'*Vache Espagnol*,' Antoine muttered. 'Zat is not stew. Zat is *boeuf en daube*.'

Phryne and William hurried over to Mr Barlow's table.

'Well, well, that was an expensive dish,' commented Phryne.

'The *daube*, it contains much wine,' observed Antoine, for the benefit of all the bystanders. 'And pearls, zey are dissolved by wine. Zere was Cleopatra, madame—she wished to give Caesar, 'er lover, ze most expensive drink in ze world. She dropped 'er earring, which contained a priceless pearl, into ze glass and pouf! It was gone.'

'You're right,' agreed Phryne. 'Jilly told me about some sailor clients of hers who were hiding smuggled pearls. There was no evidence against them because they had shoved the loose pearls into a bottle of vinegar and they were dissolved away. Jilly said that the police were quite cross about it, though not as cross as the smugglers at losing their precious cargo. I'm afraid your necklace is gone, Mrs Veale.'

'I told you not to eat that Frenchified stuff,' snapped Mr Barlow.

'Now, Herbie, don't fuss. You really ought to learn some manners,' said Mrs Veale sternly. 'Heaven knows, you're old enough. You gave them pearls to me and I lost them—well, what's to fuss about? I just got a shock when I found the string in my plate—thought it was a mouse's tail. You sit down and have some more of that red plonk and don't worry about it.'

Mr Barlow, considerably amazed, did as ordered. Antoine stood rooted to the spot with horror at the idea of anyone's expecting to find mice in his *boeuf en daube*. Meanwhile

Phryne steered William back to their table. She raised her glass to the other woman and was answered with a brief nod of the head.

The camembert arrived, accompanied by little water biscuits, and Phryne nibbled. Her escort still looked dazed.

'What happened?' he asked. 'I say, this is top-hole cheese.'

'You heard her. Her pearls fell into the wine of the *daube* and dissolved,' said Phryne artlessly.

William was not a lawyer with a large criminal practice for nothing. He knew that tone of voice.

'Phryne, what did you do?'

'I'll tell you in a moment. They're leaving.'

Mr Barlow, shepherded by Mrs Veale, was collecting his coat and hat. The blonde woman gave him a brisk pat, said, 'Off we go, dearie,' and left the Ritz, pink-faced with righteousness and fluttering with butterfly wings.

'Well,' said Phryne. 'Hold out your hands, William.'

Into his cupped palms she poured thirty-five perfectly matched pearls.

'I told you that you only had to ask her,' she said triumphantly. 'I spoke to her when we were in the ladies'. We had to find a way of doing this without arousing your sainted papa's cupidity. Antoine went along with the joke—he is an old friend of mine. I think she'll make a rather good mama, William.'

'You do?' said the flabbergasted solicitor.

'And I think the pearls'll make a rather nice contribution to the Poor Persons' Defence Fund. Your father really is a pig, as Antoine said, which gives a new twist to the old proverb. But we can still use it.'

'Phryne! Explain!'

'It's the first time,' said that young woman ruminatively, 'that I've ever stolen the pearls from the swine.'

Boeuf EN DAUBE

1¼ lb lean beef
1 tbsp flour
2 onions, sliced
1 clove garlic, crushed
2 slices bacon, diced
1 *bouquet garni* or a small bunch containing
one sprig each of thyme, chervil and parsley
2 zucchini, sliced
1 green pepper, sliced and deseeded
1 tbsp of olive oil
1 finger-sized bit of orange peel
½ lb stoned black Kalamata olives
2 cups or 1 bottle of red wine
A pinch of salt
Freshly ground black pepper

Dice the meat and coat it with flour. Fry the onions and
garlic. Throw in the meat and cook gently until it is browned.
Pour the wine and all the other ingredients into the pan, and
stir gently over low heat until it has all combined and begins
to look silky. If it looks a bit dry, pour in another 2 cups of
water, and if it still absorbs liquid add some more wine.
Put this in a very slow oven for about three hours, or
longer if your guests are always late. This peasant dish
is from the south of France.

The Body
IN THE LIBRARY

They say there is divinity in odd numbers,
either in nativity, chance or death.
William Shakespeare, *The Merry Wives of Windsor,* 5.1.3

'Bloody hell!' said Detective Inspector Jack Robinson, who never swore, and certainly not in the presence of ladies. There were two ladies present. One dead, and one alive.

'Quite,' agreed Phryne Fisher, absently.

The body was sprawled on the hearthrug. She was very dead. Her face was congested and her red dress had been ripped to rags. She was an incongruous addition to the tasteful atmosphere of the library of Robert Sanderson, MP, and Phryne caught her errant mind commenting that the red dress clashed quite frightfully with the tiled Dutch-blue hearth, whereas the corpse's cyanosed skin matched. She pulled herself together.

Jack Robinson said, 'She's been dead for hours. Rigor's set in. Could have been here all day. Room's been closed while the chimneys were swept. How she got here's another matter.'

'Couldn't have walked,' said Phryne, examining a small bare foot. 'Her feet are clean. And soft. She didn't spend all summer running around with no shoes on, and you haven't found any shoes. What does the doctor say?'

'Indeterminate cause of death,' groaned Robinson. 'Recent sexual activity. There's going to be a scandal, you know. That's why I asked you in.'

'I had been wondering.' Phryne saw with a pang that the dead girl had a corn plaster on one toe.

'Mr Sanderson is trying to pass a Private Member's Bill to regulate brothels—you know, to legalise prostitution. I think it's a good idea—you know how the girls are exploited by the pimps—but he's got a lot of enemies.'

'Who, particularly?'

'Worst one—well, the loudest one—is the Reverend Josiah Blackroot. You've probably read one of his pamphlets. The wages of sin is death, he reckons.'

'So is the salary of virtue,' murmured Phryne. 'And at least the wicked have a good time.'

'Yair, well, the nicest thing that the Rev has called Mr Sanderson is a whoremonger. And what he could do with a dead prostitute on the hearthrug—well, you can imagine.'

'Easily. That's strange,' commented Phryne. 'Look at this, Jack.'

'Glass bracelet,' said Robinson, examining it.

'Odd,' said Phryne, sitting back on her heels. 'This dress

would be expensive at seventeen and six. It's cheap art silk and ready-made. Such as remains of her underwear is fine Chinese washing silk with hand embroidery and the remnants of Valenciennes lace edging. Last time I priced it, it was three guineas an inch. On that hand is a brass wedding ring. On this wrist is a diamond bracelet with some really very nice stones. She doesn't match, Jack. It's mostly safe to assume that underwear expresses the real woman. Perhaps she's a lady's maid who has robbed her mistress's underwear drawer or a lady of light repute with a very rich protector. So what is she doing wearing a shop-bought dress and a brass ring?'

'Dunno. She ain't been doing any hard work,' said Robinson, examining the fingers. 'No pinpricks, no callouses.'

'Not a lady's maid, then. About twenty-five,' said Phryne, trying to mentally reduce the swollen contours of the face. 'Any ideas?'

'She's probably called Alice. This was stuck on her back.' He handed over a card which said 'For a good time call Alice MW 421'. 'Otherwise she's just a well-nourished female with blonde hair.'

'It is blonde, too,' mused Phryne, rubbing a tress between her fingers. 'I mean, she was born blonde, not decided to be

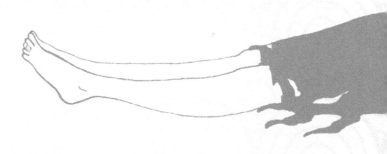

blonde. This hair is gritty. Fetch me that *Table Talk*, will you, Jack dear?'

Phryne combed out the hair over the open magazine, clamping down firmly on her inexplicable tendency to shudder. 'Well, we know how she got here. Look at this. It's coal dust. The sweep brought her in in a sack. There's a smear on her shoulder, too, and on her knees. That gives us the time. Now, we need a name—I don't believe in Alice.'

'No handbag,' said Jack Robinson gloomily. 'No tags in the clothes. You stay here, and I'll see about arresting that sweep. He might be able to tell us more.'

Phryne shook the coal dust out of *Table Talk* and found that the issue contained an interview with the Reverend Blackroot. A good-looking man. 'REPENT!' screamed the banner headline. Phryne kept reading, addressing the dead girl.

'Did you repent at last, then?' she asked, skimming down the page. 'Did someone object to your repentance? And did the Rev Josiah Blackroot promise you heaven? That is not an unusual male promise, though it seldom comes off...by God,' said Phryne, flattening the magazine under the lamp and staring at the picture and then at the corpse. 'By God, Jane Trellis-Smythe, how did you come to this?' Phryne looked at the picture. Then she looked at the sweep's card again. Then she stared into space for some minutes, biting her lip.

Phryne shoved the picture at Robinson when he returned from instructing his sergeant. He read, '"Mrs Trellis-Smythe is active in Church work and frequently helps the Reverend at his home for fallen women." That's her all right. But what's she doing here?'

'Not much. Tell me, Jack, has she been reported missing?'

'No. Her hubby's away in Japan, I think. I know because he's a friend of the Commissioner. Oh Lord, this gets worse and worse!'

'It isn't a lot of fun for Mrs Trellis-Smythe, either,' Phryne reminded him tartly. 'I have a story to tell you, Jack dear. Are you sitting comfortably? Then I'll begin. A rather foolish, bored young woman whose husband is often away takes up with a Reverend who is doing Good Works amongst the fallen women. So exciting for a nice, well-brought-up girl. Then matters advance. She may be the Rev's lover. So deliciously wicked.'

'So he kills her when she threatens to tell all to her husband?'

'Not so simple. Have you ever wondered about that home for fallen women? Here it says that there is a terrible lot of recidivism there. Did it occur to you, as it did to Mrs Trellis-Smythe, that—'

'You don't mean that the Rev is running a brothel?'

'What could be a better cover than a home for fallen women? He can even keep them all together. Anyone listening to the women would have worked it out. So when poor silly Mrs Trellis-Smythe wondered what it would be like to be a fallen woman, she put on the dress and the brass ring. Then—what? Perhaps she was smothered with the skirts of that dress, perhaps she died of a heart attack or shock. And the sweep brought her here to embarrass Mr Sanderson and put paid to all that nonsense about legal brothels. It would ruin the Rev's business.'

'So it would. But how did you know?'

'This article has his telephone number,' said Phryne. 'I found this card on the hall stand, and of course we found this stuck to her back.'

'Chimneys swept,' Jack Robinson read, and put down the first card. 'The Rev Blackroot's Home for Fallen Women, and "For a good time ring Alice" ...MW 421. They're all MW 421.'

'It was safe enough,' commented Phryne. 'The various clients would never speak to each other. They simply wouldn't know what to say.'

'Neither do I,' said Jack Robinson.

WHAT'S in *Phryne's* BAG?

The Miracle *of* ST MUNGO

Venus, wounded, rightly takes up arms gives dart for dart to the aggressor and makes him suffer in his turn the hurt he has caused.
Ovid, *The Art of Love*, Book 2

Phryne Fisher sipped. The cocktail might well be the hit of 1928. A dazzle of golden light from the Derwent shone on a shaker of gin and an elaborate ashtray-and-cigarette-box full of Balkan Sobranies.

'All right, Lucy dear,' said Phryne evenly, sitting down on her bed. 'What do you want me to do?'

'Phryne!' protested Lucy, Lady Wessex. 'The pleasure of your company...'

'Out with it, old thing,' said Phryne.

'Thank you for coming,' Lucy began, biting a thumbnail. 'I have got into a... difficulty. Everyone says you're horribly clever. It seemed like providence when

I heard you'd flown down here. And it's James, you see, I do love him, and he'd never understand, he's so upright and Scottish and...'

'A young man?' asked Phryne, blowing a smoke ring into the light.

'How did you guess? I really thought he loved me. It was madness, madness, and now he's got my locket.'

'Tell him to give it back.'

'You don't understand, he took it when we were...when I was in his rooms in Montpellier Retreat, and now he wants a hundred pounds, Phryne, and I can't ask James.'

'And if you don't pay?'

'He'll give James the locket, and it has a picture in it, of both of us together.'

'That could be explained,' commented Phryne.

Lucy wailed and tore her hair, an act which Phryne had never actually seen before. 'But it's got a quotation from Ovid on the back!'

'Oh,' said Phryne. Ovid was known for his carnal poetry.

'I tried selling some jewellery. I took that ugly great tiara into Jamieson's and they told me it was paste! Great-Grandmamma must have had it made. She was rather extravagant.'

Phryne examined the portrait on the wall. A face very similar to Lucy's: milk-and-roses, heart-shaped, dimpled, and blonde curls which covered a head entirely free, as far as Phryne could tell, of brains.

'I could lend you the money, but that's encouraging a blackmailer. What have you told James about the locket?'

'I said it fell overboard when I was out in the yacht. He was cross—the locket was my wedding present and it's been in his family since they came out from Glasgow.'

'Glasgow, eh? That could account for that alarming saint I saw on the wall downstairs, next to the flag of St Andrew and over the crossed claymores.'

'That's St Mungo, patron saint of Glasgow. He's rather a dear. St Mungo found a lady walking by the river, weeping, because her husband had found out that she had given her marriage ring to her lover. The husband killed the lover and threw the ring into the river, then ordered his wife to present herself, wearing the ring, that night at dinner or he'd kill her as well. He knew she couldn't do that. St Mungo called up a salmon and took the ring out of its mouth and gave it back to the lady. Nice miracles. He resurrected a sparrow, too. Oh, Phryne, what am I to do?'

Lucy sobbed. Phryne tugged on one golden curl.

'Pull yourself together, Lucy. Tell me about this young man.'

'His name's Percy Fellowes. He's a medical student. I met him when my brother brought his friends home. James quite approved of them, though they did sit up all night playing cards and the housekeeper complained about the mess. Then I met him crossing Arthur's circle, and then...somehow I went home with him. I don't know how it happened! For three months I was so happy. Then he grew cross and wanted me to leave my husband, and I'd never leave my dear old James, and then one morning, I got a note demanding money.'

'I've got an idea,' said Phryne. 'Leave it to me. Now, let's dress for dinner. What would be suitable for Hobart, Lucy?'

'Something with more back in it than that,' said Lucy, examining dresses. 'And more front than that. This one, Phryne.'

It will go beautifully with all that polished wood and starched linen.'

Phryne donned the scarlet tunic and watched as her maid threaded a scarlet panache into her perfectly straight, perfectly black hair. A pale, oval face, with penetrating green eyes, a firm mouth, a decided chin, and eyebrows like thin black wings. She blew herself a slightly tipsy kiss and went down to dinner.

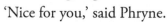

She retreated several hours later, exhausted by trying to make conversation over a crowd of Gay Young Things who reminded her that she was no longer as Gay or Young as she had once been. Phryne's partner had been an elderly and partially deaf bishop which had not made the task easier. But the food had been excellent. Phryne had eaten sole with lemon, roast beef with potatoes, carrots, Yorkshire pudding and gravy, raspberries and clotted cream, and a savoury of cheese and biscuits. With the meal she had drunk burgundy (imported, French) and after it a positively ancient port (laid down for Sir James when he was born by his wistful, gout afflicted father).

A Gay Young Thing caught at her scarlet hem as she mounted the stairs.

'I say, pretty lady, don't desert us! We're going to dance!'

'Nice for you,' said Phryne.

'Dance with me?' he pleaded.

'Not even if you dance like a dervish, my dear,' she said gently, for he was very good-looking and

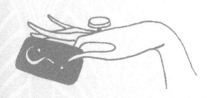

excessively young. 'But I'll sit with you for a moment,' she conceded, sinking down onto a carpeted step. 'If you fetch me an ashtray and a glass of water, I'll talk to you for a while.'

The young man vanished with a whirring noise and returned with a smoker's stand and a tray on which reposed two glasses and a jug of iced water.

'You,' Phryne told him, allowing him to light her gasper, 'will go far—possibly too far. I'm Phryne Fisher. What's your name?'

'Gerald. I'm Lucy's brother. Gosh, are you the famous Miss Fisher? The detective? You're not at all what I thought. I thought you'd be...'

'Yes?' Phryne leaned back.

'Not like you are,' he said clumsily. 'I mean, beautiful, poised, like a bird, an exotic bird, amongst these Tasmanian chickens.'

'Your compliments,' said Phryne judiciously, 'are good, but you should practise the delivery. Surely not all your contemporaries are plain?'

'Well, no, there are some fine girls amongst them, I'm sure, but Hobart's a small place. I've known them all since we were children. Everyone knows everyone here. Lucy's never brought anyone like you to the house. Only her dowdy schoolfriends... there, I've done it again, haven't I?' He laughed as Phryne laughed. Blond to the brain stem, both siblings, Phryne thought, dismissing any idea that this ingenuous young man could be in league with Percy Fellowes to gouge money out of Sir James. Not a single malicious thought had ever taken refuge under those absurdly fluffy curls.

'Are you at university?' she asked.

'Yes, I'm studying arts. No need for a profession, you know. The pater's rich as Croesus. Says if I want to spend my life writing Latin verse I can. Lots of my friends aren't. Rich, you know. Poor Tommy and people like Percy Fellowes have to do all sorts of jobs to pay the fees. Tommy's a chucker-out at the Montpellier. Lots of the chaps go there to play cards. Waste of time, in my opinion.'

'Could you take me to play cards at the Montpellier?' asked Phryne, lowering one finger to touch the glowing cheek very gently.

'Not a place for ladies...', sighed the boy, enraptured. 'But if you say so...tomorrow night?'

'Tomorrow night.' Phryne dropped a kiss on the unlined forehead and resumed her climb. She turned at the landing and saw the upturned, cherubic face still gazing upward, like a visionary drinking in his favourite saint.

———

The Montpellier was much as Phryne had expected. It stank of beer and men. The main pub was closed, but the side bar was kept open for the refreshment of seamen who came wandering along Salamanca Place in search of the usual maritime amusements. The unswept pavement was clotted with old horse dung and tar and dust. The unswept bar was lined with unclean sawdust in which reposed rat droppings, drunken sailors, and human debris too revolting to contemplate.

'Charming,' said Phryne. She found squalor interesting,

once in a while, and so far the Montpellier had not produced the bladed Apache who could be expected in the equivalent Marseilles bar. It seemed astounded almost to the point of silence by the entry of a real, live lady, dressed in a red satin dress and loaded with jewellery. Several voices called out suggestions. Phryne replied so indelicately that there was another silence. Not even the dock women swore like that.

Wisely, the pub decided that she was none of their business and the proprietors turned back to their own concerns: robbing sailors, watering beer, and calculating exactly how much turpentine could be added to the Montpellier gin without the customers actually expiring on the premises.

'They're in here,' said Gerald, leading Phryne to another side bar. This one contained a large, scarred table, an overhead electric light, ten chairs, a lot of bottles, and an assortment of dissipated young men. One caught her attention immediately. A smooth, glossy young man with patent-leather hair, a shirt collar which was still white, and a full red mouth. A vampire, thought Phryne, a bloodsucker, just the sort to attract that little goose Lucy. She smiled on the gathering. Gerald tipped a friend off his chair, dusted it, and set it down. Phryne sat.

'Cut me in?' she asked.

'We're playing poker,' said the glossy young man.

'Good,' said Phryne. 'You're Percy Fellowes, aren't you?' she added, putting a purse on the table. 'Florins?'

'Florins,' said Percy Fellowes. 'Have we met?'

'No,' said Phryne, smiling warmly upon the young snake, 'but I've heard all about you.'

'Nothing good, I hope.' Even his voice was smooth.

'Oh no,' Phryne assured him. 'Nothing good.'

For her plan to work Phryne had to lose consistently, and since luck was running her way she had to start cheating much earlier than she ordinarily would have. The cards were old and the players noticed that the lady's rings appeared to be tight. She was forever fiddling with them, especially a rose-cut diamond with sharp facets. She handled the cards clumsily, too, almost dropping them. And she managed to lose, first all of her coins and then all of her notes.

'Come home with me, Phryne,' Gerald urged, shocked at the amount of money she had lost. 'It's late.'

'No,' said Phryne. 'One more game. With you,' she said loudly to Percy Fellowes. The forefinger she pointed at him trembled. 'For a certain piece of jewellery,' she said.

The glossy head shook. 'You've nothing left to stake,' he sneered.

'I have myself,' said Phryne. The table gasped. The other players drew away. Gerald's hand fell from Phryne's arm. His sister's guest was drunk, unsteady, and about to stake her virtue on the turn of a card. And Gerald had no idea what a gentleman was supposed to do under these circumstances.

'Out you go,' said Phryne. 'This is between him and me.'

Gratefully, they left the room. Such a force of hatred was building up between the scarlet-dressed woman and their old friend—a good bloke, really, Percy Fellowes—that they didn't want to watch. But they couldn't completely tear themselves away. Phryne heard them breathing outside the door and grinned, very privately.

She chose her chair. The mirror was not behind her shoulder.

The light did not fall on her face. She shuffled the cards and laid the deck down. 'Cut for dealer,' she said. 'Stake on the table.'

'Why should I be carrying the thing with me?' he asked.

'Where would you leave it? Nothing's safe in this rat hole. Come along. I'm wagering my body on this. Show me your stake.'

Reluctantly, Percy Fellowes reached into a side pocket and extracted a heavy gold chain and locket. Phryne picked it up, took out the loose picture and read the inscription on the back of the photograph. 'Yes, that would be rather hard to explain,' she murmured. She clapped the locket closed and replaced it on the table. Then she cut the cards, revealed a red king against Percy's five of clubs, and took the deck.

'Why are you doing this?' he asked, accepting two cards.

'Because I want that locket,' said Phryne.

'Why do you want the locket? Another card, please.'

'A whim,' said Phryne. The young man examined his cards with mounting concern. Then he threw them down on the table.

'Two more,' he demanded.

Phryne, who knew perfectly well what two cards he was going to draw, passed them over. Percy noticed two things. One was that the woman opposite him, who had earlier seemed hysterical, desperate and more than a little drunk, was now collected and smiling. The other was that he had drawn the two of clubs and the nine of diamonds from a deck which he had personally stacked.

Phryne gave herself another card. She could not raise her stake any higher. She returned the puzzled stare with a cool smile. Percy requested more cards. He was beginning to sweat.

His patent-leather hair looked tarnished. Then Phryne laid down her hand.

'Ten, jack, queen, king, ace,' she said calmly.

'Can't be!' Percy grabbed the pack and scattered the cards. He ran his fingertips gently along the backs and turned to Phryne a blanched, shocked face.

'You cheated!' he whispered.

'Of course,' said Phryne. Then she added, as Percy leapt to his feet, 'And so did you, my boy. You only noticed the dents from my ring because they are in different places from your own. I use the French system,' she said with detached interest. 'Easier and faster. If you are good I may teach it to you. Don't do anything rash,' she advised, hearing the young man growl.

He reached across the table for her and froze. He was looking down the barrel of a small but serviceable pearl-handled pistol. He snarled.

'Think,' Phryne urged, secreting the locket in her garments. 'Let me get out of here without a fuss and I won't tell your friends that you are a cheat. I will also refrain from enlightening that engaging boy, Lucy's brother, as to the nature of your relations with her. Make a scene and I'll shoot you where you stand—no one in this pub is going to notice. You've won ten pounds from 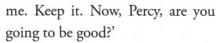 me. Keep it. Now, Percy, are you going to be good?'

 If looks killed, Phryne would have been not only dead but carbonised.

'She broke my heart,' he muttered, lurching into his chair.

'You should never entrust your heart, or other important organs, to anyone with that shade of hair or those blue eyes,' said Phryne unsympathetically. 'If you were married to her you'd be homicidal in a month. Nice girl, but a butterfly. Be thankful you got out of this with a whole skin. Nice playing with you,' she said, passing behind him and opening the door. 'Gerald? It's late. I think I'd like to go home now.'

———

'Lucy, I want you to tell me two things. One, when is your fish delivered? And two, can you get the cook out of the kitchen for about two minutes?'

'But, Phryne, have you got it? What happened? You came in terribly late.'

'Lucy, do as I say and we shall get out of this with your reputation intact,' exclaimed Phryne.

'All right, all right. The fish should be here by now. They bring it up from the harbour about eight. And I can always ask Mrs McGregor about last night's carrots. They were as hard as wood.'

'Good. Come along, I want to get this fixed before breakfast and I'm starving.'

Phryne found the tray of fresh, gleaming fish, a sharp knife and the required two minutes. She completed some minor oral surgery on a large sea bass, cleaned her

hands, replaced the knife, and was staring out the window when the cook passed her on the way back, having delivered herself of a refreshing tirade about the greengrocer. Phryne went in to breakfast—scrambled eggs with cream, fresh toast with local butter, kedgeree with crispy edges and a whole pot of coffee— with the sense of a job well done.

———

They were in the middle of morning tea when Phryne heard a shriek from the kitchen. Sir James put down his cup testily. 'What's the matter with the woman?' he demanded.

'I'll go and see,' offered Lucy. She flickered out of the morning room in a tumble of curls and lavender cotton. Phryne continued talking about Scotland with Sir James. She liked him. A nice, steady old buffer, just the thing for a flibbertigibbet like Lucy. Phryne was just extolling the glories of the Highlands when a procession came in. Lucy, looking amazed. The butler, carrying a dish. The cook, clutching her fish-gutting knife.

On the salver was a large sea bass. It looked surprised, as well it might. Spilling from its belly were innards and the gleam of gold. Sir James drew it forth. Lucy sat down abruptly and fanned herself.

'Whoever heard of such a thing?' demanded the cook. 'I was just cleaning the fish for dinner and the knife jarred on something and there it was. That'll be milady's locket what she lost overboard, I said to Mr Hughes, I said, and I was right.'

'We have been particularly blessed, Mrs McGregor,' said Sir James, looking up at the picture of St Mungo on the wall.

'Have the locket washed, will you. I would like to see it where it belongs again.'

'Oh, James!' Lucy flung herself into her husband's tolerant embrace and burst into tears.

Phryne caught Sir James' eye. He was looking straight at her over his wife's bent head as he spoke.

'Indeed, we have been particularly blessed. And I have not forgotten the stories of St Mungo, either,' he said gently, and winked.

Phryne raised her coffee-cup to him and drank a silent toast. To St Mungo, of course.

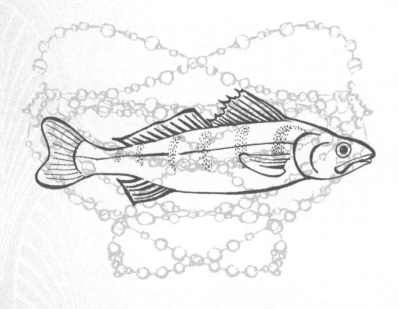

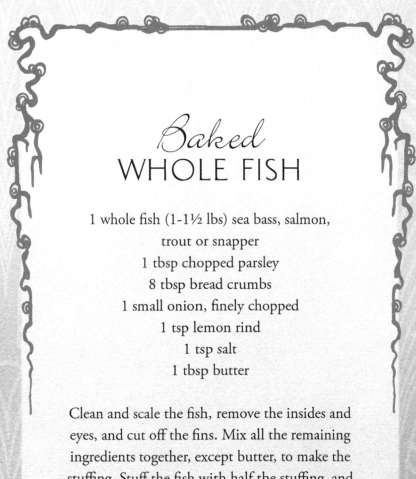

Baked
WHOLE FISH

1 whole fish (1-1½ lbs) sea bass, salmon,
trout or snapper
1 tbsp chopped parsley
8 tbsp bread crumbs
1 small onion, finely chopped
1 tsp lemon rind
1 tsp salt
1 tbsp butter

Clean and scale the fish, remove the insides and
eyes, and cut off the fins. Mix all the remaining
ingredients together, except butter, to make the
stuffing. Stuff the fish with half the stuffing, and
sprinkle the rest in a baking dish. Lay the fish
down in the baking dish and dot fish with butter,
then cover with a lid or foil and bake for ten
minutes. Take off the lid and bake for a further ten
minutes, until you can pull a bone out cleanly.

Overheard
ON A BALCONY

This was a good dinner enough, to be sure,
but not a dinner to ask a man to.

Dr Samuel Johnson
James Boswell, *Boswell's Life of Johnson*

Phryne Fisher surveyed the ranked waiters with the slightly doubtful air of a Head of State taking the salute from a very well-dressed, well-trained army.

My, she thought, they do look spruce. Each white shirt front gleamed like a pedigreed cat's fur, glossy with grooming. The black trousers were of stygian hue, and each bow tie perched at an exact angle on each neat starched collar, as though twenty black butterflies had alighted north of the waistcoats and frozen in some sudden frost. The Queenscliff Hotel's staff was under constant, quasi-military discipline.

It was the 25th of June, 1928 and Phryne was invited to celebrate Christmas. Tom Adams, the publisher, liked Australia. He liked Miss Jane, his fiancée. He approved of the beaches, the beer, the people and the writers. However, he was willing to consider any offer for the dust and the flies, and he still longed for a white Christmas. He yearned for snow, plum pudding, robins, and roast turkey. He felt that decorating a Christmas tree and eating a Christmas dinner in temperatures above 100 degrees Fahrenheit was ridiculous.

So he had arranged to put on a proper Country House Christmas feast at a time when the weather might cooperate. He had chosen for his setting an establishment so sure of itself that it had no other title but 'The Queenscliff Hotel'. Tom Adams admired arrogance, particularly when it was justified.

Phryne had motored down from Melbourne in the Hispano-Suiza with her maid Dot, a plain young woman dressed entirely in brown: a chocolate coloured coat, hat, gloves, and scarf over an ochre woollen costume. She was shivering. Dot did not like winter.

'Oh, Miss, I'm that cold!'

'One moment, Dot dear, I'll just sign the register and we shall go and sit in front of that nice fire in the salon.' She scrawled her name with a characteristic flourish and saw her baggage borne up the red-carpeted stairs by marching minions to the best room in the hotel.

Dot sat down on the edge of a leather armchair, directly in front of a blazing fire. Phryne, who did not feel the cold, leaned on the mantelpiece between the Chelsea spaniels and a huge vase of cotoneaster berries and ferns, and surveyed the room.

Tom Adams was not there. Huddled to one side of the fire was a thin, nervous blonde girl, who was staring at the open pages of a romance as though she had forgotten how to read. She was so pale as to be almost transparent. In response to Phryne's greeting, she whispered, 'Emmy Harbottle.' Her fingers were icy cold. A large, red-faced, bluff military gentleman bellowed, 'General Harbottle—call me Alex' from the chessboard. A buxom red-headed woman wearing very few garments, considering the weather, gave Phryne a languishing glance and murmured, 'Lilith Johnson.' Phryne had heard of her. She wrote convoluted novels of what would have been shocking indelicacy if they had been less obscure to the general reader. As it was, no one, including the censor, was quite certain that she could have meant what they thought she meant. Her novels enjoyed considerable sales and wide acclaim.

The General's opponent was immediately recognisable. He had long dark hair, curiously dead looking, which hung down over his disordered collar, four big silver rings on his left hand, and thick glasses. Zechariah Silk, the cubist poet. Phryne had tried to read some of his work and found it so dense with depressing imagery that she sent the book back to the library. She had it in for him especially for a fetid little offering called 'Dead Foxgloves', the first line of which had burned itself into her memory: 'Slimy-green, envenomed, desiccate petalled, the death of foxgloves'.

The poet got up, observed, 'Check and mate,' to the General in a heavily accented voice, and took Phryne's hand to kiss it. His smile was sweet and rather shy, and his mouth was warm on her wrist.

'Merry Christmas,' he said. 'I am delighted to meet you, Miss Fisher.'

She could not identify the accent—it was a rich, plummy Middle European, maybe Hungarian, perhaps Russian.

'Mr Adams has telephoned,' the waiter informed the General. 'He and the Smythe and Brenton parties will be here directly.'

'I should think so. Been waiting for the feller for an hour,' grunted the General. Losing at chess had not improved his temper.

'But you have not been bored,' observed the poet. 'You have learned not to underestimate an opponent and also a valuable lesson about the queen's side defence.'

The General snarled. Phryne sauntered away from the fire to look at the board. A very pretty attack had decimated the General's men and hemmed his beleaguered king in behind his remaining pawns, where he had been trapped. She recalled that General Harbottle had conducted at least one large battle—was it the Gallipoli campaign?—and hoped that he was more skilful with real men than he was with chess pieces. She said as much to the poet, who shrugged.

'It is a game of strategy and intelligence, Miss Fisher. You would not expect a soldier to have any knowledge of it.'

Mrs General Harbottle had got to her feet, one

hand on the back of her chair. 'Where are you off to, Emmy?' demanded her husband.

'I thought I'd go and lie down,' she faltered.

The General barked, 'I didn't bring you all this way for you to hide away from company. I'm a crock, ticker's gone bad—' he looked around the room for sympathy—'but I'm sticking it out. You're all right, Emmy. Sit.'

'But, Alexander...' she protested faintly.

He swelled and turned purple. He grabbed his wife's arm and forced her down, pinching her upper arm so that she winced. With his other hand he felt in his pocket and produced a letter. His wife blanched at the sight of it.

His manner nettled Phryne, who did not like bullies. Emmy looked ill. Phryne slid between the General and his spouse and said, 'Come along, Mrs Harbottle, we'll go up together. Travel is so fatiguing, isn't it?'

The General, scowling, had no choice but to allow his wife to take Miss Fisher's hand.

Phryne and Dot took Emmy to her room. Dot assisted her to remove her shoes and lie down, covered with a patchwork comforter. 'I'll order some tea for her, Miss, and perhaps I'd better stay.'

'All right, Dot dear, that is kind of you. If you have any trouble with the General give me a shout.

Wife-beaters are scared of women. Do you want to dine with the company?'

'Oh no, Miss, not unless you need me. The staff dinner's supposed to be really good and…that might be more fun.' Dot, who had been brought up not to criticise her social superiors, blushed a little.

'Yes, I see your point. Though the presence of those Bright Young Things will mitigate the atmosphere a little, I expect. Come and get me dressed at about seven thirty. I think I'll take a walk.'

Phryne took herself off to stroll along the pier, where she encountered the promised Bright Young Smythe girls and Brenton boys and spent an agreeable afternoon travelling to Portsea and back on the ferry *Hygeia* amongst a festive crowd, breathing in the scent of ozone and brass polish and steam.

———

Tom Adams watched her sail down the grand staircase, dressed in an Erté original. She flowed from step to step in the loose folds of the heavy red satin gown. Phryne gleamed with the expensive gloss of Famille Rose china, from her close-cut cap of shining black hair to her red brocade shoes.

She extended a scented hand for him to kiss and observed, 'Tom dear, how lovely to see you. Thank you for inviting me, and what on earth possessed you to inflict that brute of a general upon us? I don't recall doing you any harm.'

Tom Adam seemed ill-at-ease. His ordinarily rubicund complexion was pale and he had been biting his fingernails.

'I owe him...a favour,' he said with an unconvincing smile. 'Anyway, his wife's my cousin and you'll enjoy the others. Lilith is always good value and so is Silk. They should make up for one irritating general.'

'Very well, if you wish to dine with a bounder it is your business,' said Phryne, and allowed him to conduct her into the dining room.

It was a high ceilinged, wood-panelled chamber with more polished plate than the collective annual output of the Peruvian mines, and damask tablecloths starched to the rigidity of paper. Holly wreathed every table and the épergnes were full of bright berries. Tom was seated at the head of the long table with Phryne at the foot.

The guests smiled at each other. Phryne had a Brenton boy to her right and the poet to her left. He had added to the usual gentleman's evening dress a bright red cummerbund and a ribbon of some foreign order. Phryne resolved on being as bright as possible under the circumstances.

Silk only grunted when spoken to, so she engaged John Brenton on the subject of skiing, in which she had minimal interest but upon which both Brentons could be relied on to converse until whole herds of dairy cows came home.

'Last year at Baw Baw we were skiing on rocks but this year...' He closed his eyes in rapture. 'There is powder down to five hundred feet.'

'Oh, good,' murmured Phryne, wishing she was elsewhere.

The waiters served the soup. It was a delicate flavourful julienne of vegetables and its excellence moderated Brenton's snowy discourse. Beside her, the underfed poet laid his thick glasses down on the menu and slurped. Phryne looked idly, then with increasing interest, at the glasses and the menu beneath them. 'How curious!' she thought.

A political argument was developing, the storm centring around the General. While Lilith was amusing herself by attracting one of the Brenton boys in direct competition with one of the Smythe girls—Lilith was winning—the military man was proclaiming, 'These trade union chappies, disgusting, holding the country to ransom. Ought to join the army, there's no bolshie stuff there—soon beat it out of them, few years' military discipline, straighten their ideas up.'

'A lot of them were soldiers,' observed the poet, quietly.

'Not in my war.'

'Oh yes, many of them,' said Zechariah Silk.

The General swallowed a huge mouthful of turkey and chestnut stuffing and slapped his wife's hand off his arm. 'Leave me alone, Emmy. Remember the letter!' Emmy shrank back with a little cry. 'Consider your place. You came from the gutter, and you can easily go back there.'

Tom Adams said, 'Here, I say, Alex,' and an adroit waiter poured the General more wine, which he gulped. Lilith removed her gaze from the Brenton boy and directed at the General a glance so full of malice that it should have stung.

'You, Silk,' bellowed General Harbottle. 'You were a conchie, I'll bet, a yellow, lily-livered, white-feathered conchie. I had one in my regiment. We sent him into the front line pretty smartish. That's what I do with cowards!'

The poet leapt to his feet, tipping over his chair, and left the room without a word, his hair flopping across his face, his shoulders bowed.

Tom Adams protested, 'Really, General!' and the older man bared his teeth at his host in return. 'I know about you, too, Adam. I know your secret. And that slut down there—I know about her.'

'But you do not know anything about me,' observed Phryne in a clear, carrying voice as cold as one of Brenton's blizzards. 'Moderate your tone and mind your manners.'

Perhaps General Harbottle had had a governess. The ice cut through his bluster and he humphed and gulped more wine.

'Shall I go after the poet chappie?' offered a Brenton boy, and Tom Adams sighed. 'No, he'll have taken offence, and who can blame him?'

A waiter came to the table to remove the plates. Even the indefatigable Brenton had run out of conversation. In silence, they waited as a huge and perfect plum pudding was brought to the table. The waiter sliced it and Phryne nibbled a fragment or so, wishing that she had not come.

The General bolted his serving, choked, and fell balletically from his chair, which crashed to the floor on top of him. It was the most interesting thing he had done all evening.

It took some time to disentangle the chair from the General, take the patient to his room and summon a doctor from the township. And when he arrived, the General was perfectly dead.

———

Phryne perched on the arm of a chair and smoked and thought.

Everyone wanted to kill the General, except possibly the

Brentons and Smythes. Phryne observed sardonically that Amelia Smythe had collapsed into Tom Adams' arms and that Lilith had captured the Brenton of her choice and was reclining on his manly bosom. Mrs Harbottle was sitting on one corner of a sofa with Dot in attendance. She was not crying. In fact, she seemed to be relieved. Her suppressed hair was fluffing out from its band.

Clearly Tom Adams was being blackmailed, and so was Lilith. 'What dread secret was that notorious flapper hiding?' Phryne wondered. It must have been something fairly choice. Of course, the old pest might simply have had an apoplexy and died from the enormous dinner he had just eaten. She reflected that her thoughts were turning too frequently to murder. She took up a magazine and glanced though it.

Ten minutes of *Table Talk* were enough to drive her into inviting an unattached Brenton to walk along the pier with her. She was on her way out when a large policeman politely asked her to return once again to the salon to await the arrival of his sergeant. Phryne smiled at the brass buttons and asked sweetly, 'What killed the General?'

'Doctor says it was an overdose of his heart pills,' said the policeman, dazzled. 'I think it will be all right, miss.'

The salon contained a large jigsaw puzzle which was half completed, and Phryne and her attendant Brenton sat down to fit the remaining bits together.

The guests were dismissed an hour later and allowed to go to bed. Phryne reached her own room, undressed herself, and sat on the pearl coloured loveseat in the bay window, staring into the night and thinking.

There was no way that anyone could have poisoned General Harbottle at dinner. She ran through the courses one by one—the soup, the entrée, the turkey and the pudding had all been shared between the diners. Tom Adams had been sitting beside the General, and might have been able to sprinkle something onto his plate. Phryne was restless and unable to sleep. She wondered if Tom Adams felt the same.

Phryne found him on the upstairs balcony. He was leaning on the rail and she saw the glow of his cigar. 'Can't sleep? Neither can I,' he greeted her. 'What a thing, Phryne.'

'Indeed, though if I had to choose a victim, he would be high on my list. Tom, you know my profession. I can help you. Did you poison him?'

'No, by God, Phryne, what a question!' he said loudly, and she laid a hand on his arm.

'Hush, idiot, four rooms abut onto this balcony, speak quietly. What did he have on you, anyway?'

Tom Adams stared, summed up his acquaintance with Miss Fisher, and said rapidly, 'A marriage, Phryne. It's a relief to tell someone. When I was a student I married a girl in London. Recently I've been courting....'

'So you have. Does Miss Jane know about this?'

'Of course not. I'm pretty sure that the woman's dead anyway. I've got people finding out for me. But Jane...Jane's the one, amazing girl. I want to spend the rest of my life with her. And her father doesn't approve of me above half, so...'

'Was the old beast blackmailing you?'

'Well, yes, but only for things like this invitation. He wanted to go about in society. Can't imagine why. Needed new people to insult, I suppose. Well, he's gone and I didn't do it, and the relief is profound, let me tell you.'

'Then who did it?'

'It might have been an accident. Perhaps he just gulped a handful of heart pills. But I'm afraid...the person he treated worst...'

'Yes. His wife. But I don't think she'd have the nerve. What did he have on Lilith?'

Tom Adams laughed softly. 'You promise not to tell.'

'I promise,' said Phryne promptly.

'Her blameless private life.'

'Oh, Tom, don't be silly.'

'No, really.' Tom drew Phryne close so he could whisper. 'She has a husband who is a clerk in the Public Service and two very nice children. But half of her stock in trade is her femme fatale act and the General knew she couldn't afford to lose it. Who wants to read shocking novels written by a bourgeois housewife? It was a serious threat. But I can't see how she could have done it. She was too far away and moreover she was vamping the Brenton boy.'

'Yes. Has anyone seen Zechariah Silk since he flounced out?'

'Yes, he went into the small salon and was playing chess with himself. I saw him later in the evening. I'm going for a walk along the beach. Want to accompany me?'

'No thanks, Tom dear. I'll go down and see if someone can make me a cocktail.'

———

The next morning brought orders to stay in the hotel, which was no hardship, and a police surgeon who announced that the patient had died of an overdose of digitalin. The guests were searched and no one had any supply of the drug. Phryne idled the day away, dressed for dinner, and sat down to another excellent supper, irritated at her inability to solve this puzzle. She could not see the General killing himself, and he did not seem to have been a careless man.

'Perhaps he realised what a bounder he was and removed himself to spare us his company,' said Lilith from across the table, echoing Phryne's thought.

'No such luck,' rejoined Tom Adams, as the waiter reached past him to pour a delicate chicken soup into his bowl. Phryne sipped at the fragrant broth, possessed of the edges of a memory which slipped away as she tried to grasp it. Her unease lasted through two courses and coffee and persisted as she went upstairs.

There had been something about the waiter's hand as he sliced the plum pudding. Not rings or scars. Just some oddness about the colour of the skin.... She stopped abruptly and Zechariah Silk, who was behind her, stood on the hem of her red satin dress and muttered an apology. She grabbed his arm, proceeding up the carpeted stairs and through the little door onto the balcony, where she turned and faced him, her arms around his neck.

'If anyone sees us they will think we are spooning and look away,' she said into his shirt front. 'Mr Silk, you are a fraud.'

'Fraud, ma'mselle?' said the liquid, heavily accented voice, and Phryne tugged at the long hair. It came off in her hand. She pulled off the glasses. A young man with cropped black hair stared uncertainly into her green eyes.

'Yes. This party is full of them. Tom Adams has a secret wife, Miss Johnson has a hidden husband and children, and you, my dear, have a secret identity.'

'How did you know?' The voice was lighter than it had been and had a pronounced Eton accent. 'I thought I did a dashed good Zechariah Silk.'

'You did.' Phryne was enjoying his closeness. 'It was superb. But you put your glasses down on the menu and they did not magnify it. And your hair looked dead; it is not a very good wig.'

'Second-hand,' confessed the young man.

'And you murdered the General.' The body flexed in her arms and she held tight. 'It's all right, my dear, I just want to know why. And how would be nice. You took all your rings off when you doffed the wig, cummerbund and glasses and impersonated a waiter, but I saw his hand and he had patches of lighter skin on all four fingers. Unusual.' The young man sighed heavily and said into her hair, 'All right. Are you going to turn me in, Phryne?'

'Depends,' said Phryne 'Tell me all.'

'You know all.'

'Tell me how and why.'

'I read about the method in a book of notable British trials when I was imprisoned by the Turks.'

'So you were a soldier.'

'I was, and that old bastard was our commander. He sent us over the top—at Gallipoli. They all died, all my friends, but the Turks found me alive and kept me as a slave for two years.' He released Phryne and unbuttoned his soft white shirt. A bullet had carved a track across his chest.

'I spent a lot of time thinking about him, the General. He had sent us up an unclimbable hill to take an untakeable machine gun. I watched them all die, cut down around me, Phryne, all my friends. My mates—that's what the Aussies called them, mates. Fellows I'd known since I was a child. Well, I got released when the war ended, then I met the old devil in London. I was quite alone, you know—everyone I knew had been killed. I took to being Zechariah Silk, partly because no one would publish my poems if I didn't look right, and good old Silk looked perfect. I had quite a success. Then there was Emmy—we were engaged, you know, before the war. I did nothing for a long time, just watched. But the fellow kept intruding into my world, seemed to positively seek my society. I couldn't bear the way he treated her. That letter he kept talking about—it was my letter, one I'd written her before the war.'

'So you decided to poison him—how?'

'Easy. I just walked out, ran into the gents, took off the disguise and took in the pudding. I had a knife smeared on one side with the poison, and the greedy blighter gulped the stuff down. But now, Phryne, tell me how you knew.'

'About the poison? Your poem—that ghastly one about the death of foxgloves. That's where you get digitalin. Foxgloves. What's your real name?'

'Ian. Ian Roberts.' He stared out to sea, one hand on Phryne's silk-clad shoulder.

'What are you going to do now?' she asked.

'Go away. I can't tell Emmy what I did—that wouldn't be right. She's free now, though—he can't torture her anymore. I've got an offer of a job in Africa—I used to be a medical student. Lot of disease to be treated in Africa. Promise you won't tell Emmy. She must never know.'

Phryne considered the face in the half-light. It was determined, sober, beautifully made. The lips were set and the jaw firm. She moved away.

'What are you going to do?' whispered Ian Roberts, and Phryne said, 'Nothing. I am going to do nothing. Unless someone else is charged, and that doesn't seem likely.'

A figure shot past her in a whirl of white draperies. Mrs Harbottle, freed of her appalling husband, ran straight into Ian's arms and clung to him as though she would never let go.

'Oh dear,' observed Phryne. 'I forgot about the bedrooms opening onto the balcony.'

'I heard it all,' Emmy said into Ian's shirt front. 'I thought you were dead! Oh, my dear, my dear.' She kissed him, tears running down her face. 'Oh, Ian darling.'

'Emmy, no—I never meant you to know...,' he protested and she stopped his mouth with another kiss.

'I'm terribly sorry, Ian,' she babbled. 'I got married when they said you were dead—missing, believed dead, they said. I dreamed about you dead on that cliff, then Father died and Mother was ill and I didn't have any money, and the General was nice at first, he brought me flowers, and everyone was dead, Ian, all our friends....'

'Oh, my dear,' and the erstwhile Zechariah Silk's head bent over the disordered hair. 'Emmy, think. We can't start our life together with such a weight on our consciences—it would drive us apart. Oh, my dear.' He held her close, the pale hair crushed against his white shirt. 'Oh, Emmy, I love you so much.'

'I love you too, Ian. Do you forgive me for marrying the General?'

'Of course,' he said fondly.

Emmy drew herself partly out of his embrace and scolded, 'Why didn't you come back to me? You made me think you were dead, and then I didn't care what happened to me! How could you, how could you watch while that beast of a man tortured me all this time?'

'I...I didn't believe that you still wanted me,' he said helplessly. 'I thought that I wasn't good enough for you. I thought...dammit, Em, you had a house and a car and servants. I haven't a bean in the world—you don't make a living out of poetry. Forgive me,' he said, and Emmy subsided into his arms again.

'But it won't do, Em,' he said, gently pushing her away from himself with wincing effort. 'You can see it won't do, my girl. We might be happy for a few months but then as soon as we had a quarrel—and we will have quarrels, everyone does—you would think of how I killed your husband, and I would think that you might be afraid of me, and even if we didn't think like that there would always be the shadow of a dead man to poison

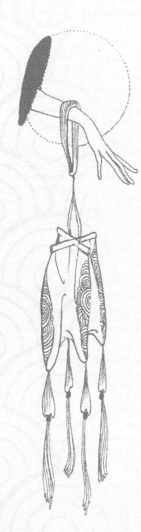

our love. You can see, can't you, Emmy, that it won't do?'

Emmy gave a stricken cry and burrowed into his embrace.

Phryne looked at the agony on Ian Roberts' face, backed by stoic resolution, and felt a pang of pity. What he said was true. The relationship based on murder could not succeed. It might have been all right in the old days when knights were bold, but even then that did not include the deliberate poisoning of a rival.

She was about to withdraw when a quiet voice observed, 'There is something you should know.'

Lilith Johnson stepped through her open window. She was draped in an expensive silk negligee and had a piece of paper in her hand. 'Before you make any hasty decisions, lovebirds, have a look at this,' she said.

Ian took the note and Phryne came close as he angled it towards the moon to read. 'I know you don't love me, Emmy,' it said in black letters. 'You are still hankering after that Roberts chap, but he's dead. You can't compete with the dead. The quack tells me that my ticker is so dicey that I may go anytime. So I'm taking the easy way out. If you marry again, Emmy, you won't have a penny. The money will all go to my brother. Goodbye. I did love you, Emmy. I really did love you.' It was signed with a bold military signature.

'It's his writing,' observed Emmy, not letting go of Ian Roberts for a moment. 'It's the General's writing.'

'Where did you get this, Miss Johnson?' asked Phryne.

Lilith Johnson lit a gasper. She looked out to sea as she spoke. 'That monster of a man was pursuing me. He thought I was an easy touch—fallen women excited him.' She puffed on her cigarette. 'He slid this under the door, with a note demanding an assignation. So you didn't kill the loathsome old beast, Mr Silk, or whoever you are. How much digitalin do you think you can get by boiling foxgloves? You just get foxglove soup. He killed himself and good riddance. Tomorrow I will give the note to the police, and we will all go home.'

Emmy vanished into a rapturous embrace. Then she sagged. The so-called

Zechariah Silk swept her up into his arms and carried her triumphantly from the balcony into her own room.

'That's not all there is to it, is it?' asked Phryne very quietly, as she leaned on the balcony with Miss Johnson. The woman smiled, her red mouth a sidelong slash in the moonlight.

'And what if...' she said deliberately, lighting another gasper and blowing a plume of smoke at the moths. 'What if I told you that a woman with a dearly loved husband and two lovely children was being blackmailed by a military ape? If I said that all of her happiness was being threatened by that bounder's knowledge of a moment of madness with a pretty boy? If I mentioned that the woman's husband is worthy but dull and very jealous, and that the soldier in question was offering her the choice between disclosure of this brief affair and a lifelong affair with him? And perhaps she felt desperate—perhaps she invited him to her room and talked to him and gave him a glass of wine in which a lot of heart pills were dissolved? She might have known that he was a self-pitying bastard and had a habit of writing suicide notes, and she might have stolen one for use at a suitable juncture. She might have been quite mad with fear. If you had overheard that story on this balcony, Miss Fisher, what would you do?'

The woman's face was set and she turned her blue eyes on Phryne. She looked haggard and resolute and one hand crushed the silken nightdress into creases. There was a pause in which the sea sounded, wash and crash, and a night bird cried with unbearable loneliness.

'I don't know what you think you can overhear on this balcony,' said Phryne, walking away from Lilith and pausing with her hand on the doorknob, 'but I didn't hear a thing.'

Soupe
JULIENNE

1 onion
2 carrots
1 parsnip
2 sticks celery
1 tbsp olive oil
1 tbsp brandy
4 cups strong chicken stock
5 peppercorns
2 bay leaves
1 sprig of thyme

Chop the onion carefully and cut all the other
vegetables into thin matchsticks. Cook the onion
in a little oil until soft, then add all the veggies, stir
them around and deglaze with a tablespoon of brandy.
Add the chicken stock
and herbs, and simmer for an hour.
Remove herbs before serving.

Six ways
to discourage the overenthusiastic suitor

1. Inform him that you have just joined a strict Christian sect which bans music, alcohol, dancing, smoking, black pepper, and sex.

2. Lead the conversation around to your sisterly feelings for him and inform him that you will always think of him as a brother.

3. Tell him of your recent reading of *The Golden Bough* and describe the sacrifice of the Summer King—in detail.

4. Steer him towards a complaisant young woman in need of a good time.

5. Pick his pocket.

6. Spill your drink down his shirt. In extreme cases, a fork in the groping hand or a cup of hot coffee in the crotch is a guaranteed distraction.

The Hours *of*
JUANA THE MAD

Memorial from the soul's eternity
To one dead deathless hour
DG Rossetti, *House of Life,* part 1

The academic cocktail party was not Phryne's idea of a good
time. She had been enticed to enter the solemn portals of
Melbourne University by the charms of a rather
spiffing young Associate Professor upon whom she
had designs. Jeoffrey Bisset had pleased Phryne on
first acquaintance by pronouncing her name
correctly (Phryne to rhyme with briny) and
displayed an unacademic interest in both
her matchless person and her Hispano-Suiza
racing car, both things of which she was fond.
He had promised, in addition, to show her
the department's treasure. It was a *Book of
Hours* made for Mad Queen Juana of Spain,

purchased in that country by a graduate of the university, and found among his effects after he had succumbed to a random bullet in the mountains of Catalonia. The university had not tried to remove his blood from the binding, in case cleaning should injure the gilding. It had a macabre interest, as well as that intrinsic in a medieval work of art.

Phryne sipped some sour, new sherry and surveyed the crowd. The wood panelled room was full of academics, packed in so close that they could hardly move. This did not in any way inhibit their flow of discourse, though the parts that Phryne could catch did not sound very scholarly.

'They say that poor Bradbury is completely broke,' shrilled one bird-like woman, pecking up peanuts from the palm of her hand. 'Not a penny left, and all his goods to be sold....'

'I shall bid for the Catullus,' said a pale young man, slicking his hair back cautiously, as though it might bite. 'He found it in the Charing Cross Road, apparently...'

'And the two of them, out taking the air, bold as brass!' whickered a horsy man in a checked coat evidently made from a blanket. 'I said, "Good morning, sir, nice morning, is this the wife?" and he bellowed at me, "Mind your own bloody business, Hoskins!" In Lygon Street, I'll have you know, on a Saturday morning!'

'Too, too distasteful,' worried a small, bald man. 'Such a nice man, frightfully good family, and takes Holy Orders even though we all said that it was not, really not, a good idea, and now there are all these wretched choirboys!'

Jeoffrey interrupted Phryne's eavesdropping just when it was getting interesting. He smiled a sweet and guileless smile down

at her from his six-four height and asked, 'You don't want any
more of that revolting fluid, do you?'

'I do not. If I want vinegar, I'll buy vinegar.'

'I've mentioned to the committee that the sherry is terrible,
but they are all teetotallers except for Connors, and with those
foul cigars he smokes he can't taste anything anyway. Never
mind. Come and see the *Book*.'

Phryne tucked her hand between his elbow and his side,
and they tacked across the room, sliding through scandalous
conversations, the tall blond man linked to the small Dutch-
doll Phryne, who wriggled in his wake.

'And then he had the nerve to say that my work was
derivative—me! Derivative!'

'Everyone knows that you are a most original writer, dear boy.
If you weren't so original, I might be able to understand you,'
murmured a beautiful, dark brown voice, soft and malicious.
It belonged to a short, gnome-like man with sharp eyes. 'Ah! A
vision!' he cried.

Phryne replied, 'Not a vision, but Phryne Fisher, and I think
I'm struck.'

'Phryne who offered to rebuild the walls of Thebes?' asked
the man, edging a little sideways to allow her to pass.

'The citizens wouldn't agree,' she said, slipping out of his
grip. 'And I hope they enjoyed their ruins. Goodbye.'

She caught up with Jeoffrey, who had just noticed that she
was no longer with him.

'Who is that small man—there—talking to the poet?'

'Gerald Street. Anglo-Saxon and Old Norse. He's a very
kind chap—pays out most of his salary to indigent students.

Anyone who shows an interest in his subject is family, but he has a tongue like a viper. Here we are. This is the library, and it might be a bit quieter. Kitty? I've brought a visitor.'

A plump and smiling middle-aged man crawled out from under a desk, removing spiderwebs from his hair, and holding a very indignant cat.

'I do beg your pardon, Bisset, but I had to find Pussy. I just saw a mouse in the tutor's room, and I want to lock her in there tonight. You've come to see the *Book*? Wait just a moment. I shall return directly.'

'Kitty?' asked Phryne.

Jeoffrey smiled. 'His name is Katz—K-A-T-Z—and he's very fond of the library cats, so he was almost guaranteed to be called Kitty. The *Book* is in the safe. You see, we look after it well.'

Phryne examined the green-painted safe and curled a lip. It had a very impressive front with a huge lock, and a back made of a sheet of tin which was peeling away from its rivets. It was the same mentality which provided a front door which could not be opened with a battering ram and a back door protected only by a 'keep out' notice. But she did not want to offend the young man.

Kitty returned, dragged out of his pocket a chain with at least seventy keys on it, and opened the safe door. There were many things in the safe, including examination papers and the dean's wife's pearls, but the *Book of Hours* of Juana of Castile was not one of them.

———

Phryne had been introduced to the emergency meeting called by a frantic dean and was now on her knees beside the open safe.

Gerald Street lounged in his chair, smoking a cigarette. Mr Katz hovered in the foreground, squeaking with dismay. The dean, Mr Connors, was pouring departmental whisky with distracted generosity for the Classics professor, John Hoskins, who was slumped over the library table, his ruddy face paled to the colour of tallow.

'This is a disaster!' he moaned. 'The *Book of Hours* stolen! And we were so careful with it!'

'Ha,' commented Phryne. 'I could crack this safe with a hairpin. What are these? I can't read Latin.'

'They are the half-term examination papers,' answered Jeoffrey, taking the bundle out of Phryne's hands and leafing through them. 'Hang on, though. This doesn't seem to belong.' He exhibited a leaf of parchment, with a couplet lettered on it in a beautiful flowing script.

'*Hac in hora sine mora corde pulsum tangite*. Anyone recognise it?'

'You should know it yourself,' snapped Hoskins. "Carmina Burana", part of the *O Fortuna*. We read them this term.'

'Excuse me, gentlemen, but what does it mean?' asked Phryne, getting up and dusting her knees. 'It seems to be the only thing in the safe that doesn't belong there, so it may be a clue.'

Hoskins gulped his whisky and his lecture-room manner began to return.

'*Hac in hora*...in this hour... *sine mora*...without delay ...*corde pulsum tangite*...touch the beat of the heart. A broad translation would be, I submit, pluck the strings of the heart, wouldn't you agree, Dean?'

'Yes, though touch is more correct, Hoskins. But what leads our distinguished guest to believe that it might be a clue, as she puts it?'

'What does *hora* mean?' asked Phryne, collaring the whisky bottle.

The Dean blinked. 'Hour.'

'And what are we looking for?'

'A *Book of Hours*, yes. But is it not more likely that the *Book* has been stolen by a common thief?'

'A very comforting thought, no doubt, but there are two problems with it.' Phryne sipped her drink. Unlike the sherry, the whisky was quite good. 'One is that a common thief would not have left those pearls and the petty cash.'

'Perhaps he did not notice them.'

'Perhaps. The other is that a common thief could not possibly sell a *Book of Hours*. Art theft is a highly skilled profession. Usually the buyer is arranged in advance. Your local tea-leaf is not going to try to sell a *Book of Hours* to the boys down the Collingwood pubs, is he? But if you think that someone crept in and stole it, gentlemen, you should send for the police.'

A shudder ran through the gathering. Phryne eyed them cynically.

'No? So you do think that one of you pinched it. Who else can walk into the library without Mr Katz watching their every move? Well then. Who needs money, and has contacts in...say, America?'

There was a silence. Finally Gerald Street butted out his gasper as though he had a personal grudge against it and laughed.

'I'd better say what we are all thinking. Our colleague Bradbury has been bankrupted. He had a system for picking horses, poor fool, and it succeeded as such systems always succeed. He is a mad gambler and...well, he has extensive debts, a wife and two little girls, and as Fine Arts professor he certainly knows people who would buy it.'

'And the Carmina couplet?' asked Phryne.

Gerald smiled a razor-edged smile at her. 'I'd say that you are suffering from an overactive imagination, Miss Fisher.'

'Very well, you solve this your way, and I'll solve it mine, and we'll see who finds the *Book*. And if I find it I want to dine at the High Table.'

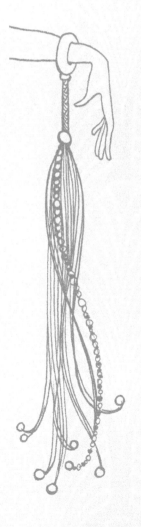

'Miss Fisher! No lady can dine at the High Table!' objected the Dean, shocked.

'This lady shall, indeed, if I find your *Book*.'

'It's a bet, Miss Fisher,' said Mr Street. 'I shall escort you myself. If you find the *Book*.' He grinned maliciously at Connors. 'The least we can do, eh, Dean?'

Mr Connors muttered an agreement, and Phryne took her leave.

Outside the red brick wall of the English Department building was a courtyard in which grew a huge Cussonia tree. Phryne stood for a moment under the gnarled branches, one hand laid on the trunk, relishing the age and strength of the tree and the shade of the abundant dark green leaves. This tree had been a sapling when the university was built, but it was not as venerable as the *Hours of Juana the Mad*. Pinned to the tree was a piece of parchment and on it was written in the same beautiful hand and in very black ink, '*Tempora a lapsa volant, fugitivis fallimur horis*'. Although Phryne could not read Latin easily, a sweating teacher had hammered the rudiments of the language into her head. She recognised 'horis' as 'hours' and she laughed. 'The game's afoot, Watson!' she said softly. She rummaged in her bag for a pencil and wrote underneath the couplet 'Quare?', which she recalled from a tedious lesson involving the Latin for 'why'.

Then she left the university, walking with her usual enjoyment through the Gothic arches of the Law Quadrangle and into Carlton for a bite to eat and some real coffee.

Jeoffrey Bisset translated the couplet, which she had copied into her notebook, at dinner that night in the Café Royale.

'"Time that is fallen is flying, we are deceived by the passing hours"—it's a medieval Latin song, from one of the vagantes, I think, the wandering scholars. Such good verse. Do you think that you can solve this, Phryne?'

'I don't know. But it's a game, and I love games. Have some more wine and tell me what you do at the university.'

'I'm an Associate Professor of English Literature and a tutor in Classics. Latin, you know, and Greek.'

'Oh. Do you like it?'

'Well, yes, it gives me time to work on my book, you know. I'm studying the poems of Alcuin. I don't think that they are sufficiently appreciated.'

'Indeed, I've never heard of him.'

'In translation they lose their magic. I am preparing new translations, attempting to keep the freshness of the verse...the dawn light now upon the sea...such a good poet, perhaps you might like to see some of them?'

'I would,' agreed Phryne. This was a very attractive man indeed, now that his enthusiasm was aroused. His blue eyes shone and his pale cheeks pinkened and his beautiful hands made broad gestures.

'I saw one of the original manuscripts, you know, in the Bodders. They say that there is a manuscript in Tours, but it belongs to a local family and they will not let it be studied.' His face was now flushed with rage. Phryne was fascinated.

'Well, it is their manuscript, you know. I suppose that they can keep it secret as long as they don't harm it.'

'Knowledge should be free!' exclaimed Jeoffrey. 'There is no excuse for keeping a work of art locked up, hidden, just for the private satisfaction of one person. It's...it's...immoral!'

'And that's what will happen to the *Hours of Juana*, you know, if it is sold in America. Some collector will gloat over it or keep it in his safe and no one will see it, until he dies. A strange passion, collecting,' commented Phryne. 'Have some more osso bucco, it's delicious.'

'In Florence and Venice there are works by Titian and Raphael which no one has seen for a hundred years, until some family goes broke and all their stuff is sold,' exclaimed the young man, helping himself to more of the rich, oniony stew. 'Dreadful! I only got into the Scuola di Farnese by bribing the doorkeeper. There were spiderwebs all over the face of the Raphael virgin.'

'Appalling,' agreed Phryne.

Jeoffrey Bisset took a huge mouthful of hot osso bucco and calmed down as he choked.

'Who do you think stole the *Book of Hours*?' asked Phryne, patting him on the back and administering water.

'I can't think that it was Bradbury, I really don't think so, but he is a gambler and gamblers cannot be trusted. They are addicts, like alcoholics. But I can't see him doing it, I've always found him a very honourable man.'

'I will find the book, Jeoffrey,' said Phryne idly, 'because I will dine at the High Table. I am determined,' she said, and passed the wine.

———

The Cussonia tree bore a new leaf, white and fluttering, when Phryne came back to it the next day. Phryne snatched it down, as she could not read it from the ground. It had been pinned high up on the trunk. This time it was not in script, but Gothic capitals, and Phryne could puzzle it out: *Quis legem dat amantibus?* 'What law for lovers?' she translated. 'Or something like that. Now what does he mean? I wonder how the faculty are getting on. Time for a threat, I think.'

She printed under the capitals, 'Render unto me, Monmouth,' pinned it to the trunk, and walked into the faculty office, where Gerald Street was draped over the secretary's desk, blowing smoke in her face and proofreading her typescript.

'That "d" is a "th", Beryl,' he snapped. 'Get it right, or the abysmal stupidity of my students will be rendered even more deep. Ah, Miss Fisher. How is the Sherlockery?'

'I will dine with you yet. How is yours?'

'Come over here.' He drew her aside, aware of Beryl's outstretched ears. 'Bradbury denies it, but that is what one would expect. He was alone in the library for a good couple of hours, too, when Kitty was busy with the new books. And can you open that safe with a hairpin?'

'Yes.'

'Show me,' requested Gerald Street, grinning, and Phryne was conducted into the misused library where Kitty was still fussing over the mice in the tutor's room.

'You will note that the front is secure,' said Phryne, feeling in her handbag and finding her strong German nailfile, 'but the back is tin and rivets. Watch.'

With little effort she lifted the sheet of tin off its rivets with the nailfile and removed the whole back of the safe. 'Remarkable!' exclaimed Professor Street. 'Can you put it back?'

Phryne twisted the nailfile, resocketed the holes in the tin over their rivets, gave the safe a sharp tap with the flat of her hand, and removed the lever.

'See?'

'Yes, I see. Very impressive. And I also see that the scratches produced by your operation on the safe are duplicated on the other side.'

'Yes, I saw that at once. He used a chisel, I think. Not as neat, but then, he probably hasn't the same experience as I have. Is that all, Professor?'

'Yes, Miss Fisher, thank you. And I look forward to dining with you,' he added.

Phryne left the room, and walked back to the tree. There was a new parchment on the branch. She pulled it down and shivered. He must have been watching me, she thought—now what?

'Dolorous Gard' said the paper, cryptically. Phryne thought while she delved for her pencil.

'Arthurian legends,' she mused. 'Two castles, Dolorous Gard and Joyous Gard, and I don't remember anything else about it. I shall have to go home and read Malory, not something a woman wants to do lightly. Now what shall I write?'

She thought deeply, trying to remember all the Latin she had been so laboriously taught.

Ubis est libus? she wrote, pinned back the notice and went home to read Malory, a prospect which did not please.

———

Extended study of medieval verse, thought Phryne at breakfast, produces a hangover almost as bad as that obtained by drinking absinthe cocktails. She tossed the crust of her toast onto the floor for her black cat to play with, dressed in a regrettable temper, and returned to the university and the Cussonia tree, which bore the usual banner of white paper.

'Not Latin again! I wish I had paid more attention to poor Miss White. How she would laugh if she saw me now! Oh. English, in fact, Chaucer. But not helpful. "A Knight there was, and that a wont thy man...he loved chivalry, truth and honour, freedom and curteseye...." What can he mean?'

She scribbled on the paper, 'Give me back that book or else!', pinned it to the tree, and sat down on a nearby bench, looking over the south lawn down to Grattan Street.

Several students were lying at ease on the grass, and some hardy souls were reading, though most appeared to be absorbing literature by the osmosis method, which involved resting one's head on the text and hoping that some of the knowledge would seep through into the sleeping skull. It was a breezy, gusty, reckless day, but Phryne could not relax and enjoy the sun. The unknown game player had given her sufficient clues to find the *Book*—he was now alarmed, and wanted to return it, wanted her to be able to find it. The rules of the game, however, did not allow him to tell her in plain words where it was, but they also did not allow him to cheat. Therefore with 'Dolorous Gard' and 'A Knight there was' she should be able to guess where the *Book* was, and she had not the faintest idea.

She lit a gasper and allowed her mind to wander. She noticed that the red brick English building had a clock tower. She looked at the stately grey pile of the Law Quadrangle. It was built in a Gothic manner, like a castle, though a small castle—rather, a Norman keep. She wondered idly why the builders had put in capitals with faces on them and what foes they expected the Law School to have to fight that they needed battlements. She mused delightedly on a mental picture of capped and gowned lawyers pouring boiling oil on the attacking working class, dropped the cigarette into her silk-clad lap, and did not even swear as she brushed it off and stamped it out.

Phryne entered the English faculty office at a run, skidded into Professor Hoskins, and grabbed his arm.

'Come along, Professor, I have something to show you. Is Professor Street in? Good, bring him too. I'll meet you in the Law cloisters in ten minutes. Where is Jeoffrey? I must have a ladder!'

She found Jeoffrey finishing a tutorial on Boethius, and he found a maintenance man who provided a ladder and they sped across the courtyard and into the Law Quadrangle, where a disturbed and puzzled group of professors awaited them.

'Miss Fisher, what is this all about?' demanded Hoskins, who had never approved of women as a sex and particularly disliked excitable ones. 'Why the ladder?'

'You shall see.' Phryne placed the ladder against the inner battlements and climbed up several rungs to deliver her lecture.

'I was given two clues to the whereabouts of your book,' she said, balancing easily. 'One was "Dolorous Gard" and one was the beginning of the description of the Knight in the *Canterbury* prologue. If one takes the English building as Joyous Gard—'

'An attribution which can only have been the product of a diseased mind,' commented Professor Street.

'Then the Law cloisters are Dolorous Gard, aren't they?'

'Possibly,' agreed Hoskins. 'But why the ladder?'

'Wait. Have a look at the capital of the pillar directly in front of me.'

The assembled professors looked. Carved into the soft grey stone was the stern face of a helmeted knight.

'Where, then, is the *Book of Hours*?' asked Mr Katz, trembling with eagerness.

In answer, Phryne scaled the ladder, heedless of the fine display of expensive undergarments which she was giving, and reached an arm over the battlements.

'I can't reach it, dammit, it's wrapped in oilskin.... Jeoffrey, come up and give me a boost.'

The tutor climbed uncertainly up the ladder and hoisted Miss Fisher on his shoulder. With the added height Phryne could see over the guttering. She bent to seize something, slipped, and almost fell, and found herself with one arm hooked around Jeoffrey Bisset's neck and the other hand clutching a parcel. With a certain difficulty and a further flourish of French knickers,

Phryne climbed down and Jeoffrey Bisset descended without hurt, shaken by such close proximity to Phryne's strong arms and her Nuit d'Amour scent.

'There's another note,' she said, pleased, as Kitty dropped to his knees to unwrap what seemed like miles of oilcloth and string and an inner layer of tissue paper.

'What does it say?'

'*Ave, formosissima,*' read Gerald Street. 'Hail, most powerful Lady! It's an invocation to Venus,' he added with a sly grin. 'And very fitting.'

'It isn't even damp,' cried Kitty, clutching the *Book* to his bosom. 'Look, Miss Fisher!'

He laid it down. Open on the lush green of the Law School's grass was an illuminated manuscript of such colour and delicacy that Phryne's breath was taken. She knelt down next to it as Kitty turned the pages with a reverent hand. Monkeys and cats danced down the side of black lettered pages; bright birds which had been dust for centuries sang loud and shrill from branches of thorns, a bunch of spring flowers which Chaucer might have picked lay dewy and complete across a windowsill through which angels were peeping, and the gentle ass ate the hat in the Christ Child's manger as the Baby clutched at his Mother's lapis-lazuli gown. It was beautiful beyond words, perfect, enamelled, the colours as fresh as yesterday and as bright as jewels.

'How could you lock this in a safe?' cried Phryne, and Hoskins said portentously, 'We won't lock it up again. I had forgotten how beautiful it is. We shall have a secure glass case and Kitty shall turn a page every day. Pick it up now, Kitty, we don't want it getting wet.'

Kitty scurried away to his library, to search every page for damage. He was almost weeping with relief, and Phryne was touched. There was a man who really loved books. To take his *Book of Hours* out of his loving custody had nearly broken his heart.

'Well, Miss Phryne, we have to thank you, and ask you to explain who stole it,' the dean said gravely.

'I shan't tell you,' Phryne replied, ordering her clothes, which had been ruffled during the climb, 'because I don't know. I played a long-distance game with the thief and he gave me the *Book*, and that will have to be enough for you.' She shook herself and put back her perfectly straight black hair from green eyes as sharp as pins. The faculty members stared at her, and sighed.

'Well, if that is your decision, Miss Fisher...' The Dean was looking on the bright side. 'Now, Hoskins, if you will give me a few moments of your time, we shall decide about the glass case. Thank you, Miss Fisher. A very precise demonstration.'

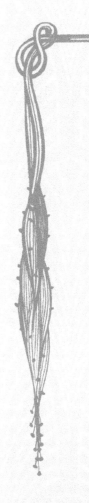

Phryne bowed and smiled, and took Jeoffrey Bisset's arm. 'Naughton's,' she commented. 'I need a drink.'

———

'You shouldn't have stolen it, Jeoffrey,' she said over a gin and tonic in the crowded pub. 'It was a huge risk. If they had called in the police your academic career would have been shot.'

'The *Book* cried out to me,' he said plaintively. 'All that beauty, locked in that green iron prison. I never meant to steal it, you know. I would have given it back. But I would never have found so...delicate a way to do it. My congratulations, Phryne. Are you going to turn me in?'

'No. When did you decide to give it back?'

'When you announced that you knew me. Who is the Monmouth that everyone knows? Geoffrey of Monmouth. I decided then that you had penetrated my game and...I put it on the roof, which is easy if you go out of a window on the second storey.'

'I see. Order me another drink, will you? It was a fine game, my dear.'

'How did you decide it was me?'

'I shall tell you later. And you have done me a favour, dear boy, because now I shall definitely dine at the High Table.'

'The food is awful, and don't touch the table wines. The port is drinkable. Dear Phryne, won't you tell me how you knew it was me?'

'There were only three people it could have been—Kitty, you or Gerald Street.'

'Yes, but how did you decide between us?'

'You are the only one that is tall. You pinned the parchment high up on the tree. The others are all not much bigger than me. Simple, eh? Like all mysteries when you know the solution.'

'*Ave, formosissima*,' said Jeoffrey Bisset.

Cocktail
DELIGHTS

CELERY BOATS

2 celery stalks
4 tbsp cream cheese
A pinch of salt
Freshly ground pepper

Wash, string and dry the celery, then cut into finger lengths. Mix the cream cheese and seasonings, then put into a piping bag and pipe into celery.

DEVILS ON HORSEBACK
(stuffed prunes)

4 rashers bacon
½ cup cooked rice
2 tbsp chutney
Salt
Pepper
½ lb prunes, pitted

Fry the bacon, and drain on kitchen paper. Mix all the ingredients, except the prunes and bacon, then stuff the prunes with the mix. Wrap bacon around each prune and secure with a toothpick.

Phryne's FAVOURITE headpieces

DEATH *shall be* DEAD

Death shal be deade, if we canne hym finde
Geoffrey Chaucer, 'The Pardoner's Tale'

'He says that someone is trying to murder him,' chuckled Detective Inspector John—'Call me Jack, Miss Fisher, everyone does'—Robinson, as the waiter refilled his glass.

He was dining with Miss Phryne Fisher, which was notable, and he was at the Café Royale, which was surprising. Phryne liked the Café Royale because it was raffish and bohemian. Jack Robinson had never been there and considered it luxurious, slightly dubious, and far above his touch. Miss Fisher had invited him and was at present engaged in deftly twirling flat green spaghetti around her fork. Jack, who had no taste for foreign food, was dissecting the best steak he had ever eaten. The lights were low, obscured with charcoal and the pungent Gauloises which the Café Royale's clients smoked. The tables were wooden, the waiters Italian and the noise subdued, except around the big log fire where three artists were arguing about Modernism.

'And is someone trying to murder him?'

'I don't know. He said he was shot at, but we couldn't find the slug. He's a cantankerous old cuss, lives all alone with his dog, and his neighbours don't like him, but why would anyone want to kill him? He hasn't got any money—at least, I don't think so. He also says that someone is trying to buy his house, and has offered him a king's ransom for it, but he won't sell.'

'That's interesting, Jack. Do go on.' Miss Fisher's green eyes gleamed and she laid down her fork and smoothed back her perfectly black, perfectly straight hair. Although Robinson knew that she was a powerful young woman, possessed of courage and a very bad temper, she looked elegant and harmless in wine-coloured wool and a close-fitting cloche decorated with green and black flowers.

'That's about all I know. He lives in Austen Street, Footscray, in a worker's cottage, and he's been there five years. It's an ordinary place, a bit run-down. He says that someone offered him hundreds of pounds for the house, and that is not likely. I reckon he's loopy—it happens to old men who live alone.'

'What's his name? And how is your steak?'

'Jackson, Albie Jackson, and the steak is the best I've ever eaten. Did I tell you I've taken up poetry?'

'Poetry, Jack?'

'Yes. Always liked it at school. Mechanics' Institute has a night class. We're beginning at the beginning. Chaucer, you know. I'd never heard of him before.'

'Good stuff,' commented Phryne, taking another mouthful of spinach fettucine. How are you managing the language?'

'Oh, it's all right, once you work out that you have to say it out loud. We're reading *The Canterbury Tales*. Sharp tongue he had, old Chaucer. Bring him to the attention of the censor if it wasn't so long ago. What about that Wyf of Bath with all those husbands?'

'She only had them one at a time,' objected Phryne. 'Have some more wine.'

'If I have any more I'll be drunk in charge of feet,' objected Jack Robinson, then conceded to the hovering waiter: 'Well, one more glass, perhaps.'

The sweet red Lambrusco from the Po Valley was much to his taste.

'And what have you been doing, Phryne?'

'Nothing much. Things are quiet. I traced a missing son for a very old family last week—no wonder he went away, his father kept locking him in the coal cellar, and you can't do that to an eighteen- year-old for too long. And I exposed a nice little fraud being worked in a shop. The owner was creaming off the profits and blaming the bookkeeper, intending to sack her and tell his partner that she had taken the money—nasty, wicked little man. Nothing else. I might go and see the snow if the weather holds.'

Outside the wind howled through the alleys. Jack Robinson

leaned back with the added contentment that bad weather gives to being inside, fully fed, near a fire.

'I suppose that you didn't send us the gen on the shopkeeper?'

'No, Jack, worse—I told his wife.'

As she was bidding her guest farewell some time later, Phryne said, 'About Albie Jackson—why not find out who owned the house before?'

Jack Robinson did not get her drift, but her ideas were usually good. He nodded, buttoned his greatcoat closely, and stepped out into the storm, running with Miss Fisher to her indecently big and red Hispano-Suiza racing car.

She dropped him at his respectable cottage in Collingwood, declined an invitation to see his orchids, and drove home to St Kilda.

———

The next morning dawned colder than a tomb, and she decided to stay in, as no cases were pending, taking to the parlour a few books, a box of Hillier's chocolates, and a glass or two of a dry Barossa vintage which she was trying for a vintner friend. It was young but sprightly and she passed the morning pleasantly before the fire, the red light washing the sea-green walls. The phone rang.

'Jack Robinson here. You remember that case we were talking about last night? Old Albie Jackson? Well, things have happened at old Albie's place. It caught fire last night. What with the rain and the local fire brigade, they put it out fast enough. But...'

'But?'

'There are three dead people in the house,' said Jack glumly. Unlike Miss Fisher, he hated mysteries. 'I don't know what to think.'

'How odd!'

'Odd isn't the word I'd use, Miss Fisher.'

A bad sign. Last night, Robinson had called her Phryne.

'One of 'em's a client of yours,' he continued. 'Thomas Mason.'

'What, that creep? His wife was my client, Jack. She wanted a divorce and we had to get it through while he was still in jail. She was afraid that he'd kill her. Oh, no...don't tell me...'

'Yeah. One of the dead 'uns is his wife. You want to have a look? We got no one else to confirm her identity.'

'Very well. What number Austen Street? I'll be there directly.'

Jack Robinson told her the number. Phryne ran upstairs to dress for the weather and found garments suitable for clambering around a half-burned house in the rain: boots, trousers, and a big woolly jumper decorated with multi-coloured parrots. She dragged on a black cloche and pulled on an airman's sheepskin-lined leather jacket.

Who could have wanted to kill poor downtrodden Mary

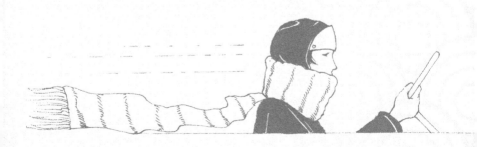

Mason except her revolting bank robber of a husband? She gunned the Hispano-Suiza down Footscray Road, with the railway yards and the clutter of hovels on Dudley Flats miserable under the rain.

Austen Street had trees, bare and sad, and she parked next to a black maria and an ambulance. Jack Robinson was at the sagging, paintless door.

'Mind the verandah; it's burnt through. In the kitchen, Miss Fisher. Things are bad.'

'Bad?' Phryne picked her way from beam to beam through to the kitchen, taking the policeman's hand. It was a gardener's hand, calloused and hard.

'The damage is worst here,' said Jack glumly. 'And burned all along the hall.'

'The door must have been open. What a dump! I mean, even before it was burnt. No one's painted the place since it was built.'

Visible and soaked with water from the firemen's hoses were piles of old newspapers, opened and mouldy cans of soup and beans, unwashed dishes caked with old meals, rags, and broken chairs, the detritus of friendless old age. It smelt of fire, now, and cold, and burning, with the musky aftertaste of squalor. Phryne walked carefully down the hall into the parlour.

Three people were sitting at a dining table, on which was a teapot, several mismatched cups, an ashtray filled with butts, a bottle of whisky and three glasses, and a flat iron which had been put down hot and had burned the table. The three were dead. One had fallen forward, his face a carnival horror, a grinning mask. Mary Mason had slumped sideways from her chair, prevented from falling by the wall, and grinned at death as though she had at last seen the joke.

'God help us, Jack!' Phryne stepped back a pace. 'What has happened to them?'

'Is that Mary Mason?'

'Yes, yes, of course. She got her *decree nisi* last week. When did her husband get out of prison?'

'Yesterday. He collected her from her boarding house. Landlady said that she was terrified, but went with him.'

'Yes, she was terrified all right. And with good reason. Who is the other...the other dead man?'

'Foxy Harris. Old mate and accomplice of Mason's.'

'Bank robbers, weren't they?'

'Yes. We never found the last lot they pinched—eight hundred quid. Now I don't suppose that we ever shall! Ah, here's the doctor.'

A small and fussy GP was escorted in over the burnt beams and made a brief examination, tutting under his breath.

'Cyanide,' he concluded. 'They were all poisoned. You observe the *ricus sardonicus*? The deathly grin. Well marked, very well marked. Probably in the whisky. I wouldn't advise you to have a tot. Dear me no, wouldn't advise it at all.'

'How long would they have taken to die?' asked Jack.

The small doctor shrugged. 'Five minutes—less, perhaps. Nasty death, cyanide, but quick, undeniably quick. Rigor is holding them in place. I'd say, with the weather as it is, time of death was last night, twelve hours or so. Not less. Hard as stone.' He tapped Mary Mason's horrifying face with a casual finger. 'If you want to move the bodies, officer, you'd better wait until tonight, or you'll find them hard to handle. Yes, well, is that all? I can certify death,' and he was out into the street before a white-faced constable called him back, and a dog began to bark.

'I was going to ask the whereabouts of Albie Jackson,' said Phryne, suppressing nausea, 'but I have a feeling that you've just found him.'

Lying broken and dead on the back verandah was an old man. Rain had soaked his hair, his shirt was torn, and a black labrador dog lay beside him with its head on the mutilated chest.

'Oh, Lord!' said Jack Robinson. 'The poor old bloke.'

He had seen, as had Phryne, the flat-iron burns on the chest. The face, however, was peaceful. The dog did not move, but barked and then howled. A constable who laid a hand on the corpse was promptly bitten and jumped back.

Jack Robinson then did something that confirmed him in Phryne's high regard. He sat down on his heels and spoke directly to the dog.

'Come on, old fellow,' he said soothingly. 'I know he was your master and you loved him, but he's dead now, dog. He's dead. You have to leave him, feller. Come here, then. Come here. You can come home with me. He's dead, mate. He doesn't need you anymore.'

Phryne felt tears prick her eyes. The dog lifted its head and stared at Jack Robinson, who held out his hand.

'Come on, then, mate. Come on.'

The black dog wavered. It got to its feet, licked the face of the corpse, and howled again. Then it pushed its nose into Jack

Robinson's hand and howled, flung itself back on the dead man, then sighed a human sigh loaded with grief, and walked over to Jack and leaned against his leg.

'Poor old bloke,' repeated Jack Robinson. 'Come on, doctor, tell us about this one.'

The doctor, keeping a wary eye on the dog, knelt next to the dead man and pushed aside the torn shirt.

'He's been tortured,' he commented. 'With a hot iron. But he hasn't been poisoned, at least not with cyanide. I'd say he died of heart failure.'

'Natural causes.'

'If you call being tortured to death natural,' snapped the doctor. 'Now if you have no more corpses on the premises, Detective Inspector, I'll be getting back to the hospital. I'll do the autopsies when you can unkink the corpses. Goodbye,' and he was gone.

'What a bedside manner,' observed Phryne. 'How his patients must love him.'

'Not particularly, Miss, but he never hears any complaints. He only deals with the dead, so he doesn't need any manners. Come on, dog,' said Jack Robinson, 'we'd better get you something to eat, eh?'

The dog, with a last look at the old man, followed him into the house.

'Go out, Jones, and buy me a leash and a couple of dishes and some dog meat,' ordered Robinson.

Phryne asked, 'What will you do with the dog?'

'I'll take him home. The kids have been asking for a dog, but the wife says that they are too much trouble. I reckon she'll have

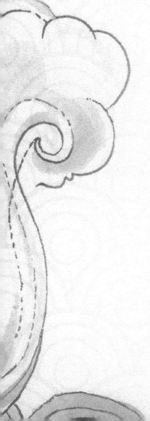

this one, though,' he smiled. 'Proper sentimental she is. And he's a good dog,' said Robinson, as the black nose was inserted confidingly into his hand. 'He's a good old mutt.'

Robinson found two unburnt chairs in the front of the house and sat down, the dog leaning against him. He motioned Miss Fisher to a chair.

'So now we've got a mystery, and a murderer to find,' he mused. 'Any ideas?'

'Not at the moment. I never saw such a horrible scene, Jack, not even when I was driving an ambulance in the Great War. They told me about the tea party, though. That must have had the same effect.'

'The tea party?'

'A group of soldiers who were sitting around a little fire making tea, and didn't hear the gas alert. They were all killed and, like these ones, they were struck dead as they sat, and the rescue party found them all in their places, one with a cup raised to his lips. I've seen a photograph of it.' The house stank of filth and bitter smoke. Phryne was beginning to feel queasy.

'Back in a moment,' she promised. She went into the street and was sick into a convenient bush. She then found the flask which she always kept in her car, and took it back to the policeman.

'Have a swig, Jack. It's my own whisky, and contains no improper substances.'

They drank in silence. It was good whisky.

'Let's look at the facts, then. The old man reported that someone was trying to kill him. He said that he had been shot at, and people were making threats against him, and we didn't take him seriously because he was a difficult old cuss and we get a lot of complaints from loonies. And he had the dog, too, so I thought he was safe enough. Then he said that someone wanted to buy his house, and I wrote him off as mad. Who'd want a dump like this, when there are hundreds of these houses, all the same?'

'There must have been something about this house rather than any other,' mused Phryne. 'What?'

'I better find out who used to own the place,' said Robinson. 'And I better organise a proper search, and soon,' he added, as the cold wind set the damaged timbers groaning, 'before the whole place comes down on our heads. Ah, here's Jones. That was quick.'

'Lady down the street has a dog, sir, and she lent me his dishes and some meat and biscuits. And I've brought some water from her place. Sir, the lady herself would like a word.'

'Good, bring her in—well done, constable.'

The young constable, recovering from the greenish pallor of the badly shaken, blushed. He put the dishes down on the floor and filled the water dish. The dog looked at Robinson.

'Go on, then,' he said encouragingly. The dog continued to stare. It did not move, although it was obviously hungry.

'Well, you mutt, don't just sit there and drool,' said Robinson.

Phryne said, 'It's been trained not to eat before it has permission. You'll have to say the right word.'

'Golly, what a case,' muttered Robinson. 'And I can't ask its late master, can I? Well, I can ask, but I won't get no answer. Go on then, Blackie! You're my guest. You're welcome.'

That was evidently the word. The dog leapt forward and buried his nose in the water dish, drinking with a great deal of splash, then wolfed down the meat and biscuits.

'That's a good dog,' observed Robinson. 'Look at him eat! How long since you last had a meal, eh, dog?'

Blackie did not reply, but licked the dish as carefully as if he was trying to remove the pattern. He came back to Robinson's side and lay down, whimpering a little, with his head on the Detective Inspector's highly polished boot.

'Hard to tell,' commented Phryne. 'All labradors eat like that. Look at the side of his head, Jack. He's hurt!'

Jack Robinson felt over the furry black skull, while the dog held still and licked at his hands.

'Been given a good old thump on the noggin',' he agreed. 'There's a big lump. A kick, perhaps, or a club. That explains why they didn't kill him.'

'Kill him?'

'Stands to reason, a good dog like this wouldn't hang about

while they tortured his master,' said Jack indignantly. 'He must have attacked one of them and they woodened him out, and he didn't recover until it was all over. Check for a dog bite on one of them in there, Jones, and bring in the lady, will you?'

Jones, swallowing dread, escorted into the room a thin and voluble lady so muffled in garments that one would have needed a shoe horn to get her out. She was wearing at least three cardigans in various colours and a pair of men's labouring boots.

'What has happened? Is the poor old man dead?' she asked in a shrill voice, setting all of Phryne's teeth on edge. 'Where is Mr Jackson? That young cop wouldn't tell me anything. Why there's Nubis,' she said, sighting the dog, which thumped its tail on the floor. 'He's all right, then. I thought so when the young man asked me for some dog food.'

'What's his name?' asked Phryne.

'Nubis. Something like that. That's what Mr Jackson called him.'

'Anubis?' hazarded Phryne. The late Mr Jackson had evidently been a man of some learning. 'It's the name of the ancient Egyptian God of the Dead. The black dog, Anubis.'

'I don't know, I'm sure. Strange man, Mr Jackson. Come down in the world, he had. Used to be a chemist, you know, a dispensing chemist, but his wife died, and then he sort of lost interest in things. She was a nice lady, used to grow geraniums. But she died three years ago, it must be, and it just broke his heart. Wouldn't let anyone help, wouldn't talk to anyone, just stayed in the house. What has happened to him?'

'He's dead, Mrs...?'

'Greene. Dead? His heart, was it? He had a bad heart.'

'He was murdered,' said Jack Robinson gently. 'Someone killed him. We are trying to find out who did it. Were you at home last night? Did you hear anything?'

'No one could hear anything over the storm we had last night. My daughter did say that she heard a car along about eleven, when she got up to put some buckets under the holes in the roof. But I didn't hear anything until the fire brigade came, about seven this morning. Murdered! What a dreadful thing!'

'Did he have any money?' asked Phryne.

Mrs Greene shook her head. 'No, not that I knew. No one ever said that he had money. But you couldn't talk to him, really. I came down a few times with a pot of soup or a cake for the poor soul, and he wouldn't let me in the house. Thanked me all nice, but he didn't want to be helped.'

Mrs Greene's eyes had an avid gleam, and Phryne reflected that a lone widower was fair prey for lonely local widows. She wouldn't have let Mrs Greene into the house, either. What a strange man, this Albie Jackson! A man of sardonic humour, who named his dog after an Egyptian god.

'Did you know the people who used to have this house?' asked Robinson.

Mrs Greene bridled. 'Me? Know them? They were criminals. Nasty people. The man was a fence, so they said. Lots of people used to call at the house, not nice people, neither. I was very pleased when they took him to jail, and she left, and then the Jacksons bought the house. She wanted a nice yard, she said, to grow her geraniums in. He used to make up things, you know, cough mixtures and things, and he was ever so good with animals. He cured my Toby of distemper, and he had a poultice which could take out splinters and bring up boils beautiful. But he wasn't a doctor. If anyone was real sick, he'd always send them to a doctor. "I'm just a chemist, Mrs Greene," he said to me once when I asked him about me rheumatics. "You need to see a doctor about your leg." Pains something cruel in this weather. What are you going to do about poor Nubis, then? I'd take him except that Toby wouldn't like it.'

'I'm taking him,' said Robinson. 'Thanks for the loan of the plates, Mrs Greene, I'll return them.'

'That's all right. I hope you get whoever done it. Poor old man!'

'Jones, show the lady out.' And Mrs Greene went, her curiosity unsatisfied and still glinting in her eyes.

———

With some cursing and a lot of manoeuvring, the ambulance men had taken the corpses away, and Phryne and Robinson were standing on the back verandah while three constables searched the house. Mason, asserted a shuddering Constable Jones, had a dog bite on his right forearm. Jones was not used to murder. Phryne, shivering in her parrot-patterned jumper and airman's jacket, reflected that neither was she.

'Let's reconstruct it. The three of them come to Mr Jackson's door late at night.

He opens it. They jump in and grab him, flattening poor old Anubis here with that hockey stick we found by the door. They bring the old man in here and tie him up. We've found the rope, it's new washing line, which indicates that they brought it with them.'

'But they didn't bring the flat iron,' commented Phryne, crossing both arms across her breast. 'It's an old one and probably dates back to Mrs Jackson. They might have just thought they could tie him up and find what they had come to find.'

'Which was the proceeds of the bank robbery, given to the fence to hold for them, and hidden in the house.'

'Yes. They tried to just buy the house but the cranky old bloke wouldn't sell.'

'Perhaps he loved the house,' said Phryne, wondering how anyone could. 'His wife lived here, you know, and died here. And Mrs Greene said that he was fond of her.'

'Yes. Perhaps. Anyway, they can't find the gelt, either because the fence took it with him or...'

'Or Mr Jackson found it, and moved it.'

'And they decided that he had moved it, maybe because they knew something from the fence. I've found out about him. Name of Carr. In Pentridge for receiving and theft and a few hundred related offences. Nasty bloke, but not violent. He's being interviewed about it now. So, they decided that Mr Jackson knew where the money was.'

'And they tried to persuade him to tell.'

'But at some point they must have loosed him, maybe to make them a cup of tea, or to get out the whisky. Just the sort of thing that the rat Mason would do, he was a nasty piece of work...'

'And he poisoned the whisky with a hefty dose of cyanide from his chemist's stock, which is still in the kitchen...'

'And then he died of heart failure when they started on him again, and they flung the body out the back, where the dog was.'

'Then they sat down to have a friendly drink before they searched the house.'

'And that was their last drink.'

'The poor old dog recovered, but he couldn't get in, and so he lay there all night next to the dead man.'

'And the fire started in the parlour, where a sweep of Mason's dying arm pushed the kero lamp onto the floor, where it smashed.'

'And the fire spread slowly because the house was wet with rain coming through the roof, and it swept down the hall, away from the parlour, because the front door blew open...'

'The fire brigade came and then it was all revealed,' Phryne completed the litany. 'What a brave man! He knew they were going to kill him, or maybe he felt his heart going, and still had enough courage and wit to poison the drink.'

'Not brave, just cranky. He wouldn't have wanted them to have their money. If he hid it, why didn't he give it to them? He didn't need it. Then they wouldn't have killed him. Just like him, to have the last laugh. If he had the money.'

Phryne gazed unseeing out into the rain-swept yard where the geraniums grew tall and ragged.

'I know where it is,' she exclaimed, and ran back into the house, Robinson and Anubis (whom he decided to call Blackie) at her heels. 'Where did the dog sleep?' she asked a puzzled constable, who was sorting through the contents of a cupboard which seemed to contain nothing but a thousand empty tobacco tins. He pointed to a pile of partially chewed blankets near the stove. Anubis suffered, it appeared, from night starvation.

Phryne pulled back the blankets and revealed a patch of unburnt flooring, in which a hole had been neatly cut. She pulled up the boards and dragged out a grey sack which still had the bank's identifying numbers stencilled in black.

'Anubis,' she said triumphantly, 'was the God of the Dead, but also the Guardian of the Hidden Treasure.'

The Guardian of the Hidden Treasure wagged his tail and whined.

———

Detective Inspector Robinson was at home, cup of tea in hand and slippers on his feet, before his own domestic hearth, anticipating a roast of lamb for dinner and watching his children play with Blackie. The dog showed a great tolerance for having fingers poked in his eyes and even Mrs Robinson had wept a few tears over his fidelity to his dead master and admitted that he was a fine, gentle animal. The telephone rang, and he padded out in his slippers to answer it, swearing that if it was another murder on a night like this he would quit the police force and become a grocer. It was not another murder. It was Phryne Fisher. 'You said that you were reading Chaucer, Jack?'

'Yes, that's right.'

'Apropos of today's events, have a look at "The Pardoner's Tale". How's Anubis?'

'Blackie. He's fine. The kids love him and the missus likes

him too. Is that all?'

'That's all. Goodnight, Jack.'

He found the collected Chaucer and sat down before the fire, listening to the rain on the roof, and located the tale. He read the unfamiliar spelling aloud, as the three young men met an old man and asked where they could find death, for he was killing their friends. 'Death shall be dead, if we can him find,' he translated. 'To find death,' said the old man, 'they had but to dig under a certain tree. There they found a bushel of gold coins: two decided to kill the one, who poisoned the wine, and thus they all died.'

> Right so they have him slain, and that anon.
> And when this was done, thus spake that one
> 'Now let us sit and drink, and make merry
> And afterward we will his body bury.'
> And with that it happened, in this case
> To take the bottle where the poison was
> And drank, and gave his fellow to drink also,
> For which anon they were slain both the two...
> Thus had these wretches their ending
> Thus ended were these homicides two
> and the false poisoner also.

Detective Inspector Robinson read the next line and could not but agree with it: 'O cursed sin, full of cursedness! Oh traitorous homicide, o wickedness!'

'Put aside your book, Jack,' said his wife from the door. 'Dinner's ready. Kids, come in to dinner. Yes, you can bring the dog, but wipe his paws! Was it a very bad case, Jack?' she asked, seeing how slowly and with what effort he got out of his chair.

'Yes, love,' he said, putting Chaucer down. 'It was a bad case. And I'm glad to be home,' said Robinson, and smiled.

Mulled ALE

½ cup honey
1 cup boiling water
1 tsp nutmeg
1 tsp cinnamon
Ale

A Chaucerian drink. Dissolve the honey
in the boiling water. Flavour this with
the nutmeg and cinnamon. Put in a large
container and fill up with strong 'real' ale.
You can turn this into 'sheep's wool' by
adding a roasted apple or two.
Warms the cockles....

Carnival

Beauty provoketh thieves sooner than gold
William Shakespeare, *As You Like It*, 1.3.106

Phryne Fisher, daringly elegant in a peach and black bloused top and a pair of palpable, scandalous trousers, mostly regretted that she had ever met Bobby Ferguson, but she had come with him because she loved all circuses and carnivals. And here it was.

The hot wind crackled through the dry grass alongside Williamstown Road. It carried not only the usual city messages—'A Far Too Male Cat Has Been Here' and 'Watch Out for the Van'—but also Turkey lolly and toffee apples, animal dung, machine oil and frying grease. She sniffed an appreciative sniff.

'Oh, yes,' she said. 'I love carnivals. Not your sort of place, I wouldn't have thought.'

Bobby did not reply. Phryne headed up the dusty path towards the lights, where the wheezing of a calliope was enchanting the night. It was playing 'Daisy, Daisy, give me your answer, do', in just the wrong key. What was the matter with the spoiled rotten son of a major banking house now? He complained about the car, her treasured Hispano-Suiza. He complained about her driving. He complained about the heat. No one had ever stopped Bobby from having anything he had set his heart on, but no one else was going to drive Phryne's car while she had breath in her body.

She decided that a little light ignoring might cure his sulks and pressed on. She was just producing her sixpence when she heard a faint scream from behind her and was in time to see Bobby transfixed with horror as something frightful rose from the ground, giving vent to a bubbling whine like a monster from a nightmare. Phryne bore Bobby up on one shoulder and grabbed a trailing rope.

'It's only a camel,' she said soothingly. 'I rode them in Arabia. I admit that this is an unusually revolting specimen of an unattractive species. Still, I believe that there are people who love them. Hello,' she said to the woman at the gate, who still held Phryne's sixpence. 'Two tickets, please. And is this your camel?'

The woman tore off two tickets and, instead of replying, shrieked, 'Bill! Them bloody camels is out!' Then she smiled and took the tether. 'You're good with camels,' she commented in a harsh rasp. 'You in the trade, maybe? One of

Wirth's dancers? Tell 'em on the merry-go-round that Mama said you was to 'ave a free go.'

'Thank you,' replied Phryne, delighted.

She passed through the gate, taking Bobby and leaving the camel, though the camel might have proved better company.

'What is the matter with you, old bean?' she asked.

'The heat. I hate the heat,' said Bobby.

'In that case you should have stayed in a nice cool hotel and drunk nice cool beer,' said Phryne. 'It's as hot as a furnace in the north, where this wind comes from.'

'And I've just realised that I've forgotten to have mother's pearl bracelet fixed. I've got it in my pocket.' Bobby, a pink young man with slicked down hair, patted his pocket, just in case any passing thief hadn't deduced where he might have put it. 'It's very valuable. Anyone could steal it.'

'Then put it in another pocket and stop talking so loudly,' advised Phryne absently. She was looking for the carousel.

'But all these people are thieves,' protested Bobby.

A slim young man in greasy overalls paused in bolting together a collection of iron pipes and scowled. The light caught his hair. It had the same blue sheen as a cock's feather. His face was all angles, sharp and defined in the harsh electric glare.

'Nonsense,' said Phryne briskly. 'A carnival has the exact same proportion of thieves as anywhere else, and I am not excepting your bank.'

The young man gave Phryne an astonished and vulnerable smile, packed up his spanner and vanished into the darkness between the lights.

The merry-go-round was old and a little tired. Phryne chose a rearing Lipizzaner stallion called Prancer and swung herself aboard. She told the attendant about Mama and he grinned.

'Come on, Bobby!' she called.

'I'll watch you,' said Bobby, fanning himself with his straw boater.

Phryne dismissed him as the carousel creaked into life and she was off through patches of coloured and flavoured light: green and wet canvas, blue and engine oil, yellow and fairy floss, red and chips frying. She stayed on, paying a penny for the extra ride, through another set of circuits. Delicious. The moving air was almost cool.

As she descended, she heard thunder. A nice drop of rain would be reviving, but she hoped it would hold off for a few hours. Wet carnivals were sad.

She led Bobby along the shaky row of sideshows. 'The Wild Man from Borneo!' announced a man attired in frock coat and someone's top hat. His voice was rich and fruity with an undertone of cigar and an overtone of port.

'The missing link!' he bellowed. 'Captured in the jungles of Malaya!'

Phryne paid and entered the booth. There was a crouched human figure, gnawing conscientiously at a haunch bone which could have come from a dinosaur. He was wearing a scanty and rather moth-eaten animal skin. His tangled hair straggled to his shoulders. He looked up at Phryne and bared his teeth. They were all filed to a point.

'Very nice,' said Phryne. 'We should introduce you to Sailor, though he might teach you bad habits.'

She was referring to the zoo's large and extremely male chimpanzee, who had been known to surprise the delicately nurtured by proving it. The wild man grinned again.

Bobby pulled at Phryne's arm. 'You don't want to see this disgusting exhibition, do you? And the next one has snakes! I hate snakes!'

Phryne thought that the Wild Man looked rather hurt. She took Bobby out of the tent.

'I do, and the next one is...?'

'The Princess of the Amazon!' bellowed the shill, tipping his top hat to the lady. 'Brought at Great Expense from the Jungles for the Edification of the Multitudes!'

This ability to speak in capitals must have been valuable, Phryne reflected, examining her change and buying admission. The lady might not have been royal but she was extensively blacked-up and her snake was magnificent.

Phryne turned to find that Bobby had been replaced by the young mechanic. She considered that the night was suddenly improving.

'Go on, Doreen, show the lady the snake,' he encouraged.

The Amazon Princess looped a few yards of boa around her comely shoulders and moved forward. The huge blunt head of the snake rose, tongue flicking.

'My name's Alan Lee,' said the mechanic. 'This is Doreen, and that's Cleopatra.'

'Pleased to meet you all. I apologise for my escort.'

'Him? Been after Anna,' said Doreen. 'Mopes about like a sick cat. Been here every night.'

'See, Miss, we don't like strangers going after our girls,'

explained the young man. He had eyes as black as ebony. It was hard to guess what he was thinking. He had shaken Phryne's hand cautiously, conscious of the grease on his own. 'The townies think they're whores. They ain't. Anna's my sister. She's going to marry Samson, our strongman. Can you take your bloke away? He might get damaged.'

'My dear Mr Lee,' said Phryne, 'Bobby isn't mine. I expect he's gone off to eat worms. I'm going to enjoy my evening. I love carnivals.'

Alan Lee smiled. 'We can tell. You want to stroke Cleopatra? Go on. She won't hurt you.'

Phryne stroked Cleopatra, who felt like a good snakeskin shoe. Not knowing the terrible thought in Phryne's mind, the snake rose a little under her hand.

'If she'd been a cat, she would have purred,' commented Alan.

The pressure to do something about Bobby was still there. Phryne sighed. 'All right, I'll try and remove Bobby—but only if you swear I can come back another night.'

His red lips parted over teeth as white as seeds. His black eyes held the promise of dark delights. If there were angels, this was a midnight one. Phryne shivered pleasantly. She gave the young man a highly combustible look and left the booth, searching for Bobby.

No great detective ability was required to locate

the pink-faced pest. He was standing in the middle of the patch, next to the shooting gallery, screaming at the top of his voice, 'I've been robbed!'

'That bloody bracelet,' muttered Phryne to herself. 'I should have taken it from him. He was telegraphing "Steal This Trinket!" on all frequencies. Oh dear.' She pushed through the gathering crowd and asked crisply, 'What's the matter, Bobby?'

'Mother's pearl bracelet—it's gone!' he screamed.

'Will you shut up,' demanded Phryne. 'You're making a scene. Have you searched all your pockets?'

Around her she could sense the growing dismay of the carnival folk. This was real trouble. No one trusted carnival people. No one was likely to believe them when they swore their innocence. Everyone knew that the gypsies stole chickens and washing. And spoke a strange language and probably didn't wash and did you see the state of that woman's fingernails? Good name ruined, permits refused ... This was a disaster. Phryne was incensed.

Phryne searched Bobby's pockets. No bracelet. He opened the black velvet case and showed it was empty. He was just about to bellow again when Phryne grabbed his shoulder and shook him.

'Will you stop yelling! When did you miss the bracelet?'

'I don't know. Just now. I got out some coins for the shooting gallery and found the case empty. It's gone!'

'All right, now. I'll find it. Be quiet. Show's over,' she said to the gaping crowd. 'Nothing more to see. The gentleman has mislaid something. Alan, start the calliope again. Off you go,' said Phryne, and such was the force of her personality that most of the onlookers lost interest and wandered away.

The one who didn't was the policeman. 'Something been stolen, sir?' he asked, getting out his official notebook. He was a blond, blue-eyed guardian of the people. He had never trusted carnivals since he had failed to win the stuffed parrot on which he had set his heart at the age of eight and later had found out about fixed fairground guns. 'Missed something? Silly of you to bring anything valuable into a carnival! We all know what carnies are like. And they are nasty, dirty places. They wouldn't be allowed if I had my way.'

'I'm Phryne Fisher,' said Phryne, holding out her hand. She had just a few moments before that detestable oaf started writing in his notebook. She had also just caught sight, for the first time, of Samson the strongman, who must have been seven feet tall and was inhaling as though he had asthma.

'I'm a private investigator. Shall I give my good friend Detective Inspector Robinson your regards? I don't believe we need to waste your valuable time on my escort's lost property.'

She gave him a full-beam three hundred watt dazzling smile, which usually worked its magic on the recipient. Not this time, though. The policeman did not take her hand. He said mulishly, 'Gentleman says he's been robbed. I heard him.'

'The gentleman hasn't the brain of a peahen.'

Bobby felt that he was being ignored. 'I had it in my pocket!

And there's the case, empty! What will Mother say? It's worth four hundred pounds!'

The carnies paled and the policeman stood to attention in the presence of money. Damn. Now it was official. Phryne walked away into the dark between two stalls and Alan Lee came to her side.

'It looks bad!' he exclaimed. 'Who could have robbed him? I ain't seen any of the local dips. We always gets Samson to see 'em off. They're bad for business.'

Samson rippled a few muscles and looked down modestly. A slim, elegant girl sat on the shooting gallery bench, scowling at Bobby.

'That's Anna,' said Alan.

The shooting gallery shone. Not very new rifles were laid out on the counter. Targets wobbled across the back: tin ducks. On a board were the prizes—kewpie dolls, Chinese porcelain fresh from Abbotsford, glass rings and Woolworths pearls, hanging singly on hooks. Why was Bobby making this scene? Something jarred on Phryne. What thief took the jewel and left the case? Of course. This was Bobby's own doing. He had staged this scene: just take out the bracelet, distract Anna, and hang it on a hook. And either blackmail Anna or ruin the carnival. Simple. Phryne reflected that merchant banking really was bad for the soul.

'I'm afraid,' said Phryne, 'that even from here, amongst those trinkets, I can see a sheen only produced by irritating an oyster.'

'Not Anna,' said Alan Lee. 'She's no thief.'

'I don't believe it either,' said Phryne. 'Now we need a diversion.'

'What if I just break his neck?' asked Samson reasonably. 'I could do it easy. Like snapping a daffodil.'

'Thanks anyway, Samson. Not with that cop there taking notes,' replied Alan.

'Go get the Wild Man,' said Phryne. 'Er...does he speak English?'

'Tom? He's from Footscray.'

'And ask the Princess of the Amazon if Cleopatra would like an outing. Bobby,' said Phryne vengefully, 'hates snakes.'

———

The policeman was still taking notes. Anna Lee, frightened and disdainful, was sitting on the shooting gallery bench, affecting not to notice.

'I felt in my pocket for a penny to give a child—'

'Could the child have picked your pocket, sir?'

'It was only a small child,' said Bobby.

'Might have been a midget. You never know in a carnival. Hells bells!' he exclaimed. 'What's that?'

Hooting and leaping through the crowd came the Wild Man, Alan Lee in close pursuit. Tom bounced and gibbered with aplomb, turned a neat somersault and leapt into the shooting gallery where he tried to groom Anna's hair. She pushed him away and he bounced down again, snarling now, menacing Bobby and the policeman. They backed away. So did Phryne. She almost had her hands on the bracelet when they turned to face her again. Phryne cursed under her breath.

Alan Lee, stockwhip in hand, cracked it. The Wild Man

uttered a shriek and ran back to his nice safe booth with the gypsy behind him. The crowd stirred and muttered. This was turning out to be a more interesting evening than they had expected.

'The camels are out!' shouted Phryne, losing patience. Both Bobby and the policeman looked away. In a second she had the little bundle of beads in hand. When they looked back, Phryne Fisher had slid away into the darkness.

The constable decided to arrange a search. Phryne heard Bobby say to Anna, 'I've got you now, girl. Me or jail,' he said. 'Now you have to come with me when I snap my fingers.'

'Snap, then,' replied Anna, voice dripping with scorn.

'By God, I will! Constable!'

The policeman was not having a good evening. Finding witnesses was harder than he thought. He returned.

'I've found the bracelet!' Bobby exclaimed. Phryne thought how unattractive he was, red with frustrated passion and dripping with sweat. 'I wondered where someone might hide it and I thought, what about the prize board? This girl stole them,' he said, unhooking without looking at his object. 'See? Mother's pearls!'

'No, they ain't,' said the policeman. 'They ain't worth tuppence.'

Bobby stared at the Woolworths pearls. 'Then where are Mother's pearls?' he cried.

'Here,' said Phryne Fisher, fervently hoping that it was true. She put the string into his hot hand. 'You dropped them near the carousel. You really are careless, Bobby. Now shall we just tell this nice policeman what you have really been up to?'

'No,' said Alan Lee, laying a hand on Phryne's arm. 'No trouble, lady.'

'Then we will allow him to carry on with his very useful task of keeping the world safe from carnivals,' agreed Phryne.

The disgusted constable moved away. Samson lifted Bobby off his feet by his collar with no apparent effort.

'You horrible little insect,' said Phryne dispassionately. 'Still, I suppose it is educational to find out that you can't have everything you want. And just in case you want to cause any more trouble,' she told Bobby, 'we are going to lock you up, just for a while, while I enjoy the carnival. I won't say that Doreen might leave one of her snakes in the booth,' she said with quiet venom. 'I'll just let you find out for yourself.'

Doreen was walking through the crowd, carrying Cleopatra, who was pleased to be out of her tent. Bobby fell to his knees. Phryne took pity on him.

'Or perhaps you would prefer to give them all the money in your pockets, a promise never to return, and flee the scene?'

Bobby shed three pound notes, a folded ten-pound note, seven shillings, three pence and two farthings and ran for his life. As he ran, Anna reached out a hand and snapped her fingers in his face.

———

Phryne was cool at last. Supper was over, the others had gone back to their caravans. Tom had turned out to be a cheery man who had been shipwrecked in Borneo, which gave him a new career. Doreen had inherited her snakes from her mum, who had married

a grocer in Tumbarumba. Phryne had patted one snake and scotched another. A day full of incident.

The lights were out. Across the huddle of booths the rain sluiced, washing away the stains of anger and appetite and fear. Camels hooted and bubbled, surprising local owls. Alan Lee was behind her and she leaned back into his salty, soapy scent. She could feel every defined muscle in his chest.

'You could stay the night,' he stated. Phryne laughed and turned into his embrace, kissing the strong throat and the hollow of the collarbone. His hands slid down her sides.

'I think I might,' she said softly. 'I have always...loved...the carnival.

KERRY GREENWOOD

LEMONADE

2 cups caster sugar
3 cups boiling water
3 lemons, juice and zest
extra lemon slices, mint and borage flowers

Dissolve the sugar in the water, add the zest
and juice, and stir. When cold, add lemon
slices and decorations. This recipe can be
made using any citrus fruit
—just add the sugar.

The *Camberwell* WONDER

Mordre wol out, that see we day by day
Geoffrey Chaucer, 'The Nun's Priest's Tale'

The constable straightened up, and held out a gentleman's starched collar. It was slightly greenish from the moss it had lain in. There was a dark splotch of dried blood across the whole length of the back. He exhibited it to Detective Inspector Robinson, who nodded.

'What have you got to say about this, eh, Stevie?'

The big man nodded. A glint of what might have been intelligence gleamed in his sullen eyes. He said slowly, 'I killed Mr Clarke. I killed him.'

And all the way down to Russell Street and on every subsequent enquiry, that was all he would say.

——————

It had been a disagreeable night, and Phryne Fisher fought off her escort with more force and less finesse than she usually showed. The young man was clumsy, having battered her toes to pulp while dancing with her at the Green Mill; she feared that her satin train was damaged beyond repair, and he had probably marked her dress with his hot, sweaty hands.

'Let me go or I'll break your arm,' she advised him. 'Good-night, Mr Clarke.' She did not necessarily wait until her own door was closed before she added, 'And good riddance!' She stalked into her parlour and flung herself down into a sea-blue easy chair.

'Dot, get me some slippers, my shoes are ruined, and my feet, too,' she exclaimed, examining her toes ruefully. 'That's the last time I do favours for people! "Take the poor boy out, Phryne, you might be able to do something with him, terribly good family, you know."' She spat indelicately into the fireplace. 'Hell and damnation, look at this satin!'

'Likely it will clean,' said Dot equably. 'How about a nice cup of warm milk?'

'Get me a small glass of green chartreuse,' requested Phryne, more civilly, for she was fond of her assistant. 'The drinks at the Moulin Vert really are frightful. But weak. You couldn't get drunk on them in a millennium. The management are foundation members of the Temperance League Against Alcohol. What an evil temper I have. It's not the poor boy's fault that his father is a loony and his mother hasn't spoken to him for years.'

'What, Mr Clarke? I saw that name in the paper,' said Dot, handing over the glass.

'Oh, you must have heard of him, Dot. Man's got a mania

for rehabilitating the retarded. Staffs his whole estate with the feeble-minded. Supposed to be a charitable man, but in my opinion he is purely cynical. If his staff are dim, they work hard, and I bet they don't get holidays and union rates. Met him once at some bazaar that Lady Rose Maillart was sponsoring, and I didn't like him, Dot. I've never trusted men with the kind of social smile that never reaches the eyes. And his wife— now called Parvarti—was captured by some Indian sect and floats around in ochre robes, which clash dreadfully with her complexion, chanting mantras or sutras or whatever they are. Dreadful people. And their son just trampled my toes like the corn beneath the harrow and made a very obvious grab for my... er ...attributes. Oh well, curse the lot of them. At least I'm home in one piece. What are you looking for, Dot?'

'Toad,' corrected Dot absently. 'It's a toad beneath the harrow. Here we are, Miss. Listen: "Mr Clarke the Philanthropist missing. Gardener confesses to Murder".'

'Good Lord!'

'That's about it, Miss.' Dot crossed herself. 'It says that the boy confessed freely to having murdered his master but won't say anything else. Excuse me, Miss Phryne, there's the phone, and the Butlers are out. Who could it be, at this time of night?'

Phryne sipped her liqueur and scanned the newspaper for any further information. Where was the body? How had this murder been committed? She felt a pang of guilt for her dislike of the deceased. His philanthropy appeared to have been fatal.

Dot appeared in the doorway. 'Lady Rose, Miss Phryne.'

'Oh, gosh.' Phryne padded barefoot out to the phone. The

tiles were icy under her feet. 'Phryne Fisher,' she said into the receiver.

'Phryne, you must come here right away!' demanded the cool, high voice. 'I have a commission for you.'

'Lady Rose, it's past midnight!'

'And what should that matter to a fine healthy girl? When I was your age I was dancing until four and breakfasting in Covent Garden at dawn on fresh strawberries! No stamina, that's what's wrong with you. Too many cocktails and cigarettes and not enough huntin'.'

'Give me a good reason why it can't wait until morning,' groaned Phryne. 'I've been dancing with the Clarke boy and it might be days before I can walk again.'

'That hobbledehoy! My dear, that was self-sacrificing of you. Tomorrow then. At nine. Sharp.'

'Sharp,' agreed Phryne, and hung up.

'What did she want, Miss? Here are your slippers.'

'Give me an arm up the stairs, there's a dear. I expect that it is the Clarke murder. Lady Rose knows that family very well. But what she wants me to do about it, Dot old bean, I haven't the faintest idea.'

———

Nine sharp found Phryne ringing the front door bell of Lady Rose's bijou Toorak residence, a small and absurd building like an iced cake. Lady Rose's maid let her in, took her coat, and confided, 'She's in a real state, Miss. Don't cross her if you can help it. It's the Clarke murder. I never did like that Mr Clarke. Nasty eyes. And they say he was involved in some shady dealings—import and export, you know.' Miss Penleigh was an inveterate and poisonous gossip. 'They say that he was bringing in all sorts of odd cargoes. Through this door, Miss. And be careful.'

Warned, Phryne trod delicately. The tiny but fiery Lady Rose was sitting on her Empire sofa, embracing as much of a huge woman in a wrapper and a drab dress as she could encompass. She glared up at Phryne.

'There you are. This is Mrs Slade. She is my cleaner. Comes in every day for the rough scrubbing. She's been working for me for thirty years. Eh, Slade?'

The large woman gave an affirmative sob.

'She has a family, Phryne. A layabout husband who is no use to anyone and a silly daughter who is a mannequin and a son called Stevie. He's twenty now, but his mind never grew up. Slade says his father dropped him on his head. He's a good boy, kind and pleasant, but he's a child.'

'And he murdered Mr Clarke,' said Phryne.

Mrs Slade gave a wail of anguish and turned up a face sodden with tears and wrinkled like an old apple. 'He'd never harm anyone, never! He wouldn't hurt a fly! Only time I ever saw him angry was when some boys were tormenting three kittens. He hoisted them up and dropped them, but the kittens he cradled in his hands and nursed like a mother. He wouldn't hurt anyone! And he loved Mr Clarke. My Dan, he said that we'd have to put Stevie away, he was getting so big and all. Then it was a blessing when Mr Clarke offered him a job. Not much pay, of course, but all found and he could come home at night.'

'But he says he killed Mr Clarke,' objected Phryne, sitting down to ease her feet. 'And they found his collar with blood on it.'

The woman's face set into stubborn lines. 'I don't believe it. Someone's been putting words into his mouth. He never done it. Not my Stevie.'

'Well, Phryne?' snapped Lady Rose.

Phryne sighed. 'I'll try, but it's going to be difficult, with a confession.'

'Everything worth doing is difficult,' said the small woman fiercely. 'Get along with you, girl, and solve the riddle. I never did like that Joshua Clarke,' she added, meditatively.

'Can you take me to see the house?'

'Of course. We shall go there directly. Don't worry, Slade,' she said, extracting herself from the sofa, 'we will get your boy back.'

Mrs Slade surveyed Phryne in her fashionable morning dress of wine-coloured wool and the Dutch-doll face with black hair swinging forward over her cheeks. She shook her head slowly.

'Thank you, Miss, I'm sure,' she muttered doubtfully. 'I'll get back to me scrubbing.'

'Come along, Phryne,' ordered Lady Rose. 'Penleigh! My coat! I'm going out.'

As Miss Penleigh dressed her employer in a fur coat which had seen better years, Phryne asked her, 'Tell me more about Mr Clarke's business—do you know any more?'

'Penleigh always knows more than she says—that's why she is so amusing,' declared Lady Rose. 'What about his business?'

'He was supposed to have got a load of watches from Hong Kong and smuggled them through customs,' said Penleigh, animated by their interest. 'And some clocks, I believe. They say he also deals in wine and tobacco, and none of it ain't paid duty.'

'Interesting,' said Lady Rose. 'But not helpful. Back directly, Penleigh. My, Phryne, what a large car, and so very red! When I was a girl, I would have been considered fast for driving in it.' She hopped into the car with delight. 'But now I'm old, I can be as fast as I like, and I do find it refreshing. Camberwell, Phryne, it's a big mansion, and he can afford it if he's dealing in smuggled wine. I wonder about that Châteauneuf-du-Pape I bought from him! How intriguing to think that it might have been illegal!'

Phryne steered the Hispano-Suiza, her treasure, carefully past lumbering delivery trucks and onto a broad road.

'What about Mrs Clarke?'

'Oh, quite dotty, dear, always has been. I was a girl with her older sisters, and they were all a little eccentric, but Calliope was definitely, well, a little touched, even when she was at school. Has enthusiasm, you know. For botany, I recall, and bird-

watching, and she always threw herself bodily into
her current fascination. Luckily she tires easily, and
then there is a brief period of calm, then she's away
with the fairies again. Calls herself Parvarti now. Poor
Calliope.'

'Did they all have names like that?'

'Oh yes, there was Eudora and Euterpe and Psyche
and...now what was the brother's name? Are we going
to hit that tram?'

'No.'

'Oh, good. Xerxes, that was it. Died young, I seem
to remember.'

'Of acute nomenclature,' diagnosed Phryne.

Lady Rose laughed her parrot laugh until they drew
up outside a huge house. A bouncy and enthusiastic boy
threw open the massive iron gates and Phryne steered
the red car through. She tossed a penny to the boy, who
grinned a Cheshire cat grin and patted the bonnet.

'Pretty,' he yelled. 'Pretty car, pretty lady! Pretty,
pretty!'

Phryne drove on. 'Are all the staff potty?' she
asked, a little shaken by the gatekeeper.

Lady Rose had not turned a hair on her well-
groomed silver head. 'No, dear, I believe that the
butler and his wife, the housekeeper, are quite with
us, and so is the steward.'

'Steward?'

'Yes, the head keeper, I suppose you could call
him. He keeps an eye on all of the...others. A superior

man, with an eye which could open oysters. Where shall we leave the car?'

'Here,' said Phryne. 'Next to the police car. Hello, Sergeant,' she called to a large policeman. 'Is Jack Robinson on this case?'

'Yes, Miss Fisher,' said Sergeant Day affably. He had liked Phryne ever since she delivered a child molester wrapped in brown paper to the Queenscliff police station. 'And it will take a while, too.'

'Have you found a body yet?'

'No, nothing more than the collar.'

'Has it gone to the laboratory?'

'Why should it?'

'To find out whether it's human blood. Precipitin test, you know. You'll look very silly if it turns out to be rabbit.'

'I'll send it,' promised the sergeant. 'Inspector Robinson's inside, Miss. Are you involved?'

'Yes, I'm to restore your murderer to his mother's loving arms.'

'Good luck, Miss Fisher.'

Phryne and Lady Rose mounted steps, which had been scrubbed white, and were admitted to the house by a grim butler. He took their names into an inner room and a moment later escorted them wordlessly to the door.

'Miss Fisher and Lady Rose Maillart,' he announced, turned on his heel and left.

'Jack! How nice to see you!' cried Phryne, as a

puzzled detective inspector rose from a couch and took her hand. There was a bundle of yellow garments on the floor.

'Oh, Calliope, do get up!' exclaimed Lady Rose irritably. 'Sit on a chair like a Christian and talk to us, or I shall lose my temper with you.'

The bundle stirred, put out a thin arm, and Phryne helped her into a chair. She shook back tangled grey hair and said meekly, 'Rose, you are so forceful.'

'That's more than I could do,' murmured Jack Robinson. 'She's been sitting there all morning chanting and refusing to answer me. I reckon the whole place is loony.'

Phryne patted his arm. 'What do you want to know?'

'When she last saw her husband.'

Lady Rose took her cue. 'Well, Calliope, when did you last see Joshua?'

'In eternity there is no time...' Mrs Clarke caught the look in Lady Rose's blue eyes and stammered, 'Yesterday morning. He had a meeting with some businessmen and then he was supposed to be back for lunch and he never came, but he does that, sometimes, and sometimes even if he comes I am meditating on the infinite and I don't lunch when I'm meditating on the infinite, but he always comes home to sleep and he never came, and the maid said his bed hadn't been slept in and then I called the police and they found that collar and then Stevie said...he said...'

She ran down, like a gramophone. She stared hopefully at Lady Rose.

'Was he worried about anything? Any of these business matters?' asked the policeman, and she answered, 'Oh, Joshua would never talk to me about business. He was pleased about something, though. Lately he'd been losing patience with the staff, and they do try so hard, poor things, and said he was thinking of breaking up the establishment and settling in a smaller house, he said, and I said that I wouldn't like that, because I need space, you know, to...'

'Contemplate the infinite, we know. Really, Calliope, you are the silliest creature I ever met! Was he intending to leave you?'

'Leave me?' The vague eyes, half closed, were shocked into opening wide. 'How could he? This is my house, Rose, and he hasn't any money, at least, I don't know what money he has, but it can't be much because he's always asking me to sign cheques for more, but he seemed happier lately...yes, happier. He sang in the bath.'

'What did he sing?' asked Phryne, without any clear idea of why she was asking. Jack Robinson gave her a censorious look.

'French songs.' Calliope Clarke hummed in a surprisingly tuneful voice, then sang the words, *'Je donnerais Versailles, Paris et Saint-Denis, le tours de Notre-Dame et...et...'*

Phryne finished the song. *'Et le clocher de mon pays.* That's "Auprès de ma Blonde". Did he usually sing?'

'Oh, no, no, not for years...' Calliope's attention, engaged like a faulty gear, was slipping.

Lady Rose shook her. 'The nice policeman wants to ask some more questions, Calliope.'

'Nothing more, madam, just permission to search the house.'

'Of course.' Calliope sat down on the floor again, crossed her legs and began to chant. Jack Robinson led the way into the hall.

'Dear, dear, she's pottier than ever,' sighed Lady Rose. 'You go and search, Phryne, and I'll sit with her a little. Perhaps some tea.'

The hard-faced man was at her elbow. 'Tea, Lady Rose? I shall order it immediately.'

'Thank you.' Lady Rose went back into the drawing room and Phryne detained the man.

'Are you the butler?'

'No, Miss, the steward. The butler is indisposed.'

'Take us to Mr Clarke's rooms, please.'

'If I could give the order for tea first? Annie!' He tinkled a little bell and a very clean maid ran to him. 'Tea, Annie, for Mrs Clarke and a visitor, and be careful with the tray, mind! Now, Mr Clarke's rooms are this way.'

Very well-appointed rooms, too. Leather-bound books covered the walls, the desk was a massive slab of walnut, and the carpet both Persian and precious. It was all in perfect order and smelt of beeswax.

'This room has been cleaned,' accused Jack Robinson. The steward nodded.

Phryne poked about then asked suddenly, 'What was in the wastepaper basket?'

'I'm sure I don't know, Miss.'

'Where is your rubbish put?'

'In the bin, Miss. Burnables in the incinerator.'

'Show me,' demanded Phryne.

The steward glanced at Detective Inspector Robinson for his cue, and the policeman nodded. Resignedly the steward led the way through the hidden region of the house, into a cold, scrubbed passage lined with American cloth and out the back door into the kitchen garden. There Phryne picked her way through a wilderness of peasticks and fallow asparagus beds until she was led to a brick incinerator.

'Take off the lid,' she requested, and delved inside, sneezing as ashes  crept into her nose. She emerged a moment later to ask, 'Did Mr Clarke smoke cigars?' and received an affirmative. Bits of paper were in both hands when she came into view again, and she sorted them rapidly. Brochures and shipping lists, a partly destroyed book, and a mass of paper which looked as if it had been torn from a notebook, covered in figures in a neat, cramped hand.

'Good. Go and get me a bag, will you—that sack will do.'

The bemused steward assisted Miss Fisher in transferring the waste paper into a sugar sack. He noticed that she retained one scrap in her hand as she ran back to the house, leaving him to toil behind with the sack.

'Jack, Jack, where are you? Come on, we have to hurry. I've got some things to confirm, but you must go forth and do battle with the heathen. Quick, there's no time to lose. It's eleven already!'

Jack Robinson, who had found nothing out of the ordinary in the study, seized Miss Fisher by the elbows, judging her hysterical, but she twisted free.

'I'm fine, Jack, really. Take this paper, see? The pencil mark.

In the second column. Now get down there, and I'll see you at Russell Street—hurry!'

Jack was still staring at the scrap of paper in his hand when he heard the front door slam behind Lady Rose, Phryne Fisher, and the sugar bag. Then he ran after her towards his car, calling for Sergeant Day and all the horsepower at his disposal.

———

Lady Rose sorted through the papers as Phryne drove at an electrifying pace straight down Canterbury Road.

'His business certainly seems to have been smuggling, dear, as Penleigh suggested—she knows everything, that woman. These columns of figures are accruing—a bank account, perhaps. The shipping list numbers agree with this list, and I expect that these are numbers of watches, or weights of tobacco, and this is certainly wine. Nothing else is measured in litres. He has been running a thriving business.'

'What's the last figure on the accruing column?' asked Phryne, flicking the big car past a dray and waving at the cursing driver. Lady Rose held out the list. She refused to wear glasses.

'Sixty-four thousand nine hundred and eleven pounds, three shillings and fourpence. Where are we going?'

'To your house to pick up Mrs Slade. Can you read the title of that wad of print?'

'Torn out of a book, evidently. It's rather tattered, but if this piece fits in there...yes, it's from a book called *Famous Historical Puzzles* and the chapter heading is...the Camden...no, that bit is missing. What is this all about, Phryne?'

'See if you can find the other bit.'

Lady Rose rummaged. 'Fancy, it had slipped down onto the floor. Yes, there, and to think I was never good at jigsaw puzzles when I was a girl! "The Camden Wonder". Would you like to tell me what is happening?'

'"The Camden Wonder" has always been a favourite puzzle of mine,' said Phryne. 'I knew the answer to the riddle as soon as I saw that torn book. Imagine. It is just after the Civil War in England. A certain gentleman, who has had shady dealings with both sides, vanishes one night. All that is found of him is a torn shirt, stained with blood, and one shoe. A nice touch, that. The steward of his house confesses out of the blue that he, his mother, and his brother murdered the gentleman. Both mother and brother deny it fiercely, beg their relative to come to his senses, but it goes to trial. The gentleman has been gone for a year. Then the steward changes his story, tries to withdraw his confession, says that he doesn't know what happened to the gentleman. Here we are—can you go and get Mrs Slade? And we'll continue the story on the way.'

Lady Rose was only gone for a moment before she returned, dragging the tear-stained Mrs Slade with her and cramming her into the car as though she was stuffing a cushion. 'We are going to Russell Street, Mrs Slade, and if Jack Robinson has behaved like his namesake, I think you shall have your son back today. To continue,' Phryne addressed Lady Rose, 'the steward withdrew his confession, but they were all tried anyway.'

'What, without the body? I thought that you had to have a body.'

'Do you think so too, Mrs Slade?'

The big woman nodded. 'Stands to reason. Got to have a corpse. Have they found Mr Clarke, Miss?'

'I hope so. So you both think that you cannot be tried for murder without the body?'

Lady Rose and Mrs Slade nodded.

'Right. Russell Street. All change. Wait for me,' said Phryne, dropping them at the door of the police headquarters, 'I have to put the car away.'

With magnificent assurance, Phryne parked the Hispano-Suiza in the street next to a sign which said 'Chief Inspector's Vehicle Only' before ushering her companions into the police station.

———

'We want to see Stevie Slade. Detective Inspector Robinson has given me leave,' said Phryne to the duty policeman. They were conducted to a small room where Mrs Slade's huge offspring was sitting on a chair, a hulking lump of misery. His eyes brightened when he saw his mother.

'Oh, Mum! Are they gonna let me out?'

'I don't know, son, I'm sure. Talk to the lady.'

Mrs Slade dropped into another chair. Phryne surveyed Stevie Slade. He was huge, at least six foot four, with a gentle, foolish smile on his turnip head. He was favouring one arm. 'Show me your arm, Stevie,' Phryne said quietly. There was a long cut on the forearm. Phryne was suddenly so angry that it was an effort to speak.

'Mr Clarke is your friend, isn't he, Stevie?'

Stevie nodded.

'But Mr Clarke cut your arm, didn't he?'

Another nod.

'What did he say, Stevie? That it was a joke he was playing on Mrs Clarke?'

'Joke,' agreed Stevie, grinning a wide grin. 'Joke.'

'So he was going to vanish, and you were to confess to having killed him, and you wouldn't be in any trouble because there has to be a body for anyone to be convicted of murder?'

Stevie nodded again, his eyes widening at the lady's perspicacity.

'But you wouldn't hurt him, would you, Stevie? Even though he cut your arm to bloody his collar?'

'Didn't hurt much,' said Stevie. 'I asked Mum about the body, and she said that Mr Clarke was right.'

'My God, he did ask me,' said Mrs Slade, clutching the collar of her wrapper. 'He did ask me, the innocent!'

'But the joke's over now, Stevie,' said Phryne, sick with disgust. 'Mr Clarke wants you to tell the truth, now.'

'Joke's over?' asked Stevie. They all nodded.

'I didn't like saying it, Mum, because it was a lie, and you always said liars would go to hell,' said Stevie Slade at last, and his mother dived across the cell to cradle his head against her breast.

'You stay here, Mrs Slade,' said Phryne through her teeth. 'By the sound of that shouting, I should say that Jack Robinson has caught his man. And I want to meet him.'

She left the cell, told the policeman at the door that he no longer had a murderer to guard, and strode down the corridor towards a fair-sized argument. A strident male voice dominated. Lady Rose scuttled at Phryne's heels, agog with curiosity.

'You have no right to drag me off my boat just before sailing!' objected a small, furious gentleman in overcoat and hat. 'It's outrageous. Do you know who I am?'

'You are Joshua Clarke,' said Phryne Fisher, in a voice which would have frozen nitrogen. 'And you are a murderer.'

This silenced Mr Clarke.

'Jack, this gentleman had a joke with his poor retarded gardener. The boy was to say that he had killed Mr Clarke, and everyone knows that you can't be tried for murder without a body, so he was in no danger. He was so fond of the gentleman that he allowed him to cut his arm with a razor to provide human blood for the clue of the collar. Then Mr Clarke would pop up and say "April Fool" and everyone would laugh. But Mr Clarke wasn't going to pop up. Mr Clarke was heading for France with all of his ill-gotten gains and as much of her estate as he could convince his poor silly wife to give him.'

'And in pleasant company, too,' grinned Jack Robinson. 'A Miss Gladys Worth. Typist. Or so she says. He didn't tell her about his wife. She's creating something awful at the front desk.'

'There was one thing he didn't tell Stevie, either,' spat Phryne. 'You can be tried for murder without a body. In "The Camden Wonder" the three were hanged, and the gentleman came back after three years and found all his accomplices neatly removed to heavenly judgment. You intended Stevie Slade to be hanged, Mr Clarke, and that's attempted murder, isn't it, Detective Inspector?'

'Oh yes, it's attempted murder all right. And your law is correct, Miss Fisher. No need for a corpus if there's enough circumstantial evidence and a confession. Now, sir, don't make a fuss. Just you come this way, and we'll find you a nice cell. Sign Slade out, will you, Sergeant Day? He can go home. Sorry he's been troubled. No charges.'

'It was a joke!' protested Mr Clarke, turning a sweating face to Phryne and attempting a light laugh. 'Just a harmless little joke, that's all!'

'You bastard,' said Phryne. 'You malicious, smug, hypocritical bastard. How long have you been hatching this plot? When did you start milking your wife's estate? And when did you decide that poor Stevie Slade was expendable? I hope they hang you,' she concluded.

'It was a joke!' Mr Clarke struggled with the constable, who was escorting him towards the custody sergeant to be booked in. 'How dare you speak to me like that!'

Lady Rose laid a warning hand on Phryne's arm. Stevie Slade was coming down the corridor, his mother in tow, having been released. Catching sight of his erstwhile master, Stevie laughed massively, and called, 'Joke's over, Mr Clarke! Good joke, but joke's over, Mr Clarke!'

His laughter followed Mr Clarke all the way to his cell.

'Good joke, Mr Clarke,' said Phryne with unconcealed venom. 'Good joke, Mr Clarke, but it's over.'

Come, SABLE NIGHT

But in her heart a cold December
Thomas Morley, 'April is in My Mistress' Face'

1928 was a good year for madrigals.

The Honourable Miss Phryne Fisher surveyed the crowd of singers, drawn from the Glee Club and the Women's Choir, as they moved through patches of sunlight in her sea-green parlour, shoes clicking on the polished boards. It was a summer's day, still cool enough to make the sunshine welcome, and they were worth looking at. So was Phryne, in a golden afternoon dress with silk embroidered bees, her Dutch-doll hair as shiny as embroidery floss. She had invited the Madrigal Choir to her bijou residence for their rehearsal. She provided the refreshments and they provided the music—and the scandal. Phryne had taken the day off. She was not detecting anything at the moment.

Phryne watched the distribution of champagne cup and listened to the low voice of the large bass who stood behind her. Claude Greenhill, engaging, calm, and the best informed gossip in the Western World, was providing a situation report. Phryne's neat black head came up to his first waistcoat button.

'Lawrence has done something outrageous,' commented Claude dispassionately. Phryne watched the tall, blond, athletic scion of the Newhouse-Gore fortune as he divided his attention between two adoring young women.

'Lawrence is always outrageous,' she replied. 'He treats the Women's Choir as a harem, always has—and his success, I have to say, is remarkable. I don't know how Diane stands him.'

'She doesn't have to endure him anymore,' whispered Claude.

'Oh? Come to her senses, has she? I wouldn't have thought it—she seemed quite besotted with him. He does have a clean-cut, Captain of the Boats charm, you have to admit.'

Diane Hart was sitting by the window. The light set her long red hair aflame and bronzed her grass-green dress. A bunch of red roses lay on her lap, and she was staring at Lawrence with an expression which Phryne could not read.

'I admit the charm, but this is going too far,' said Claude, taking a gulp of champagne cup. 'He's dumped Diane and taken up with Violet.'

'Oh dear,' said Phryne lamely. Violet was Diane's younger sister, mouse to her bright scarlet. 'How do you know?'

'Diane spent most of last night telling me about it.' Claude made a gesture which mimed wringing out the shoulder of his white shirt. 'I suppose that they can transfer the wedding plans to the sister. The funeral baked meats, that sort of thing.'

'The dress won't fit,' said Phryne. 'Lord, lord. Any more gossip, Claude?'

'Oh, yes. Poor Alexandra is devastated. She's always been Button B in that ménage, and now she's pipped at the post. Violet looks sweet enough, but she's got a will of adamant. Our Lawrence won't be dropping in to Alexandra's house for tea and sympathy anymore. And she really did love him.'

Phryne noticed Alexandra. She had plaited her long black hair into a punitive queue and was on her third cocktail. Her dark eyes were shadowed with grief.

'Damn Lawrence, why will he do it?' said Phryne suddenly. 'He's rich enough to buy all the companionship he needs. Must he reap the Women's Choir like wheat?'

'He's not as bad as Victor,' said Claude.

'This is true. Victor is a rakehell, a Casanova, a totally unreliable cold hungry bastard,' agreed Phryne. 'But he lays all his marked cards on the table. No young woman, however self-deluded, could think that Victor really liked or appreciated her.'

'There's one who does,' said Claude, angling his chin to indicate a drooping figure leafing through a photograph album. Jane, who had been a fiery proponent of Free Love, with all her fire gone and a suspicious bulge at her waist.

Victor caught Phryne looking at her and advanced with a plate of cheese straws, expostulating. 'Miss Fisher, you shouldn't believe all you hear.'

'Oh?' Phryne disliked Victor's practised smile even more than usual. He was slim and dark and moved like a dancer. His eyes were blue and knowing. 'Why shouldn't I?'

'You know Causeless Claude—gossips like an old woman.'

Phryne grinned. 'I know Claude, Victor, and I know you.'

His smile faded. Claude leaned over her and collected a handful of cheese straws. He was opening his mouth to speak when Lawrence clapped his hands and bellowed, 'I've got an announcement to make.'

Silence fell. He was the centre of attention, always where he felt he ought to be. He took the hand of the girl standing next to him and said, 'Violet has agreed to be my wife. Congratulate me.'

There was some scattered applause. Violet looked up at the blond Adonis with such an expression of perfect trust that Phryne's mouth dried. He patted her shoulder.

'Champagne,' said Victor. He produced an opened bottle of Moët and two glasses. 'To the bride and groom!' he said, and watched as Lawrence and Violet, laughing, drank.

'You're all invited to sing at the wedding,' said Lawrence, grinning.

The assembled choristers toasted them. Talk broke out in an excited babble. Alexandra looked crushed and bit the end of her plait.

Diane, now sitting by the fireplace, came up to the happy couple and thrust her bouquet of red roses into Lawrence's hands. 'I hope you'll be very happy,' she murmured.

'That's good of you, old girl. No hard feelings?' Phryne heard Lawrence ask in a condescending tone, as she and Claude came up to add their congratulations.

'None,' said Diane in a tight voice.

Phryne marvelled that Lawrence seemed to instantly accept her statement. After all, it had only been six months since the same man had announced that Diane was going to marry him, and with the same panache as he showed now. Lawrence's fingers closed around the stems as he leaned to kiss his fiancée's sister on the cheek.

'Ouch,' he said, shaking his hand. 'These roses have thorns!' he told Phryne, insulted that they should dare to prick him.

Phryne took the flowers and handed them to a waitress, saying, 'Put these in water, will you?'

'Time to start singing.' Arthur Dauphin, the chorus master, decided to intervene before anyone said anything they might later regret. 'It's only two weeks to the concert. Claude's got the music. This is the order in which we will sing the madrigals. Don't shuffle them. Nothing worse than a choir which rustles. All right, come along, please, ladies and gentlemen.'

Phryne sat down out of the way and watched the inchoate gathering resolve itself into groups of sopranos, altos, tenors, and basses. Sleek Arthur raised his hands, and they began to sing warm-up exercises. Collaring a glass of the champagne, Phryne surveyed the choir. They were very young, mostly good-looking, and although they were shaken and excited by Lawrence's announcement, they were relatively disciplined and professional. Even Alexandra had shelved her broken heart. Diane among the sopranos drew in a deep breath. Claude among the basses was concentrating on low notes while Lawrence was mopping his brow, possibly in relief at having escaped a scene.

Victor among the tenors was ogling an alto on whom he had his eye. She was blushing.

They opened their music and began 'Now is the month of Maying, when merry lads are playing.'

'Tenors, you are flat. That's a major third,' said Arthur, slicking back his hair. 'Sopranos, pay attention to the timing. Timing is of the essence in madrigals. All right. Now, the next song, "Fyer, fyer". Crisply, now.'

They completed the song with only minimal grumbling from the conductor: 'Ay me, ay me, I sit and cry me, and call for help alas! But none comes nigh me.'

'Sopranos, that was an interesting interpretation, but I prefer Thomas Morley's version. Let's get on. Page four, please.'

'Come, sable night,' they sang, so sadly that Phryne was moved. 'Put on thy mourning stole...and only Amyntas wastes his heart in wailing. In wailing...' the carefully pitched voices rose in exquisite harmony 'in wailing...' Arthur's hand flicked at the basses. Their voices rose. 'In wail—'

With excellent timing, Lawrence Newhouse-Gore's voice hit the top note, stuck, and failed. In failing, he fell, sprawled among the surprised choir. A stockingless medical student called Anne bent over the prone figure, felt for a pulse, and shot a look at Phryne.

'He's dead,' she told her hostess quietly.

'Lawrence!' screamed Alexandra. She clawed for the body and was held back in the firm embrace of three sympathetic friends. Diane did not move a muscle. Victor, into the sudden silence, laughed. Claude raised both eyebrows. Everyone else stood astonished, at a loss for a response.

Arthur's was possibly uncharitable. 'Damn, the concert's in two weeks.'

This was the signal for the choir to start reacting. Phryne watched them with interest. Those who usually screamed and cried duly screamed and cried and were comforted by those who usually comforted. Claude had wrapped his arms around an alto half his height who was snuffling into his chest. Violet had retreated from the body, shocked into blankness, and someone had found her a chair and a drink. Her sister Diane did not come to her side. In fact, she did not even turn to look at the fallen man.

Phryne took charge. 'Well, we'd better call a doctor—no offence, Anne dear. Claude, Jack, can you lift him?' Claude and Jack, another large bass, disengaged their petitioners and bent to heave up the long form of Lawrence Newhouse-Gore and laid him on the couch. Phryne and Anne inspected him.

The face was dusky with blood and swollen, and his lips were blue. He was definitely dead. Phryne untied her golden scarf and covered his face.

'Arthur, I think you should move the choir into the drawing room,' said Phryne. 'There's nothing to be done for you now, Lawrence,' she said to the impassive death-mask. 'I think we'd better keep singing.'

'Take your music, everyone,' ordered Arthur, gathering up the reins. 'Come along. We musn't give way,' he added, ushering the last soprano out of the room.

Phryne, sitting by the body, heard them begin the next madrigal, raggedly and out of tune. 'Oyez, has any found a lad? Take him quick before he flieth.' But by the time they came

to the next song they had recovered most of their skill. 'Sleep fleshly birth...thy doleful obit keeping'.

Summoned away from his Sunday dinner, a cross local doctor was announced. Dr McAdam had been looking forward to roast lamb and minted peas and had promised his wife he would not be called away, just for a couple of hours. He was elderly and displeased. But he examined the dead man expertly and quickly.

'Anaphylactic shock,' he said crisply. 'He was allergic to something. Very allergic. What did he have to eat or drink?'

'Er...well, some egg and mustard cress sandwiches, some caviar, a glass or two of champagne...I don't really know,' Phryne replied.

'Strawberries?' snapped the doctor.

'Yes, there were strawberries.'

'Well, that's it then. I'll certify death.' He scribbled busily. 'These are the undertakers I use, though doubtless his people will make their own arrangements. Coroner will have to sit on him, of course. Pity, really. He's very young. Good afternoon, Miss Fisher.'

He bustled off to his interrupted lunch and Phryne was again alone with the dead young man. Anne came in and sat down with her.

'The doctor said he died of anaphylactic shock. What's that?'

'Oh, was that it?' asked the young woman. 'Yes, that explains the cyanosis. No one knows how it works, but some people are so sensitive to some foods—strawberries are one of them, mustard, but it can be anything—that their whole body reacts. Their throat swells up, their lungs fill with fluid, and they suffocate.'

'But Lawrence must have known that he was allergic—he wouldn't have eaten whatever it was,' protested Phryne.

'It can sneak up on you. Like bee stings. One bee sting just creates a swelling, the next makes you really ill, and the third can kill. What are you going to do about the body?'

'I've had his parents called. They told me to order an undertaker so I've done that. And I thought it was going to be such a relaxing day. You're very cool, Anne.'

'If I started to get worried about every corpse I saw, I'd be a wreck. It's not as though I liked Lawrence. Sorry, old chum,' said the medical student, laying Phryne's scarf back over the puffed and horrible face.

Next door, the choir was singing 'Weep, weep mine eyes, a thousand deaths I die.'

Phryne asked, 'Could someone have given him the substance—ground up, so that he wouldn't recognise it?'

'Could have. What are you thinking of?'

'Can you go and cut Victor out of the crowd for me, Anne? And Claude.'

'All right.' Anne seemed not much interested. Phryne wondered if this callousness was real or affected. Anne had been mentioned as one of Lawrence's many conquests.

Phryne contemplated death. Here was a beautiful young man who had every reason to assume that the world would continue to conform to his desires, through a suitable marriage and the production of pattern children to an honourable career until a replete old age. And he was dead, faster than she could snap her fingers. Snatched out of the world. Phryne lifted the cooling hand and laid it on the immaculate breast.

Victor and Claude came out of the drawing room, closing the door on 'Death do thy worst, I care not'. 'I say, Phryne,' Victor began excitedly, 'is old Lawrence really dead?'

'He's really dead and I'm wondering if you really killed him,' replied Miss Fisher.

Victor went as pale as his screen-idol's tan would allow. 'What do you mean?' he demanded.

'Apparently he died of a violent allergy to some substance,' said Phryne firmly. 'That bottle of wine, Victor. Where did you open it?'

'Just outside the room. I wanted it to be ready and I didn't want the pop to be heard before he made his announcement.'

'Unconvincing,' said Phryne, pulling the palpitating tenor down to sit between her and Claude. The bass nodded. 'Very unconvincing.'

'What did you put in that otherwise unexceptionable wine, Victor?' she demanded. Victor looked into green eyes as cold as jade and faltered.

'Nothing, nothing, I swear.'

'Why don't I believe you? How well did you know Lawrence?'

'We were old friends, used to go out together, you know that.' Victor was sweating.

'Used to go out together? Or stay in together?'

'I don't know what you're suggesting,' bridled Victor.

Claude shook his head sadly. 'Yes, you do. Not a new suggestion, either. Not that we mind. Some of Miss Fisher's best friends are practitioners of the love that dare not speak its name. Come on, Vic, this is serious. Was Lawrence your lover?'

'How dare you!' Victor blustered. Both pairs of eyes considered him, grey and green. He collapsed. 'Yes, yes, once or twice. He didn't really like me, you know. How did you know?'

'I always suspect young men who make such a show of their manliness. You protest too much, Victor. Now, about that bottle of wine. Did you know that Lawrence was allergic to some food? What was it?'

'I never knew ... he ate what he liked, always.' Victor squirmed, then said, 'He was allergic to bee stings, though. He must have been stung, that's it, no one killed him, it's an accident. I'm glad he's dead. He had a letter of mine. He wanted me...he wanted me to...'

'Tell us,' said Phryne, grasping the shaking hands.

Victor gasped, 'He wanted me to marry Diane. Take her off his hands, make her a good husband. She likes me well enough, but I couldn't—I couldn't...'

He burst into tears, leaning his forehead on Phryne's bosom. She held him for a moment, then pushed him gently away. Not even for pity could she really bear Victor this close. He stank of Californian Poppy and fear.

'There, there, now blow your nose and sit up. Go and wash your face, Victor. The bathroom's through there.'

'Do you think he did it?' asked the bass, seriously.

'I don't know. We'll know if he comes back. He's scared enough to bolt. That's why I am giving him the chance.'

'He might be faking. And we still don't know why he opened the bottle outside the room.'

The choir began on the next madrigal, 'Adieu sweet Amaryllis for since to part your will is...' as Victor returned, mopped-up and red-eyed.

'There's something I want you to do, Victor.'

'Yes, anything.' Victor was eager to please this woman, who was in possession of knowledge which could ruin him.

'Jane. She's in a bad way. I want you to resolve her future, Victor. Settle quite a lot of money on her. I'm not asking you to marry her,' said Phryne gently but inexorably. 'But you must take care of her. And abandon all this philandering. You don't like women, you know. Go and find someone you can love.'

Victor straightened. For a moment his customary sneer visited his lips. Then it fled and he said brokenly, 'As you wish, Miss Fisher.'

Claude lit Miss Fisher's gasper and his own. Phryne sent Victor into the rehearsal to find Violet and Alexandra.

They came out together, holding hands. Alexandra was half embracing Violet, who looked exquisitely uncomfortable. Phryne asked, 'Did you know that Lawrence was allergic to something?'

Both heads, dark and mouse, shook. They looked at her solemnly, like two good children unfairly battered by fate. The fact of Lawrence's death had not sunk in. They were still shocked and numb. Phryne wanted to talk to them before they woke to a world without Lawrence in it and recognised their loss. She had never had much patience with hysterics.

'He would have told me, he told me everything,' said Violet.

'I thought the same,' said Alexandra. 'When he was with me he talked, sometimes we talked all night.'

'Diane might know,' said Violet. 'She's—she's not happy about all this, about him and me. I don't know how much she loved him, you know. She never said. But Lawrie said.... She wanted to go to the Sorbonne, he said she could go to Paris, she's always wanted to go there, it's her dream. Ever since we were children. She's so clever. She ought to have been a man. Mother said—oh God, I have to tell Mother, we have to cancel the wedding, all the arrangements...oh, Lawrence...'

Alexandra bore up Violet's drooping weight and said, 'We neither of us know anything, Phryne. I'd better take Violet home.'

'Not yet. Go back into the rehearsal. You needn't sing— sit down on the couch with this cognac and have a drink or three. You're doing well, Alexandra. I'm proud of you.' Phryne smiled into the tear-wet eyes. Alexandra murmured something, hoisted Violet, and went back into the drawing room, where the choir was beginning on the penultimate madrigal, 'Hark All Ye Lovely Saints Above'. Phryne listened: 'Diana hath agreed with love, his fiery weapon to remove.'

'Well, it doesn't look like they knew about it,' commented

Claude Greenhill, butting out his cigarette.

'No, Claude dear, but you did,' said Phryne, suddenly enlightened. She seized Claude by the earlobe and led him, protesting, into the alcove where a view of the assembled choristers could be had.

'Phryne, what's this all about?' he said, doing 'outraged innocence' quite well.

'You're the librarian, aren't you?' she demanded, dragging his face down to hers. His grey eyes were watering with pain and he smelt of wine and tobacco smoke, musky and attractive.

'Ouch, yes!'

'So you arranged the music in the order in which it would be sung,' she continued, keeping hold of the offending lobe.

'Dammit, Miss Fisher,' he protested, then grunted, 'I did.'

'Stay still unless you want to go through life in a mono-aural state. So you were responsible for "Now is the Month of Maying", "Fyer, Fyer", "Come, Sable Night", "Oyez", "Sleep Fleshly Birth", "Weep weep mine eyes", "Adieu Sweet Amaryllis" and "Hark All Ye Lovely".'

'Well actually, Morley, Ward, Tomkins, Ramsey, Wilbey and Weelkes were, but—ouch!...I put them in that order, yes.'

'To spell out a message to the hearer. One particular hearer, I suspect.'

She released him and he straightened up, rubbing his ear.

'What message?' he bluffed.

'The one that identified the murderer. You knew this was going to happen, Claude. Why didn't you prevent it?'

'No, I didn't know.' He was offended. 'I didn't think that

she'd do it. She's been breathing fire and brimstone about it, screaming that she'd kill him. So I...challenged her, perhaps. Any of the choir who were paying attention could have noticed it. I thought I'd shock her out of it.'

'But you didn't.'

'No, it appears not.'

'Merry lads are playing. And call for help. Put on thy mourning stole. Oyez has any found a lad; Take him quick before he flieth. Thy doleful obit keeping. A thousand deaths I die. Death do thy worst I care not. Adieu sweet Amaryllis and Diana hath agreed with love his fiery weapon to remove. She must have known he was allergic to bee stings. She pressed a bunch of roses into his hand. One of the thorns pricked him. You can see it—the whole hand has swelled. She was furious at being jilted and...oh Lord, I wonder if he left her any money?'

The large bass was pale. 'Yes, he changed his will when he was going to marry her. He's worth a fortune.'

'Wills made in expectation of marriage are vitiated if the marriage does not take place,' said Phryne.

'Yes, but does she know that? He borrowed her Sorbonne money, you know. Short on his allowance—he always was. But she never got it back.'

'You know, I'm beginning to feel that he had it coming to him,' sighed Phryne. 'All she had to do was to smear that rose thorn with bee venom—which only requires one to dissect a bee—and it's pretty, Claude, a really pretty plan. The problem with most poisons is making sure that the right person gets the bit of cake or whatever. In this case, if that thorn had pricked anyone else they wouldn't have been killed.'

'What are we going to do?'

'We haven't any proof. The bee venom, if it was there, would have been washed off when the roses were put in the vase.' She lifted the bunch and scrutinised the stems. They seemed quite clean. 'Nice roses. She must have bought them specially.'

Phryne looked through the little window at the choir. Diane Hart was standing among the sopranos, pitching her voice carefully and without strain, to judge by her expression. A faint smile lingered around her mouth.

'It's a good idea, generally, not to offend women with that shade of Titian hair,' mused Phryne. 'What do you think of your part in all of this, Claude?'

'I...rather wish I hadn't done it,' admitted the bass.

'Hmm.' Phryne leaned back against Claude. He was superlatively comfortable to lean against and Phryne could understand the popularity of his shoulder among the distraught. Equally, there was a sharp mind and a sense of moral outrage which made Claude a dangerous enemy. There was more behind the arrangement of songs than just an attempt to shock Diane Hart.

'We can't prove any of this, Claude. In fact, I almost wish that you hadn't known about it. I'm no good at ethics. Lawrence made a complete blackguard of himself and to some extent invited revenge—you might almost feel that someone had to get him, sometime. But I wish it hadn't been here in my house. Gosh, I sound like Lady Macbeth. Well, if Diane killed him, I fear that she is going to go free. I expect she'll get her Sorbonne money back out of the estate. She's got away with a near-perfect murder.'

'We could tell the police,' said Claude distastefully.

'And they'd laugh in our face. Besides, do we want to tell anyone? Dammit, Claude, I hate dilemmas.'

'There's nothing to be done,' he insisted. 'There'll be an inquest, maybe it will come out there.'

'Not a chance. Known allergy and what if no one noticed the bee? It was a hot day and the windows were open. Drat.' Phryne lit another cigarette and threw herself back against the bass hard enough to make him sway and grab her.

The choir were concluding 'The Silver Swan'.

'Farewell all joys, oh death come close my eyes. More geese than swans now live, more fools than wise.'

'Miss Fisher...' gasped Claude. 'Phryne, look!'

Phryne turned in his embrace to follow the pointing finger. Her eyes widened comically, then she started to laugh. Claude joined in after a moment, and they reeled, clasped in a close embrace, slipping down onto the Persian rug where they laughed until they cried.

Drunkenly, unsteadily, out of the velvety heart of Diane's red roses, a bee was crawling.

Welsh RAREBIT

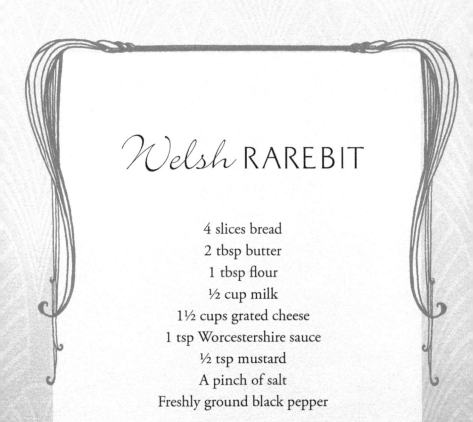

4 slices bread
2 tbsp butter
1 tbsp flour
½ cup milk
1½ cups grated cheese
1 tsp Worcestershire sauce
½ tsp mustard
A pinch of salt
Freshly ground black pepper

Toast the bread and spread with half the butter.
Melt the other half in a saucepan, then add flour,
mixing well. Add the milk and stir until boiling.
Remove saucepan from heat and add cheese and
flavourings, continuing to stir until cheese is
melted. Spread mixture on toast and grill until
golden. Serve cut into fingers.

Glossary

American cloth: early form of linoleum.

Art silk: artificial silk which brought silk stockings within a working-class budget.

Ballyragged: harassed, pestered.

Bijou: French for jewel; dainty and precious.

Blighter: reprehensible person.

Californian Poppy: a hair oil.

Cloche: a close-fitting felt hat, globular in shape.

Corker/corking: wonderful.

Dip: a pickpocket.

Docket: a criminal record.

Épergne: large silver or china bowl which obstructs table conversation. Usually filled with flowers.

Erté: one of Phryne's favourite fashion designers, and designer for the Ballets Russes.

Famille Rose: ancient Chinese porcelain.

Flapper: originally a schoolgirl with her hair in a braid down her back; later a fashionable woman with short skirts, short hair and no corset.

Flat stony motherless: entirely without capital of any kind.

Floris: very lovely brand of fragrances, cosmetics and hair tonic, still in operation in Soho.

Free love (1928 style): living together without marriage.

Gees: horses.

Gussied-up: dressed for a party.

Hellenic beverage: Phryne's very strong Greek coffee.

Jacks: police.

Knut: a dandy.

Mash: brew the tea.

Mozz: to 'put the mozz' on someone/thing is to put a curse on it.

Natural: a 'natural' is a child with some congenital cognition fault; also used as emphasis 'a natural-born bastard'.

Out of the top drawer: from the best families.

Plackets: petticoat pockets, separate from the garment, or the slits in skirts made so that they could be reached.

Poitou: a French fashion designer.

Queue (in relation to hair): a long plait.

Rakehell: a bibulous and loose-living gentleman.

Raree show: a carnival or sideshow.

Scotch, to: to frustrate or foil.

Shill: a person who hangs around a carnival sideshow and draws in customers.

Silvertail: a rich person.

Sly grog: illegal sales of alcohol outside drinking hours.

Spooning: kissing and caressing.

Sugar sack: calico sacks, used for clothing the poor.

Thimble-rigger: offers a game with three cups and a ball which you cannot win.

Three-card trick: also known as 'find the lady', the object is to guess which card is the queen. See 'thimble rigger' for your chances of success.

Tickety boo: excellent.

Turkey lolly: spun sugar or fairy floss.

Two-bob watch: not a reliable source of information.

Valenciennes: very good Belgian lace.

Voluntary (of an organ): a piece played as the organist wishes.

Wet arse and no fish: an unsuccessful venture.

Withdrawing room: a parlour in a hotel.

Zinc: the counter in a French bistro.

Zone: a gemmed belt or girdle.

PETER BROOK

The Empty Space

PENGUIN BOOKS

PENGUIN CLASSICS

Published by the Penguin Group
Penguin Books Ltd, 80 Strand, London WC2R 0RL, England
Penguin Group (USA) Inc., 375 Hudson Street, New York, New York 10014, USA
Penguin Group (Canada), 90 Eglinton Avenue East, Suite 700, Toronto, Ontario, Canada M4P 2Y3
(a division of Pearson Penguin Canada Inc.)
Penguin Ireland, 25 St Stephen's Green, Dublin 2, Ireland (a division of Penguin Books Ltd)
Penguin Group (Australia), 250 Camberwell Road, Camberwell, Victoria 3124, Australia
(a division of Pearson Australia Group Pty Ltd)
Penguin Books India Pvt Ltd, 11 Community Centre, Panchsheel Park, New Delhi – 110 017, India
Penguin Group (NZ), 67 Apollo Drive, Rosedale, North Shore 0632, New Zealand
(a division of Pearson New Zealand Ltd)
Penguin Books (South Africa) (Pty) Ltd, 24 Sturdee Avenue, Rosebank, Johannesburg 2196, South Africa

Penguin Books Ltd, Registered Offices: 80 Strand, London WC2R 0RL, England

www.penguin.com

First published by McGibbon & Kee 1968
Published in Pelican Books 1972
Reprinted in Penguin Books 1990
Published in Penguin Modern Classics 2008

3

Printed in England by Clays Ltd, St Ives plc

978-0-141-18922-2

For my father

CONTENTS

ACKNOWLEDGEMENT

This book is based upon a series of four lectures
originally delivered by Peter Brook as the first of the
Granada Northern Lectures, under the title of
'The Empty Space: The Theatre Today'. The
lectures were heard at the universities of Hull, Keele,
Manchester and Sheffield.

1

THE
DEADLY
THEATRE

I can take any empty space and call it a bare stage. A man walks across this empty space whilst someone else is watching him, and this is all that is needed for an act of theatre to be engaged. Yet when we talk about theatre this is not quite what we mean. Red curtains, spotlights, blank verse, laughter, darkness, these are all confusedly superimposed in a messy image covered by one all-purpose word. We talk of the cinema killing the theatre, and in that phrase we refer to the theatre as it was when the cinema was born, a theatre of box office, foyer, tip-up seats, footlights, scene changes, intervals, music, as though the theatre was by very definition these and little more.

I will try to split the word four ways and distinguish four different meanings – and so will talk about a Deadly Theatre, a Holy Theatre, a Rough Theatre and an Immediate Theatre. Sometimes these four theatres really exist, standing side by side, in the West End of London, or in New York off Times Square. Sometimes they are hundreds of miles apart, the Holy in Warsaw and the Rough in Prague, and sometimes they are metaphoric: two of them mixing together within one evening, within one act. Sometimes within one single moment, the four of them, Holy, Rough, Immediate and Deadly intertwine.

The Deadly Theatre can at first sight be taken for granted, because it means bad theatre. As this is the form of theatre we see most often, and as it is most closely linked to the despised, much-attacked commercial theatre it might seem a waste of

time to criticize it further. But it is only if we see that deadliness is deceptive and can appear anywhere, that we will become aware of the size of the problem.

The condition of the Deadly Theatre at least is fairly obvious. All through the world theatre audiences are dwindling. There are occasional new movements, good new writers and so on, but as a whole, the theatre not only fails to elevate or instruct, it hardly even entertains. The theatre has often been called a whore, meaning its art is impure, but today this is true in another sense – whores take the money and then go short on the pleasure. The Broadway crisis, the Paris crisis, the West End crisis are the same: we do not need the ticket agents to tell us that the theatre has become a deadly business and the public is smelling it out. In fact, were the public ever really to demand the true entertainment it talks about so often, we would almost all be hard put to know where to begin. A true theatre of joy is non-existent and it is not just the trivial comedy and the bad musical that fail to give us our money's worth – the Deadly Theatre finds its deadly way into grand opera and tragedy, into the plays of Molière and the plays of Brecht. Of course nowhere does the Deadly Theatre install itself so securely, so comfortably and so slyly as in the works of William Shakespeare. The Deadly Theatre takes easily to Shakespeare. We see his plays done by good actors in what seems like the proper way – they look lively and colourful, there is music and everyone is all dressed up, just as they are supposed to be in the best of classical theatres. Yet secretly we find it excruciatingly boring – and in our hearts we either blame Shakespeare, or theatre as such, or even ourselves. To make matters worse there is always a deadly spectator, who for special reasons enjoys a lack of intensity and even a lack of entertainment, such as the scholar who emerges from routine performances of the classics smiling because nothing has distracted him from trying over and confirming his pet

theories to himself, whilst reciting his favourite lines under his breath. In his heart he sincerely wants a theatre that is nobler-than-life and he confuses a sort of intellectual satisfaction with the true experience for which he craves. Unfortunately, he lends the weight of his authority to dullness and so the Deadly Theatre goes on its way.

Anyone who watches the real successes as they appear each year will see a very curious phenomenon. We expect the so-called hit to be livelier, faster, brighter than the flop – but this is not always the case. Almost every season in most theatre-loving towns, there is one great success that defies these rules; one play that succeeds not despite but because of dullness. After all, one associates culture with a certain sense of duty, historical costumes and long speeches with the sensation of being bored; so, conversely, just the right degree of boringness is a reassuring guarantee of a worthwhile event. Of course, the dosage is so subtle that it is impossible to establish the exact formula – too much and the audience is driven out of its seats, too little and it may find the theme too disagreeably intense. However, mediocre authors seem to feel their way unerringly to the perfect mixture – and they perpetuate the Deadly Theatre with dull successes, universally praised. Audiences crave for something in the theatre that they can term 'better' than life and for this reason are open to confuse culture, or the trappings of culture, with something they do not know, but sense obscurely could exist – so, tragically, in elevating something bad into a success they are only cheating themselves.

If we talk of deadly, let us note that the difference between life and death, so crystal clear in man, is somewhat veiled in other fields. A doctor can tell at once between the trace of life and the useless bag of bones that life has left; but we are less practised in observing how an idea, an attitude or a form can pass from the lively to the moribund. It is difficult to define

but a child can smell it out. Let me give an example. In France there are two deadly ways of playing classical tragedy. One is traditional, and this involves using a special voice, a special manner, a noble look and an elevated musical delivery. The other way is no more than a half-hearted version of the same thing. Imperial gestures and royal values are fast disappearing from everyday life, so each new generation finds the grand manner more and more hollow, more and more meaningless. This leads the young actor to an angry and impatient search for what he calls truth. He wants to play his verse more realistically, to get it to sound like honest-to-God real speech, but he finds that the formality of the writing is so rigid that it resists this treatment. He is forced to an uneasy compromise that is neither refreshing, like ordinary talk, nor defiantly histrionic, like what we call ham. So his acting is weak and because ham is strong, it is remembered with a certain nostalgia. Inevitably, someone calls for tragedy to be played once again 'the way it is written'. This is fair enough, but unfortunately all the printed word can tell us is what was written on paper, not how it was once brought to life. There are no records, no tapes – only experts, but not one of them, of course, has firsthand knowledge. The real antiques have all gone – only some imitations have survived, in the shape of traditional actors, who continue to play in a traditional way, drawing their inspiration not from real sources, but from imaginary ones, such as the memory of the sound an older actor once made – a sound that in turn was a memory of a predecessor's way.

I once saw a rehearsal at the Comédie Française – a very young actor stood in front of a very old one and spoke and mimed the role with him like a reflection in a glass. This must not be confused with the great tradition, say, of the Noh actors passing knowledge orally from father to son. There it is meaning that is communicated – and meaning

never belongs to the past. It can be checked in each man's own present experience. But to imitate the externals of acting only perpetuates manner – a manner hard to relate to anything at all.

Again with Shakespeare we hear or read the same advice – 'Play what is written'. But what is written? Certain ciphers on paper. Shakespeare's words are records of the words that he wanted to be spoken, words issuing as sounds from people's mouths, with pitch, pause, rhythm and gesture as part of their meaning. A word does not start as a word – it is an end product which begins as an impulse, stimulated by attitude and behaviour which dictates the need for expression. This process occurs inside the dramatist; it is repeated inside the actor. Both may only be conscious of the words, but both for the author and then for the actor the word is a small visible portion of a gigantic unseen formation. Some writers attempt to nail down their meaning and intentions in stage directions and explanations, yet we cannot help being struck by the fact that the best dramatists explain themselves the least. They recognize that further indications will most probably be useless. They recognize that the only way to find the true path to the speaking of a word is through a process that parallels the original creative one. This can neither be by-passed nor simplified. Unfortunately, the moment a lover speaks, or a king utters, we rush to give them a label: the lover is 'romantic', the king is 'noble' – and before we know it we are speaking of romantic love and kingly nobility or princeliness as though they are things we can hold in our hand and expect the actors to observe. But these are not substances and they do not exist. If we search for them, the best we can do is to make guesswork reconstructions from books and paintings. If you ask an actor to play in a 'romantic style' he will valiantly have a go, thinking he knows what you mean. What actually can he draw on? Hunch, imagination and a scrap-

book of theatrical memories, all of which will give him a vague 'romanticness' that he will mix up with a disguised imitation of whatever older actor he happens to admire. If he digs into his own experiences the result may not marry with the text; if he just plays what he thinks is the text, it will be imitative and conventional. Either way the result is a compromise: at most times unconvincing.

It is vain to pretend that the words we apply to classical plays like 'musical', 'poetic', 'larger than life', 'noble', 'heroic', 'romantic', have any absolute meaning. They are the reflections of a critical attitude of a particular period, and to attempt to build a performance today to conform to these canons is the most certain road to deadly theatre – deadly theatre of a respectability that makes it pass as living truth.

Once, when giving a lecture on this theme, I was able to put it to a practical test. By luck, there was a woman in the audience who had neither read nor seen King Lear. I gave her Goneril's first speech and asked her to recite it as best she could for whatever values she found in it. She read it very simply – and the speech itself emerged full of eloquence and charm. I then explained that it was supposed to be the speech of a wicked woman and suggested her reading every word for hypocrisy. She tried to do so, and the audience saw what a hard unnatural wrestling with the simple music of the words was involved when she sought to act to a definition:

> Sir, I love you more than words can wield the matter;
> Dearer than eyesight, space, and liberty;
> Beyond that can be valued, rich or rare;
> No less than life, with grace, health, beauty, honour;
> As much as child e'er loved, or father found;
> A love that makes breath poor, and speech unable;
> Beyond all manner of so much I love you.

Anyone can try this for himself. Taste it on the tongue. The words are those of a lady of style and breeding accus-

tomed to expressing herself in public, someone with ease and social aplomb. As for clues to her character, only the façade is presented and this, we see, is elegant and attractive. Yet if one thinks of the performances where Goneril speaks these first lines as a macabre villainess, and looks at the speech again, one is at a loss to know what suggests this – other than preconceptions of Shakespeare's moral attitudes. In fact, if Goneril in her first appearance does not play a 'monster', but merely what her given words suggest, then all the balance of the play changes – and in the subsequent scenes her villainy and Lear's martyrdom are neither as crude nor as simplified as they might appear. Of course, by the end of the play we learn that Goneril's actions make her what we call a monster – but a real monster, both complex and compelling.

In a living theatre, we would each day approach the rehearsal putting yesterday's discoveries to the test, ready to believe that the true play has once again escaped us. But the Deadly Theatre approaches the classics from the viewpoint that somewhere, someone has found out and defined how the play should be done.

This is the running problem of what we loosely call style. Every work has its own style: it could not be otherwise: every period has its style. The moment we try to pinpoint this style we are lost. I remember vividly when shortly after the Pekin Opera had come to London a rival Chinese Opera Company followed, from Formosa. The Pekin Company was still in touch with its sources and creating its ancient patterns afresh each night: the Formosan company, doing the same items, was imitating its memories of them, skimping some details, exaggerating the showy passages, forgetting the meaning – nothing was reborn. Even in a strange exotic style the difference between life and death was unmistakable.

The real Pekin Opera was an example of a theatrical art where the outer forms do not change from generation to

generation, and only a few years ago it seemed as though it were so perfectly frozen that it could carry on for ever. Today, even this superb relic has gone. Its force and its quality enabled it to survive way beyond its time, like a monument – but the day came when the gap between it and the life of the society around it became too great. The Red Guards reflect a different China. Few of the attitudes and meanings of the traditional Pekin Opera relate to the new structure of thought in which this people now lives. Today in Pekin the emperors and princesses have been replaced by landlords and soldiers, and the same incredible acrobatic skills are used to speak of very different themes. To the Westerner this seems a wicked shame and it is easy for us to shed cultivated tears. Of course, it is tragic that this miraculous heritage has been destroyed – and yet I feel that the ruthless Chinese attitude to one of their proudest possessions goes to the heart of the meaning of living theatre – theatre is always a self-destructive art, and it is always written on the wind. A professional theatre assembles different people every night and speaks to them through the language of behaviour. A performance gets set and usually has to be repeated – and repeated as well and accurately as possible – but from the day it is set something invisible is beginning to die.

In the Moscow Art Theatre, in Tel Aviv in the Habimah, productions have been kept going for forty years or more: I have seen a faithful revival of Vakhtangov's twenties' staging of *Princess Turandot*; I have seen Stanislavsky's own work, perfectly preserved: but none of these had more than antiquarian interest, none had the vitality of new invention. At Stratford where we worry that we don't play our repertoire long enough to milk its full box office value, we now discuss this quite empirically: about five years, we agree, is the most a particular staging can live. It is not only the hair-styles, costumes and make-up that look dated. All the different ele-

ments of staging – the shorthands of behaviour that stand for certain emotions; gestures, gesticulations and tones of voice – are all fluctuating on an invisible stock exchange all the time. Life is moving, influences are playing on actor and audience, and other plays, other arts, the cinema, television, current events, join in the constant rewriting of history and the amending of the daily truth. In fashion houses someone will thump a table and say 'boots are definitely in' : this is an existential fact. A living theatre that thinks it can stand aloof from anything so trivial as fashion will wilt. In the theatre, every form once born is mortal; every form must be reconceived, and its new conception will bear the marks of all the influences that surround it. In this sense, the theatre is relativity. Yet a great theatre is not a fashion house; perpetual elements do recur and certain fundamental issues underlie all dramatic activity. The deadly trap is to divide the eternal truths from the superficial variations; this is a subtle form of snobbery and it is fatal. For instance, it is accepted that scenery, costumes, music are fair game for directors and designers, and must in fact be renewed. When it comes to attitudes and behaviour we are much more confused, and tend to believe that these elements if true in the writing can continue to express themselves in similar ways.

Closely related to this is the conflict between theatre directors and musicians in opera productions where two totally different forms, drama and music, are treated as though they were one. A musician is dealing with a fabric that is as near as man can get to an expression of the invisible. His score notes this invisibility and his sound is made by instruments which hardly ever change. The player's personality is unimportant : a thin clarinettist can easily make a fatter sound than a fat one. The vehicle of music is separate from music itself. So the stuff of music comes and goes, always in the same way, free of the need to be revised and reassessed. But

the vehicle of drama is flesh and blood and here completely different laws are at work. The vehicle and the message cannot be separated. Only a naked actor can begin to resemble a pure instrument like a violin and only if he has a completely classical physique, with neither paunch nor bandy legs. A ballet dancer is sometimes close to this condition and he can reproduce formal gestures unmodified by his own personality or by the outer movement of life. But the moment the actor dresses up and speaks with his own tongue he is entering the fluctuating territory of manifestation and existence that he shares with the spectator. Because the musician's experience is so different, he finds it hard to follow why the traditional bits of business that made Verdi laugh and Puccini slap his thighs seem neither funny nor illuminating today. Grand opera, of course, is the Deadly Theatre carried to absurdity. Opera is a nightmare of vast feuds over tiny details; of surrealist anecdotes that all turn round the same assertion: nothing needs to change. Everything in opera must change, but in opera change is blocked.

Again we must beware of indignation, for if we try to simplify the problem by making tradition the main barrier between ourselves and a living theatre we will again miss the real issue. There is a deadly element everywhere; in the cultural set-up, in our inherited artistic values, in the economic framework, in the actor's life, in the critic's function. As we examine these we will see that deceptively the opposite seems also true, for within the Deadly Theatre there are often tantalizing, abortive or even momentarily satisfying flickers of a real life.

In New York, for instance, the most deadly element is certainly economic. This does not mean that all work done there is bad, but a theatre where a play for economic reasons rehearses for no more than three weeks is crippled at the outset. Time is not the be-all and end-all; it is not impossible to get

an astonishing result in three weeks. Occasionally in the theatre what one loosely calls chemistry, or luck, brings about an astonishing rush of energy, and then invention follows invention in lightning chain reaction. But this is rare: common sense shows that if the system rigidly excludes more than three weeks' rehearsal most of the time, most things suffer. No experimenting can take place, and no real artistic risks are possible. The director must deliver the goods or be fired and so must the actor. Of course time can also be used very badly; it is possible to sit around for months discussing and worrying and improvising without this showing in any way whatsoever. I have seen Shakespearian productions in Russia so conventional in approach that two full years of discussion and study of archives give no better a result than scratch companies get in three weeks. I met an actor who rehearsed Hamlet for seven years and never played it because the director died before it was finished. On the other hand, productions of Russian plays rehearsed in the Stanislavsky manner over years still reach a level of performance of which we can only dream. The Berliner Ensemble uses time well, they use it freely, spending about twelve months on a new production, and over a number of years they have built up a repertoire of shows, every one of which is remarkable – and every one of which fills the theatre to capacity. In simple capitalist terms, this is better business than the commercial theatre where the scrambled and patched shows so seldom succeed. Each season on Broadway or in London a large number of expensive shows fold within a week or two against the rare freak that scrapes through. None the less, the percentage of disasters hasn't jolted the system or the belief that somehow it will all work out in the end. On Broadway ticket prices are continually rising and, ironically, as each season grows more disastrous, each season's hit makes more money. As fewer and fewer people go through the doors,

larger and larger sums cross the ticket office counter, until eventually one last millionaire will be paying a fortune for one private performance for himself alone. So it comes about that what is bad business for some is good business for others. Everyone moans and yet many want the system to go on.

The artistic consequences are severe. Broadway is not a jungle, it is a machine into which a great many parts snugly interlock. Yet each of these parts is brutalized; it has been deformed to fit and function smoothly. This is the only theatre in the world where every artist – by this, I mean designers, composers, lighting electricians, as well as actors – needs an agent for his personal protection. This sounds melodramatic, but in a sense everyone is continually in danger; his job, his reputation, his way of life is in daily balance. In theory, this tension should lead to an atmosphere of fear, and, were this the case, its destructiveness would be clearly seen. In practice, however, the underlying tension leads just as directly to the famous Broadway atmosphere, which is very emotional, throbbing with apparent warmth and good cheer. On the first day of rehearsal of *House of Flowers*, its composer Harold Arlen arrived wearing a blue cornflower, with champagne and presents for us all. As he hugged and kissed his way round the cast, Truman Capote who had written the libretto whispered darkly to me, 'It's love today. The lawyers'll be in tomorrow'. It was true. Pearl Bailey had served me with a 50,000-dollar writ before the show reached town. For a foreigner it was (in retrospect) all fun and exciting – everything is covered and excused by the term 'show business' – but in precise terms the brutal warmth directly relates to the lack of emotional finesse. In such conditions there is rarely the quiet and security in which anyone may dare expose himself. I mean the true unspectacular intimacy that long work and true confidence in other people brings about – on Broadway, a crude gesture of self-exposure is easy to come

by, but this has nothing to do with the subtle, sensitive inter-relation between people confidently working together. When the Americans envy the British, it is this odd sensibility, this uneven give and take that they mean. They call it style, and regard it as a mystery. When you cast a play in New York and you are told that a certain actor 'has style', this usually means an imitation of an imitation of a European. In the American theatre, people talk seriously of style, as though this was a manner that could be acquired – and the actors who have played the classics and have been flattered by critics into believing that they have 'it', do everything to perpetuate the notion that style is a rare something that a few gentleman actors possess. Yet America could easily have a great theatre of its own. It possesses every one of the elements; there is a strength, courage, humour, cash and a capacity for facing hard facts.

One morning I stood in the Museum of Modern Art look-ing at the people swarming in for one dollar admission. Almost every one of them had the lively head and the indi-vidual look of a good audience – using the simple personal standard of an audience for whom one would like to do plays. In New York, potentially, there is one of the best audiences in the world. Unfortunately, it seldom goes to the theatre.

It seldom goes to the theatre because the prices are too high. Certainly it can afford these prices, but it has been let down too often. It is not for nothing that New York is the place where the critics are the most powerful and the toughest in the world. It is the audience, year after year, that has been forced to elevate simple fallible men into highly priced experts because, as when a collector buys an expensive work, he cannot afford to take the risk alone: the tradition of the expert valuers of works of art, like Duveen, has reached the box office line. So the circle is closed; not only the artists, but also the audience, have to have their protection men – and

most of the curious, intelligent, nonconforming individuals stay away. This situation is not unique to New York. I had a closely related experience when we put on John Arden's *Sergeant Musgrave's Dance* in Paris at the Athenée. It was a true flop – almost all the Press was bad – and we were playing to virtually empty houses. Convinced that the play had an audience somewhere in the town, we announced that we would give three free performances. Such was the lure of complimentary tickets that they became like wild premières. Crowds fought to get in, the police had to draw iron grilles across the foyer, and the play itself went magnificently, as the actors, cheered by the warmth of the house, gave their best performance, which in turn earned them an ovation. The theatre which the night before had been a draughty morgue now hummed with the chatter and buzz of success. At the end, we put up the house lights and looked at the audience. Mostly young, they were all well dressed, rather formal, in suits and ties. Françoise Spira, directress of the theatre, came on the stage.

'Is there anyone here who could not afford the price of a ticket?'

One man put up his hand.

'And the rest of you, why did you have to wait to be let in for free?'

'It had a bad Press.'

'Do you believe the Press?'

Loud chorus of 'No !'

'Then, why ...?'

And from all sides the same answer – the risk is too great, too many disappointments. Here we see how the vicious circle is drawn. Steadily the Deadly Theatre digs its own grave.

Or else we can attack the problem the other way round. If good theatre depends on a good audience, then every audience has the theatre it deserves. Yet it must be very hard for specta-

tors to be told of an audience's responsibility. How can this be faced in practice? It would be a sad day if people went to the theatre out of duty. Once within a theatre an audience cannot whip itself into being 'better' than it is. In a sense there is nothing a spectator can actually do. And yet there is a contradiction here that cannot be ignored, for everything depends on him.

When the Royal Shakespeare Company's production of *King Lear* toured through Europe the production was steadily improving and the best performances lay between Budapest and Moscow. It was fascinating to see how an audience composed largely of people with little knowledge of English could so influence a cast. These audiences brought with them three things: a love for the play itself, real hunger for a contact with foreigners and, above all, an experience of life in Europe in the last years that enabled them to come directly to the play's painful themes. The quality of the attention that this audience brought expressed itself in silence and concentration: a feeling in the house that affected the actors as though a brilliant light were turned on their work. As a result, the most obscure passages were illuminated; they were played with a complexity of meaning and a fine use of the English language that few of the audience could literally follow, but which all could sense. The actors were moved and excited and they proceeded to the United States, prepared to give to an English-speaking audience all that this focus had taught them. I was forced to go back to England and only caught up with the company a few weeks later in Philadelphia. To my surprise and dismay much of the quality had gone from their acting. I wanted to blame the actors, but it was clear that they were trying as hard as they could. It was the relation with the audience that had changed. In Philadelphia, the audience understood English all right, but this audience was composed largely of people who were not interested in the play; people

who came for all the conventional reasons – because it was a
social event, because their wives insisted, and so on. Undoubtedly, a way existed to involve this particular audience in
King Lear, but it was not our way. The austerity of this production which had seemed so right in Europe no longer made
sense. Seeing people yawn, I felt guilty, realizing that something else was demanded from us all. I knew that were I doing
a production of King Lear for the people of Philadelphia I
would without condescension stress everything differently –
and, in immediate terms, I would get it to work better. But
with an established production on tour I could do nothing.
The actors, however, were instinctively responding to the new
situation. They were underlining everything in the play that
could arrest the spectator – that is to say, when there was a
bit of exciting action or a burst of melodrama, they exploited
it, they played louder and cruder and of course whipped past
those intricate passages that the non-English audience had
so enjoyed – which, ironically, only an English-speaking
audience could have appreciated to the full. Eventually our
impresario took the play to the Lincoln Centre in New York –
a giant auditorium where the acoustics were bad and the audience resented its poor contact with the stage. We were put
in this vast theatre for economic reasons : a simple illustration
of how a closed circle of cause and effect is produced, so that
the wrong audience or the wrong place or both conjure
from the actors their coarsest work. Again, the actors, responding to the given conditions, had no choice; they faced
the front, spoke loudly and quite rightly threw away all that
had become precious in their work. This danger is built into
every tour, because in a sense few of the conditions of the
original performance apply – and contact with each new
audience is often a matter of luck. In the old days, the stroll-
ing players naturally adapted their work to each new place;
elaborate modern productions have no such flexibility. In

fact, when we played 'US', the Royal Shakespeare Theatre's group-happening-collaborative spectacle on the Vietnam war, we decided to refuse all invitations to tour. Every element in it had come into being just for the particular cross-section of London that sat in the Aldwych Theatre in 1966. The fact that we had no text wrought and set by a dramatist was the condition of this particular experiment. Contact with the audience, through shared references, became the substance of the evening. Had we a shaped text, we could have played in other places, without one we were like a happening – and in the event, we all felt that something was lost in playing it even through a London season of five months. One perform-ance would have been the true culmination. We made the mistake of feeling obliged to enter our own repertoire. A repertoire repeats, and to repeat something must be fixed. The rules of British censorship prevent actors adapting and improvising in performance. So in this case, the fixing was the beginning of a slide towards the deadly – the liveliness of the actors waned as the immediacy of the relation with their public and their theme lessened.

During a talk to a group at a university I once tried to illus-trate how an audience affects actors by the quality of its attention. I asked for a volunteer. A man came forward, and I gave him a sheet of paper on which was typed a speech from Peter Weiss's play about Auschwitz, The Investigation. As the volunteer took the paper and read it over to himself the audience tittered in the way an audience always does when it sees one of its kind on the way to making a fool of himself. But the volunteer was too struck and too appalled by what he was reading to react with the sheepish grins that are also customary. Something of his seriousness and concentra-tion reached the audience and it fell silent. Then at my request he began to read out loud. The very first words were loaded with their own ghastly sense and the reader's response to

them. Immediately the audience understood. It became one with him, with the speech – the lecture room and the volunteer who had come on to the platform vanished from sight – the naked evidence from Auschwitz was so powerful that it took over completely. Not only did the reader continue to speak in a shocked attentive silence, but his reading, technically speaking, was perfect – it had neither grace nor lack of grace, skill nor lack of skill – it was perfect because he had no attention to spare for self-consciousness, for wondering whether he was using the right intonation. He knew the audience wanted to hear, and he wanted to let them hear : the images found their own level and guided his voice unconsciously to the appropriate volume and pitch.

After this, I asked for another volunteer, and gave him the speech from *Henry V* which lists the names and numbers of the French and English dead. When he read this aloud, all the faults of the amateur actor appeared. One look at the volume of Shakespeare had already set off a series of conditioned reflexes to do with speaking verse. He put on a false voice that strove to be noble and historical, mouthed his words roundly, made awkward stresses, got tongue-tied, stiff, and confused, and the audience listened inattentive and restless. When he had done, I asked the audience why they could not take the list of dead at Agincourt as seriously as the description of death at Auschwitz. This provided a lively exchange.

'Agincourt's in the past.'

'But Auschwitz is in the past.'

'Only fifteen years.'

'So how long's it got to take?'

'When's a corpse a historical corpse?'

'How many years make killing romantic?'

After this had gone on for some time, I proposed an experiment. The amateur actor was to read the speech again,

stopping for a moment after each name: the audience was to
endeavour silently in the pause to recall and put together its
impressions of Auschwitz and Agincourt, to try to find a
way of believing that these names were once individuals, as
vividly as if the butchery had occurred in living memory. The
amateur began to read again and the audience worked hard,
playing its part. As he spoke the first name, the half silence
became a dense one. Its tension caught the reader, there was
an emotion in it, shared between him and them and it turned
all his attention away from himself on to the subject matter
he was speaking. Now the audience's concentration began to
guide him: his inflexions were simple, his rhythms true: this
in turn increased the audience's interest and so the two-way
current began to flow. When this was ended, no explanations
were needed, the audience had seen itself in action, it had
seen how many layers silence can contain.

Of course, like all experiments, this was an artificial one:
here, the audience was given an unusually active role and as a
result it directed an inexperienced actor. Usually, an experienced actor reading a passage like this will impose a
silence on an audience that is in proportion to the degree of
truth he brings to it. Occasionally, an actor can completely
dominate any house, and so, like a master matador, he can
work the audience the way he pleases. Usually, however, this
cannot come from the stage alone. For instance, both the
actors and myself found *The Visit* and *Marat/Sade* more rewarding to play in America than in England. The English
refused to take *The Visit* on its own terms; the story told of
the ruthlessness latent in any small community, and when
we played in the English provinces, to virtually empty
houses, the reaction of those who came was 'it's not real', 'it
couldn't happen', and they enjoyed it or disliked it on the
level of fantasy. The *Marat/Sade* was liked in London not so
much as a play about revolution, war and madness as a dis-

play of theatricality. The opposing words 'literary' and 'theatrical' have many meanings, but in the English theatre, when used as praise, they all too often describe ways of warding off contact with disturbing themes. The American audience reacted to both plays much more directly, they accepted and believed the propositions that man is greedy and murderous, a potential lunatic. They were caught and held by the material of the drama, and in the case of *The Visit* they often did not even comment on the fact that the story was being told to them in a somewhat unfamiliar, expressionistic way. They simply discussed what the play had said. The great Kazan–Williams–Miller hits, Albee's *Virginia Woolf*, summoned audiences that met the cast in the true shared territory of theme and concern – and they were powerful events, the circle of performance was riveting and complete.

In America, in powerful waves, comes a recognition of the deadly, and a strong reaction against it. Years ago, the Actors' Studio came into being to give a faith and continuity to those unhappy artists who were being so rapidly thrown in and out of work. Basing a very serious and systematic study on a portion of Stanislavsky's teaching, the Actors' Studio developed a very remarkable school of acting that corresponded perfectly to the needs of the playwrights and public of the time. Actors still had to give results in three weeks, but they were sustained by the school's tradition and they did not come empty-handed to the first rehearsal. This background of teaching gave a strength and integrity to their work. The Method Actor was trained to reject cliché imitations of reality and to search for something more real in himself. He then had to present this through the living of it, and so acting became a deeply naturalistic study. 'Reality' is a word with many meanings, but here it was understood to be that slice of the real that reflected the people and the problems around

the actor, and it coincided with the slices of existence that the writers of the day, Miller, Tennessee Williams, Inge, were trying to define. In much the same way Stanislavsky's theatre drew its strength from the fact that it corresponded to the needs of the best Russian classics, all of which were cast in a naturalistic form. For a number of years in Russia, the school, the public and the play had made a coherent whole. Then Meyerhold challenged Stanislavsky, proposing a different style of playing, in order to capture other elements of 'reality'. But Meyerhold disappeared. In America today, the time is ripe for a Meyerhold to appear, since naturalistic representation of life no longer seems to Americans adequate to express the forces that drive them. Now Genet is discussed, Shakespeare re-evaluated, Artaud quoted : there is a lot of talk about ritual : and all this for very realistic reasons, as many concrete aspects of American living can only be captured along these lines. Just a short time ago, the English were full of envy for the vitality of the American theatre. Now the pendulum swings towards London, as though the English hold all the keys. Years ago I saw a girl at the Actors' Studio approaching a speech of Lady Macbeth's by pretending to be a tree: when I described this in England it sounded quite comic, and even today many actors have yet to discover why odd-sounding exercises are so necessary. In New York, however, the girl did not need to learn about group work and improvisations, she had accepted these, and she needed to understand about the meanings and demands of form; standing with her arms in the air trying to 'feel', she was pouring her ardour and energy uselessly in the wrong direction.

All this brings us back to the same problem. The word theatre has many sloppy meanings. In most of the world, the theatre has no exact place in society, no clear purpose, it only exists in fragments : one theatre chases money, another chases glory, another chases emotion, another chases politics, another

chases fun. The actor is bundled from pillar to post – confused and consumed by conditions outside his control. Actors may sometimes seem jealous or trivial, yet I have never known an actor who did not want to work. This wish to work is his strength. It is what enables professionals everywhere to understand each other. But he cannot reform his profession alone. In a theatre with few schools and no aims, he is usually the tool, not the instrument. Yet when the theatre does come back to the actor, the problem is still not solved. On the contrary, deadly acting becomes the heart of the crisis.

The dilemma of the actor is not unique to commercial theatres with inadequate rehearsal time. Singers and often dancers keep their teachers by them to the end of their days: actors once launched have nothing whatsoever to help them to develop their talents. If this is seen most alarmingly in the commercial theatre, the same applies to permanent companies. After he reaches a certain position the actor does no more homework. Take a young actor, unformed, undeveloped, but bursting with talent, full of latent possibilities. Quite rapidly he discovers what he can do, and, after mastering his initial difficulties, with a bit of luck he may find himself in the enviable position of having a job which he loves, doing it well while getting paid and admired at the same time. If he is to develop, the next stage must be to go beyond his apparent range, and to begin to explore what really comes hard. But no one has time for this sort of problem. His friends are little use, his parents are unlikely to know much about his art, and his agent, who may be well-meaning and intelligent, is not there to guide him past good offers of good parts towards a vague something else that would be even better. Building a career and artistic development do not necessarily go hand in hand; often the actor, as his career grows, begins to turn in work that gets more and more similar. It is a wretched story, and all the exceptions blur the truth.

How does the average actor spend his days? Of course, it's a wide range : from lying in bed, drinking, going to the hairdresser, to the agent, filming, recording, reading, sometimes studying; even, latterly, toying a bit with politics. But whether his use of time is frivolous or earnest is beside the point : little that he does relates to his main preoccupation – not to stand still as an actor – which means not to stand still as a human being, which means work aimed at his artistic growth – and where can such work take place? Time after time I have worked with actors who after the usual preamble that they 'put themselves in my hands' are tragically incapable however hard they try of laying down for one brief instant even in rehearsal the image of themselves that has hardened round an inner emptiness. On the occasions that it is possible to penetrate this shell, it is like smashing the picture on a television set.

In England, it seems suddenly that we have a marvellous new breed of young actors – we feel we are witnessing two lines of men in a factory facing opposite directions : one line shuffles out grey, tired; the other strides forward fresh and vital. We get the impression that one line is better than the other, that the lively line is made of better stock. This is partly true, but in the end the new shift will be as tired and grey as the old; it is an inevitable result of certain conditions that have not yet changed. The tragedy is that the professional status of actors over the age of thirty is seldom a true reflection of their talents. There are countless actors who never have the chance to develop their inborn potential to its proper fruition. Naturally, in an individualist profession, false and exaggerated importance is given to exceptional cases. Outstanding actors, like all real artists, have some mysterious psychic chemistry, half conscious and yet three-quarters hidden, that they themselves may only define as 'instinct', 'hunch', 'my voices', that enables them to develop their vision

and their art. Special cases may follow special rules: one of the greatest actresses of our time who seems in rehearsal to be observing no method whatsoever actually has an extraordinary system of her own which she can only articulate in nursery language. 'Kneading the flour today, darling,' she has said to me. 'Putting it back to bake a bit longer', 'Need some yeast now', 'We're basting this morning'. No matter: this is precise science, just as much as if she gave the terminology of the Actors' Studio. But her ability to get results stays with her alone: she cannot communicate it in any useful way to the people around her, so while she is 'cooking her pie' and the next actor is just 'doing it the way he feels it', and the third, in drama school language, is 'searching for the Stanislavskian super-objective', no real working-together between them all is possible. It has long been recognized that without a permanent company few actors can thrive indefinitely. However, it must also be faced that even a permanent company is doomed to deadliness in the long run if it is without an aim, and thus without a method, and thus without a school. And by a school, naturally I don't mean a gymnasium where the actor exercises his limbs in limbo. Flexing muscles alone cannot develop an art; scales don't make a pianist nor does fingerwork help a painter's brush: yet a great pianist practises finger exercises for many hours a day, and Japanese painters spend their lives practising to draw a perfect circle. The art of acting is in some ways the most exacting one of all, and without constant schooling, the actor will stop half-way.

So when we find deadliness, who is the culprit? Enough has been said publicly and privately to make the critics' ears burn, to make us believe that it is from them that the worst deadliness really stems. Over the years we moan and grumble about 'the Critics' as though it were always the same six men hurtling by jet, from Paris to New York, from art show to concert to play, always committing the same monumental

errors. Or as though they were all like Thomas à Becket – the
jolly, whoring friend of the King who the day he became
Cardinal turned as disapproving as all his predecessors : critics
come and go, yet those who are criticized generally find
'them' the same. Our system, the newspapers, the reader's
demands, the notice dictated by phone, the problems of space,
the quantity of rubbish in our playhouses, the soul-destroying
effect of doing the same job often and too long, all conspire to
prevent a critic from exercising his vital function. When the
man in the street goes to the theatre he can claim just to serve
his own pleasure. When a critic goes to a play, he can say he
is just serving the man in the street, but it is not accurate. He
is not just a tipster. A critic has a far more important role, an
essential one, in fact, for an art without critics would be
constantly menaced by far greater dangers.

For instance, a critic is always serving the theatre when he
is hounding out incompetence. If he spends most of his time
grumbling, he is almost always right. The appalling difficulty
of making theatre must be accepted : it is, or would be, if
truly practised, perhaps the hardest medium of all : it is merciless, there is no room for error, or for waste. A novel can
survive the reader who skips pages, or entire chapters; the
audience, apt to change from pleasure to boredom in a wink,
can be lost, irrevocably. Two hours is a short time and an
eternity : to use two hours of public time is a fine art. Yet this
art with its frightening exigencies is served largely by casual
labour. In a deadly vacuum there are few places where we
can properly learn the arts of the theatre – so we tend to drop
in on the theatre offering love instead of science. This is what
the unfortunate critic is nightly called to judge.

Incompetence is the vice, the condition and the tragedy of
the world's theatre on any level : for every good light comedy
or musical or political revue or verse play or classic that we
see there are scores of others that most of the time are betrayed

by a lack of elementary skills. The techniques of staging, designing, speaking, walking across a stage, sitting – even listening – just aren't sufficiently known; compare the little it takes
– except luck – to get work in many of the theatres of the
world with the minimum level of skill demanded say in piano
playing: think of how many thousands of music teachers in
thousands of small cities can play all the notes of the most
difficult passages of Liszt or sight-read Scriabin. Compared
with the simple ability of musicians most of our work is at
amateur level most of the time. A critic will see far more incompetence than competence in his theatregoing. I was once
asked to direct an opera at a Middle Eastern opera house
which wrote frankly in its letter of invitation 'our orchestra
has not all the instruments and plays some wrong notes but
our audiences so far have not noticed'. Fortunately, the critic
does tend to notice and in this sense, his angriest reaction is
valuable – it is a call for competence. This is a vital function,
but he has still another one. He is a pathmaker.

The critic joins in the deadly game when he does not accept
this responsibility, when he belittles his own importance. A
critic is usually a sincere and decent man acutely aware of
the human aspects of his job; one of the famous 'Butchers of
Broadway' was said to have been tormented by the knowledge
that on him alone depended people's happiness and future.
Still, even if he is aware of his power of destruction, he under-
rates his power for good. When the *status quo* is rotten – and
few critics anywhere would dispute this – the only possibility
is to judge events in relation to a possible goal. This goal
should be the same for artist and critic – the moving towards
a less deadly, but, as yet, largely undefined theatre. This is
our eventual purpose, our shared aim, and noting all the sign-
posts and footprints on the way is our common task. Our
relations with critics may be strained in a superficial sense:
but in a deeper one the relationship is absolutely necessary:

like the fish in the ocean, we need one another's devouring talents to perpetuate the sea bed's existence. However, this devouring is not nearly enough : we need to share the endeavour to rise to the surface. This is what is hard for all of us. The critic is part of the whole and whether he writes his notices fast or slow, short or long, is not really important. Has he an image of how a theatre could be in his community and is he revising this image around each experience he receives? How many critics see their job this way?

It is for this reason that the more the critic becomes an insider, the better. I see nothing but good in a critic plunging into our lives, meeting actors, talking, discussing, watching, intervening. I would welcome his putting his hands on the medium and attempting to work it himself. Certainly, there is a tiny social problem – how does a critic talk to someone whom he has just damned in print? Momentary awkwardnesses may arise – but it is ludicrous to think that it is largely this that deprives some critics of a vital contact with the work of which they are a part. The embarrassment on his side and ours can easily be lived down and certainly a closer relation with the work will in no way put the critic into the position of connivance with the people he has got to know. The criticism that theatre people make of one another is usually of devastating severity – but absolutely precise. The critic who no longer enjoys the theatre is obviously a deadly critic, the critic who loves the theatre but is not critically clear what this means is also a deadly critic : the vital critic is the critic who has clearly formulated for himself what the theatre could be – and who is bold enough to throw this formula into jeopardy each time he participates in a theatrical event.

The worst problem for the professional critic is that he is seldom asked to expose himself to scorching events that change his thinking : it is hard for him to retain his enthu-

siasm, when there are few good plays anywhere in the world. Year after year, there is rich new material pouring into the cinema; yet all the theatres can do is make an unhappy choice between great traditional writing or far less good modern works. We are now in another area of the problem, also considered to be central : the dilemma of the deadly writer.

It is woefully difficult to write a play. A playwright is required by the very nature of drama to enter into the spirit of opposing characters. He is not a judge; he is a creator – and even if his first attempt at drama concerns only two people, whatever the style he is still required to live fully with them both. The job of shifting oneself totally from one character to another – a principle on which all of Shakespeare and all of Chekhov is built – is a super-human task at any time. It takes unique talents and perhaps ones that do not even correspond with our age. If the work of the beginner-playwright often seems thin, it may well be because his range of human sympathy is still unstretched – on the other hand, nothing seems more suspect than the mature middle-aged man of letters who sits down to invent characters and then tell us all their secrets. The French revulsion against the classic form of the novel was a reaction from the omniscience of the author: if you ask Marguerite Duras what her character is feeling she will often reply, 'How do I know?'; if you ask Robbe Grillet why a character has made a certain action he could answer, 'All I know for sure is that he opened the door with his right hand'. But this way of thinking hasn't reached the French theatre, where it is still the author who at the first rehearsal does a one-man show, reading out and performing all the parts. This is the most exaggerated form of a tradition that dies hard everywhere. The author has been forced to make a virtue of his specialness, and to turn his literariness into a crutch for a self-importance that in his heart he knows is not justified by his work. Maybe a need for privacy is a deep part of an

author's make-up. It is possible that it is only with the door closed, communing with himself, that he can wrestle into form inner images and conflicts of which he would never speak in public. We do not know how Aeschylus or Shakespeare worked. All we know is that gradually the relationship between the man who sits at home working it all out on paper and the world of actors and stages is getting more and more tenuous, more and more unsatisfactory. The best English writing is coming out of the theatre itself: Wesker, Arden, Osborne, Pinter, to take obvious examples, are all directors and actors as well as authors – and at times they have even been involved as impresarios.

None the less, whether scholar or actor, too few authors are what we could truly call inspiring or inspired. If the author were a master and not a victim one could say that he had betrayed the theatre. As it is, one can say that he is betraying by omission – the authors are failing to rise to the challenge of their times. Of course, there are exceptions, brilliant, startling ones, here and there. But I am thinking again of the quantity of new creative work poured into films compared with the world's output of new dramatic texts. When new plays set out to imitate reality, we are more conscious of what is imitative than what is real: if they explore character, it is seldom that they go far beyond stereotypes; if it is argument they offer, it is seldom that argument is taken to arresting extremes; even if it is a quality of life that they wish to evoke, we are usually offered no more than the literary quality of the well-turned phrase; if it is social criticism they are after, it seldom touches the heart of any social target; if they wish for laughter, it is usually by well-worn means.

As a result, we are often forced to choose between reviving old plays or staging new plays which we find inadequate, just as a gesture towards the present day. Or else to attempt to initiate a play – as, for example, when a group of actors and

writers in the Royal Shakespeare Theatre, wanting a play on Vietnam that did not exist, set out to make one, using techniques of improvisation and authorless invention to fill the vacuum. Group creation can be infinitely richer, if the group is rich, than the product of weak individualism – yet it proves nothing. There is eventually a need for authorship to reach the ultimate compactness and focus that collective work is almost obliged to miss.

In theory few men are as free as a playwright. He can bring the whole world on to his stage. But in fact he is strangely timid. He looks at the whole of life, and like all of us he only sees a tiny fragment; a fragment, one aspect of which catches his fancy. Unfortunately he rarely searches to relate his detail to any larger structure – it is as though he accepts without question his intuition as complete, his reality as all of reality. It is as though his belief in his subjectivity as his instrument and his strength precludes him from any dialectic between what he sees and what he apprehends. So there is either the author who explores his inner experience in depth and darkness, or else the author who shuns these areas, exploring the outside world – each one thinks his world is complete. If Shakespeare had never existed we would quite understandably theorize that the two can never combine. The Elizabethan Theatre did exist, though – and awkwardly enough we have this example constantly hanging over our heads. Four hundred years ago it was possible for a dramatist to wish to bring the pattern of events in the outside world, the inner events of complex men isolated as individuals, the vast tug of their fears and aspirations, into open conflict. Drama was exposure, it was confrontation, it was contradiction and it led to analysis, involvement, recognition and, eventually, to an awakening of understanding. Shakespeare was not a peak without a base, floating magically on a cloud: he was supported by scores of lesser dramatists, naturally with lesser and lesser

talents – but sharing the same ambition for wrestling with what Hamlet calls the forms and pressures of the age. Yet a neo-Elizabethan theatre based on verse and pageantry would be a monstrosity. This compels us to look at the problem more closely and try to find out what exactly the special Shakespeare qualities are. One simple fact emerges at once. Shakespeare used the same unit that is available today – a few hours of public time. He used this time span to cram together, second for second, a quantity of lively material of incredible richness. This material exists simultaneously on an infinite variety of levels, it plunges deep and reaches high : the technical devices, the use of verse and prose, the many changing scenes, exciting, funny, disturbing, were the ones the author was compelled to develop to satisfy his needs : and the author had a precise, human and social aim which gave him reason for searching for his themes, reason for searching for his means, reason for making theatre. We see the present-day author still locked in the prison of anecdote, consistency and style, conditioned by the relics of Victorian values to think ambition and pretension dirty words. How desperately he needs both. If only he were ambitious, if only he were to comb the sky ! For as long as he is an ostrich, an isolated ostrich, this can never happen. Before he can raise his head he too must face the same crisis. He too must discover what he believes a theatre to be.

Naturally, an author can only work with what he has got and cannot leap out of his sensibility. He cannot talk himself into being better or other than he is. He can only write about what he sees and thinks and feels. But one thing can amend the instrument at his disposal. The more clearly he recognizes the missing links in his relationships – the more accurately he experiences that he is never deep enough in enough aspects of life, nor deep enough in enough aspects of the theatre, that his necessary seclusion is also his prison – the more then can

E.S. – 3

he begin to find ways of connecting strands of observation
and experience which at present remain unlinked.

Let me try to define more precisely the issue that confronts
the writer. The theatre's needs have changed, yet the difference is not simply one of fashion. It is not as though fifty
years ago one type of theatre was in vogue while today the
author who feels the 'pulse of the public' can find his way to
the new idiom. The difference is that for a long time playwrights have very successfully traded on applying to the
theatre values from other fields. If a man could 'write' – and
writing meant the ability to put together words and phrases
in a stylish and elegant manner – then this was accepted as a
start towards good writing in the theatre. If a man could
invent a good plot, good twists, or what's described as 'understanding human nature' these were all considered to be at
least stepping-stones towards fine playwriting. Now the luke-
warm virtues of good craftsmanship, sound construction,
effective curtains, crisp dialogue have all been thoroughly
debunked. Not least, the influence of television has been to
accustom viewers of all classes all over the world to make
instant judgement – at the moment they catch sight of a shot
on the screen – so that the average adult continually situates
scenes and characters unaided, without a 'good craftsman'
helping with exposition and explanation. The steady discredit-
ing of non-theatre virtues is now beginning to clear the way
for other virtues. These are in fact more closely related to the
theatre form and also they are more exacting ones. Because if
one starts from the premise that a stage is a stage – not a
convenient place for the unfolding of a staged novel or a
staged poem or a staged lecture or a staged story – then the
word that is spoken on this stage exists, or fails to exist, only
in relation to the tensions it creates on that stage within the
given stage circumstances. In other words, although the
dramatist brings his own life nurtured by the life around him

into his work – the empty stage is no ivory tower – the choices he makes and the values he observes are only powerful in proportion to what they create in the language of theatre. Many examples of this can be seen wherever an author for moral or political reasons attempts to use a play as the bearer of a message. Whatever the value of this message, in the end it only works according to values that belong to the stage itself. An author today can easily cheat himself if he thinks that he can 'use' a conventional form as a vehicle. This was true when conventional forms still had life for their audience. Today when no conventional forms stand up any more, even the author who doesn't care about theatre as such, but only about what he is trying to say, is compelled to begin at the root – by facing the problem of the very nature of dramatic utterance. There is no way out – unless he is prepared to settle for a second-hand vehicle that's no longer in working order and very unlikely to take him to where he wants to go. Here the author's real problem and the director's real problem go hand in glove.

When I hear a director speaking glibly of serving the author, of letting a play speak for itself, my suspicions are aroused, because this is the hardest job of all. If you just let a play speak, it may not make a sound. If what you want is for the play to be heard, then you must conjure its sound from it. This demands many deliberate actions and the result may have great simplicity. However, setting out to 'be simple' can be quite negative, an easy evasion of the exacting steps to the simple answer.

It is a strange role, that of the director : he does not ask to be God and yet his role implies it. He wants to be fallible, and yet an instinctive conspiracy of the actors is to make him the arbiter, because an arbiter is so desperately wanted all the time. In a sense the director is always an imposter, a guide at night who does not know the territory, and yet has no choice

– he must guide, learning the route as he goes. Deadliness often lies in wait when he does not recognize this situation and hopes for the best, when it is the worst that he needs to face.

Deadliness always brings us back to repetition : the deadly director uses old formulae, old methods, old jokes, old effects, stock beginnings to scenes, stock ends; and this applies equally to his partners, the designers and composers, if they do not start each time afresh from the void, the desert and the true question – why clothes at all, why music, what for? A deadly director is a director who brings no challenge to the conditioned reflexes that every department must contain.

For half a century at least, it has been accepted that the theatre is a unity and that all elements should try to blend – this has led to the emergence of the director. But it has largely been a matter of external unity, a fairly external blending of styles so that contradictory styles do not jar. When we consider how the inner unity of a complex work can be expressed we may find quite the reverse – that a jarring of externals is quite essential. When we go further and consider the audience – and the society from which the audience comes – the true unity of all these elements may best be served by factors that by other standards seem ugly, discordant and destructive.

A stable and harmonious society might need only to look for ways of reflecting and reaffirming its harmony in its theatres. Such theatres could set out to unite cast and audience in a mutual 'yes'. But a shifting, chaotic world often must choose between a playhouse that offers a spurious 'yes' or a provocation so strong that it splinters its audience into fragments of vivid 'nos'.

Lecturing on these themes has taught me a great deal. I know that at this point someone always leaps up in the

audience to ask whether (a) I think that all theatres that are
not up to the loftiest standards should be closed or (b) whether
I think it's a bad thing for people to enjoy themselves at a good
entertainment or (c) what about amateurs?

My reply usually is that I would never like to be a censor,
ban anything or spoil anyone's fun. I have the greatest regard
for the repertory theatres, and for groups all through the
world struggling against great odds to sustain the level of
their work. I have the greatest respect for other people's
pleasure and particularly for anyone's frivolity, I came to the
theatre myself for sensual and often irresponsible reasons.
Entertainment is fine. But I still ask my questioners whether
they really feel on the whole that theatre gives them what
they expect or want.

I don't particularly mind waste, but I think it's a pity not to
know what one is wasting. Some old ladies use pound notes
as bookmarks: this is silly only if it is absent-minded.

The problem of the Deadly Theatre is like the problem of
the deadly bore. Every deadly bore has head, heart, arms,
legs; usually, he has a family and friends; he even has his
admirers. Yet we sigh when we come across him – and in this
sigh we are regretting that somehow he is at the bottom instead of the top of his possibilities. When we say deadly, we
never mean dead: we mean something depressingly active,
but for this very reason capable of change. The first step towards this change is facing the simple unattractive fact that
most of what is called theatre anywhere in the world is a
travesty of a word once full of sense. War or peace, the
colossal bandwagon of culture trundles on, carrying each
artist's traces to the evermounting garbage heap. Theatres,
actors, critics and public are interlocked in a machine that
creaks, but never stops. There is always a new season in hand
and we are too busy to ask the only vital question which
measures the whole structure. Why theatre at all? What for?

Is it an anachronism, a superannuated oddity, surviving like an old monument or a quaint custom? Why do we applaud, and what? Has the stage a real place in our lives? What function can it have? What could it serve? What could it explore? What are its special properties?

In Mexico, before the wheel was invented, gangs of slaves had to carry giant stones through the jungle and up the mountains, while their children pulled their toys on tiny rollers. The slaves made the toys, but for centuries failed to make the connection. When good actors play in bad comedies or second-rate musicals, when audiences applaud indifferent classics because they enjoy just the costumes or just the way the sets change, or just the prettiness of the leading actress, there is nothing wrong. But none the less, have they noticed what is underneath the toy they are dragging on a string? It's a wheel.

2

THE
HOLY
THEATRE

I am calling it the Holy Theatre for short, but it could be called The Theatre of the Invisible-Made-Visible : the notion that the stage is a place where the invisible can appear has a deep hold on our thoughts. We are all aware that most of life escapes our senses : a most powerful explanation of the various arts is that they talk of patterns which we can only begin to recognize when they manifest themselves as rhythms or shapes. We observe that the behaviour of people, of crowds, of history, obeys such recurrent patterns. We hear that trumpets destroyed the walls of Jericho, we recognize that a magical thing called music can come from men in white ties and tails, blowing, waving, thumping and scraping away. Despite the absurd means that produce it, through the concrete in music we recognize the abstract, we understand that ordinary men and their clumsy instruments are transformed by an art of possession. We may make a personality cult of the conductor, but we are aware that he is not really making the music, it is making him – if he is relaxed, open and attuned, then the invisible will take possession of him; through him, it will reach us.

This is the notion, the true dream behind the debased ideals of the Deadly Theatre. This is what is meant and remembered by those who with feeling and seriousness use big hazy words like nobility, beauty, poetry, which I would like to re-examine for the particular quality they suggest. The theatre is the last forum where idealism is still an open question:

many audiences all over the world will answer positively from their own experience that they have seen the face of the invisible through an experience on the stage that transcended their experience in life. They will maintain that *Oedipus* or *Berenice* or *Hamlet* or *The Three Sisters* performed with beauty and with love fires the spirit and gives them a reminder that daily drabness is not necessarily all. When they reproach the contemporary theatre for its kitchen sinks and cruelties, this, honourably, is what they are trying to say. They remember how during the war the romantic theatre, the theatre of colours and sounds, of music and movement, came like water to the thirst of dry lives. At that time, it was called escape and yet the word was only partially accurate. It was an escape, but also a reminder : a sparrow in a prison cell. When the war was over, the theatre again strove even more vigorously to find the same values.

The theatre of the late '40s had many glories : it was the theatre of Jouvet and Bérard, and of Jean-Louis Barrault, of Clavé at the ballet, *Don Juan, Amphitryon, La Folle de Chaillot, Carmen,* John Gielgud's revival of *The Importance of Being Earnest, Peer Gynt* at the Old Vic, Olivier's *Oedipus,* Olivier's *Richard III, The Lady's not for Burning, Venus Observed;* of Massine at Covent Garden under the birdcage in *The Three-cornered Hat* just as he had been fifteen years before – this was a theatre of colour and movement, of fine fabrics, of shadows, of eccentric, cascading words, of leaps of thought and of cunning machines, of lightness and of all forms of mystery and surprise – it was the theatre of a battered Europe that seemed to share one aim – a reaching back towards a memory of lost grace.

Walking along the Reeperbahn in Hamburg on an afternoon in 1946, whilst a damp dispiriting grey mist whirled round the desperate mutilated tarts, some on crutches, noses mauve, cheeks hollow, I saw a crowd of children pushing ex-

citedly into a night club door. I followed them. On the stage
was a bright blue sky. Two seedy, spangled clowns sat on a
painted cloud on their way to visit the Queen of Heaven.
'What shall we ask her for?' said one. 'Dinner,' said the other
and the children screamed approval. 'What shall we have for
dinner?' 'Schinken, leberwurst ...' the clown began to list
all the unobtainable foods and the squeals of excitement
were gradually replaced by a hush – a hush that settled
into a deep and true theatrical silence. An image was being
made real, in answer to the need for something that was not
there.

In the burnt-out shell of the Hamburg Opera only the
stage itself remained – but an audience assembled on it whilst
against the back wall on a wafer-thin set singers clambered
up and down to perform *The Barber of Seville*, because
nothing would stop them doing so. In a tiny attic fifty people
crammed together while in the inches of remaining space a
handful of the best actors resolutely continued to practise
their art. In a ruined Düsseldorf, a minor Offenbach about
smugglers and bandits filled the theatre with delight. There
was nothing to discuss, nothing to analyse – in Germany that
winter, as in London a few years before, the theatre was responding to a hunger. What, however, was this hunger? Was
it a hunger for the invisible, a hunger for a reality deeper than
the fullest form of everyday life – or was it a hunger for the
missing things in life, a hunger, in fact, for buffers against
reality? The question is an important one, because many
people believe that in the very recent past there still was a
theatre with certain values, certain skills, certain arts that we
perhaps wantonly have destroyed or cast aside.

We mustn't allow ourselves to become the dupes of
nostalgia. The best of the romantic theatre, the civilized
pleasures of the opera and the ballet were in any event gross
reductions of an art sacred in its origins. Over the centuries

the Orphic Rites turned into the Gala Performance –
slowly and imperceptibly the wine was adulterated drop by
drop.

The curtain used to be the great symbol of a whole school of
theatre – the red curtains, the footlights, the idea that we were
all children again, the nostalgia and the magic were all of a
piece. Gordon Craig spent his life railing against the theatre
of illusion, but his most treasured memories were of painted
trees and forests and his eyes would light up as he described
effects of *trompe l'oeil*. But the day came when the same red
curtain no longer hid surprises, when we no longer wanted –
or needed – to be children again, when the rough magic
yielded to a harsher common-sense; then the curtain was
pulled down and the footlights removed.

Certainly, we still wish to capture in our arts the invisible
currents that rule our lives, but our vision is now locked to
the dark end of the spectrum. Today the theatre of doubting,
of unease, of trouble, of alarm, seems truer than the theatre
with a noble aim. Even if the theatre had in its origins rituals
that made the invisible incarnate, we must not forget that
apart from certain Oriental theatres these rituals have been
either lost or remain in seedy decay. Bach's vision has been
scrupulously preserved by the accuracy of his notations: in
Fra Angelico we witness true incarnation; but for us to
attempt such processes today, where do we find the source?
In Coventry, for instance, a new cathedral has been built,
according to the best recipe for achieving a noble result.
Honest, sincere artists, the 'best', have been grouped together
to make a civilized stab at celebrating God and Man and
Culture and Life through a collective act. So there is a new
building, fine ideas, beautiful glass-work – only the ritual is
threadbare. Those Ancient and Modern hymns, charming
perhaps in a little country church, those numbers on the wall,
those dog-collars and the lessons – they are sadly inadequate

here. The new place cries out for a new ceremony, but of course it is the new ceremony that should have come first – it is the ceremony in all its meanings that should have dictated the shape of the place, as it did when all the great mosques and cathedrals and temples were built. Goodwill, sincerity, reverence, belief in culture are not quite enough : the outer form can only take on real authority if the ceremony has equal authority – and who today can possibly call the tune? Of course, today as at all times, we need to stage true rituals, but for rituals that could make theatre-going an experience that feeds our lives true forms are needed. These are not at our disposal, and conferences and resolutions will not bring them our way.

The actor searches vainly for the sound of a vanished tradition, and critic and audience follow suit. We have lost all sense of ritual and ceremony – whether it be connected with Christmas, birthdays or funerals – but the words remain with us and old impulses stir in the marrow. We feel we should have rituals, we should do 'something' about getting them and we blame the artists for not 'finding' them for us. So the artist sometimes attempts to find new rituals with only his imagination as his source : he imitates the outer form of ceremonies, pagan or baroque, unfortunately adding his own trappings – the result is rarely convincing. And after the years and years of weaker and waterier imitations we now find ourselves rejecting the very notion of a holy stage. It is not the fault of the holy that it has become a middle-class weapon to keep children good.

When I first went to Stratford in 1945 every conceivable value was buried in deadly sentimentality and complacent worthiness – a traditionalism approved largely by town, scholar and Press. It needed the boldness of a very extraordinary old gentleman, Sir Barry Jackson, to throw all this out of the window and so make a true search for true values

possible once more. And it was at Stratford years later, at the official luncheon to celebrate Shakespeare's 400th birthday, that I saw a clear example of the difference between what a ritual is and what it could be. It was felt that Shakespeare's birthday called for a ritual celebration. The only celebration anyone could vaguely remember was related to a feast, and a feast today means a list of people from Who's Who, assembled round Prince Philip, eating smoked salmon and steak. Ambassadors nodded to one another and passed the ritual red wine. I chatted with the local MP. Then someone made a formal speech, we listened politely – and rose to our feet to toast William Shakespeare. At the moment the glasses clinked – for not more than a fraction of a second, through the common consciousness of everyone present and all for once concentrating on the same thing – passed the notion that four hundred years ago such a man had been, and that this was what we were assembled for. For a breath of time the silence deepened, a touch of meaning was there – an instant later it was brushed away and forgotten. If we understood more about rituals, the ritual celebration of an individual to whom we owe so much might have been intentional, not accidental. It might have been as powerful as all his plays, and as unforgettable. However, we do not know how to celebrate because we do not know what to celebrate. All we know is the end result: we know and we like the feel and sound of celebrating through applause, and this is where we get stuck. We forget that there are two possible climaxes to a theatre experience. There is the climax of celebration in which our participation explodes in stamping and cheering, shouts of hurrah and the roar of hands, or else, at the other end of the stick, the climax of silence – another form of recognition and appreciation for an experience shared. We have largely forgotten silence. It even embarrasses us; we clap our hands mechanically because we do not know what else to do, and

we are unaware that silence is also permitted, that silence also is good.

It is only when a ritual comes to our own level that we become qualified to deal in it: the whole of pop music is a series of rituals on a level to which we have access. Peter Hall's vast and rich achievement in his cycle of Shakespeare's *Wars of the Roses* drew on assassination, politics, intrigue, war: David Rudkin's disturbing play *Afore Night Come* was a ritual of death, *West Side Story* a ritual of urban violence; Genet creates rituals of sterility and degradation. When I took a tour of *Titus Andronicus* through Europe this obscure work of Shakespeare touched audiences directly because we had tapped in it a ritual of bloodshed which was recognized as true. And this leads to the heart of the controversy that exploded in London about what were labelled 'dirty plays': the complaint was that the theatre today is wallowing in misery; that in Shakespeare, in great classical art, one eye is always on the stars, that the rite of winter includes a sense of the rite of spring. I think this is true. In a sense I agree wholeheartedly with our opponents – but not when I see what they propose. They are not searching for a holy theatre, they are not talking about a theatre of miracles: they are talking of the tame play where 'higher' only means 'nicer', being noble only means being decent. Alas, happy endings and optimism can't be ordered like wine from cellars. They spring whether we wish it or not from a source and if we pretend there is such a source readily at hand we will go on cheating ourselves with rotten imitations. If we recognize how desperately far we have drifted from anything to do with a holy theatre we can begin to discard once and for all the dream that a fine theatre could return in a trice if only a few nice people tried harder.

More than ever, we crave for an experience that is beyond the humdrum. Some look for it in jazz, classical music, in

marijuana and in LSD. In the theatre we shy away from the holy because we don't know what this could be – we only know what is called the holy has let us down. We shrink from what is called poetic because the poetic has let us down. Attempts to revive poetic drama have too often led to something wishy-washy or obscure. Poetry has become a meaningless term, and its association with word-music, with sweet sounds, is a hangover of a Tennysonian tradition that has somehow wrapped itself round Shakespeare, so that we are conditioned by the idea that a verse play is half way between prose and the opera, neither spoken nor sung, yet with a higher charge than prose – higher in content, higher somehow in moral value.

All the forms of sacred art have certainly been destroyed by bourgeois values but this sort of observation does not help our problem. It is foolish to allow a revulsion from bourgeois forms to turn into a revulsion from needs that are common to all men: if the need for a true contact with a sacred invisibility through the theatre still exists, then all possible vehicles must be re-examined.

I have sometimes been accused of wanting to destroy the spoken word, and indeed in this absurdity there's a grain of sense. In its fusion with the American idiom our ever-changing language has rarely been richer, and yet it does not seem that the word is the same tool for dramatics that it once was. Is it that we are living in an age of images? Is it even that we must go through a period of image-saturation, for the need for language to re-emerge? This is very possible, for today writers seem unable to make ideas and images collide through words with Elizabethan force. The most influential of modern writers, Brecht, wrote full and rich texts, but the real conviction of his plays is inseparable from the imagery of his own productions. Yet in the desert one prophet raised his voice. Railing against the sterility of the theatre before the war in

France an illuminated genius, Antoine Artaud, wrote tracts describing from his imagination and intuition another theatre – a Holy Theatre in which the blazing centre speaks through those forms closest to it. A theatre working like the plague, by intoxication, by infection, by analogy, by magic; a theatre in which the play, the event itself, stands in place of a text.

Is there another language, just as exacting for the author as a language of words? Is there a language of actions, a language of sounds – a language of word-as-part-of-movement, of word-as-lie, word-as-parody, of word-as-rubbish, of word-as-contradiction, of word-shock or word-cry? If we talk of the more-than-literal, if poetry means that which crams more and penetrates deeper – is this where it lies? Charles Marowitz and I instituted a group with the Royal Shakespeare Theatre called the Theatre of Cruelty to investigate these questions and to try to learn for ourselves what a holy theatre might be.

The title was by way of homage to Artaud, but it did not mean that we were trying to reconstruct Artaud's own theatre. Anyone who wishes to know what 'Theatre of Cruelty' means should refer directly to Artaud's own writings. We used his striking title to cover our own experiments, many of which were directly stimulated by Artaud's thought – although many exercises were very far from what he had proposed. We did not start at the blazing centre, we began very simply on the fringes.

We set an actor in front of us, asked him to imagine a dramatic situation that did not involve any physical movement, then we all tried to understand what state he was in. Of course, this was impossible, which was the point of the exercise. The next stage was to discover what was the very least he needed before understanding could be reached: was it a sound, a movement, a rhythm – and were these interchangeable – or had each its special strengths and limitations? So we worked by imposing drastic conditions. An actor must

communicate an idea – the start must always be a thought or a wish that he has to project – but he has only, say, one finger, one tone of voice, a cry, or the capacity to whistle at his disposal.

An actor sits at one end of the room, facing the wall. At the other end is another actor, looking at the first one's back, not allowed to move. The second actor must make the first one obey him. As the first one has his back turned, the second has no way of communicating his wishes except through sounds, for he is allowed no words. This seems impossible, but it can be done. It is like crossing an abyss on a tightrope: necessity suddenly produces strange powers. I have heard of a woman lifting a huge car off her injured child – a feat technically impossible for her muscles in any predictable conditions. Ludmilla Pitoeff used to go on stage with her heart pounding in a way that in theory should have killed her every night. With this exercise, many times we also observed an equally phenomenal result: a long silence, great concentration, one actor running experimentally through a range of hisses or gurgles until suddenly the other actor stood and quite confidently executed the movement the first one had in mind.

Similarly these actors experimented in communication through tapping with a finger-nail: starting from a powerful need to express something and again using only one tool. Here it was rhythm – on another occasion it was the eyes or the back of the head. A valuable exercise was to fight in pairs, taking and giving back every blow, but never being allowed to touch, never moving the head, nor the arms, nor feet. In other words a movement of the torso is all that is allowed: no realistic contact can take place, yet a fight must be engaged physically and emotionally and carried through. Such exercises should not be thought of as gymnastics – freeing muscular resistance is only a by-product – the purpose all the time is to increase resistance – by limiting the alternatives – and then using this

resistance in the struggle for a true expression. The principle is the one of rubbing two sticks together: this friction of un-yielding opposites makes fire – and the other forms of com-bustion can be obtained in the same way. The actor then found that to communicate his invisible meanings he needed concentration, he needed will; he needed to summon all his emotional reserves; he needed courage; he needed clear thought. But the most important result was that he was led inexorably to the conclusion that he needed form. It was not enough to feel passionately – a creative leap was required to mint a new form which would be a container and a reflector for his impulses. That is what is truly called an 'action'. One of the most interesting moments was during an exercise in which each member of the group had to act a child. Naturally, one after the other did an 'imitation' of a child by stooping, wriggling, or squawking – and the result was painfully em-barrassing. Then the tallest of the group came forward and without any physical change at all, with no attempt to imitate baby talk, he presented fully, to everyone's complete satisfaction, the idea that he had been called upon to carry. How? I can't describe it; it happened as direct communication, only for those present. This is what some theatres call magic, others science, but it's the same thing. An invisible idea was rightly shown.

I say 'shown' because an actor making a gesture is creating both for himself, out of his deepest need, and for the other person. It is hard to understand the true function of spectator, there and not there, ignored and yet needed. The actor's work is never for an audience, yet always is for one. The onlooker is a partner who must be forgotten and still constantly kept in mind: a gesture is statement, expression, communication and a private manifestation of loneliness – it is always what Artaud calls a signal through the flames – yet this implies a sharing of experience, once contact is made.

Slowly we worked towards different wordless languages: we took an event, a fragment of experience and made exercises that turned them into forms that could be shared. We encouraged the actors to see themselves not only as improvisers, lending themselves blindly to their inner impulses, but as artists responsible for searching and selecting amongst form, so that a gesture or a cry becomes like an object that he discovers and even remoulds. We experimented with and came to reject the traditional language of masks and make-ups as no longer appropriate. We experimented with silence. We set out to discover the relations between silence and duration : we needed an audience so that we could set a silent actor in front of them to see the varying lengths of attention he could command. Then we experimented with ritual in the sense of repetitive patterns, seeing how it is possible to present more meaning, more swiftly than by a logical unfolding of events. Our aim for each experiment, good or bad, successful or disastrous, was the same : can the invisible be made visible through the performer's presence?

We know that the world of appearance is a crust – under the crust is the boiling matter we see if we peer into a volcano. How can we tap this energy? We studied Meyerhold's bio-mechanical experiments, where he played love scenes on swings, and in one of our performances a Hamlet threw Ophelia on to the knees of the audience, while he swung above their heads on a rope. We were denying psychology, we were trying to smash the apparently water-tight divisions between the private and the public man – the outer man whose behaviour is bound by the photographic rules of every-day life, who must sit to sit, stand to stand – and the inner man whose anarchy and poetry is usually expressed only in his words. For centuries, unrealistic speech has been universally accepted, all sorts of audiences have swallowed the convention that words can do the strangest things – in a

monologue, for instance, a man stays still but his ideas can
dance where they will. Vaulting speech is a good convention,
but is there not another? When a man flies over the audience's head on a rope, every aspect of the immediate is put
in jeopardy – the circle of spectators that is at ease when the
man speaks is thrown into chaos: in this instant of hazard
can a different meaning appear?

In naturalistic plays the playwright contrives the dialogue
in such a way that while seeming natural it shows what he
wants to be seen. By using language illogically, by introducing the ridiculous in speech and the fantastic in behaviour, an
author of the Theatre of the Absurd opens up for himself
another vocabulary. For instance, a tiger comes into the
room, but the couple take no notice; the wife speaks, the
husband answers by taking off his pants and a new pair floats
in through the window. The Theatre of the Absurd did not
seek the unreal for its own sake. It used the unreal to make
certain explorations, because it sensed the absence of truth
in our everyday exchanges, and the presence of the truth in
the seemingly far-fetched. Although there have been some remarkable individual works stemming from this approach to
the world, as a recognizable school the Absurd has reached
an impasse. Like so much that is novel in texture, like much
concrete music, for instance, the surprise element wears thin,
and we are left to face the fact that the field it covers is sometimes very small. Fantasy invented by the mind is apt to be
lightweight, the whimsicality and the surrealism of much of
the Absurd would no more have satisfied Artaud than the
narrowness of the psychological play. What he wanted in his
search for a holiness was absolute: he wanted a theatre that
would be a hallowed place; he wanted that theatre served by
a band of dedicated actors and directors who would create out
of their own natures an unending succession of violent stage
images, bringing about such powerful immediate explosions

of human matter that no one would ever again revert to a
theatre of anecdote and talk. He wanted the theatre to contain all that is normally reserved for crime and war. He
wanted an audience that would drop all its defences, that
would allow itself to be perforated, shocked, startled, and
raped, so that at the same time it could be filled with a powerful new charge.

This sounds tremendous, yet it raises a nagging doubt. How
passive does this make the spectator? Artaud maintained
that only in the theatre could we liberate ourselves from the
recognizable forms in which we live our daily lives. This
made the theatre a holy place in which a greater reality could
be found. Those who view his work with suspicion ask how
all-embracing is this truth, and secondly, how valuable is the
experience? A totem, a cry from the womb : these can crack
through walls of prejudice in any man : a howl can certainly
reach through to the guts. But is this revealing, is this contact
with our own repressions creative, therapeutic? Is it really
holy – or is Artaud in his passion dragging us back to a
nether world, away from striving, away from the light – to
D. H. Lawrence, Wagner; is there even a fascist smell in the
cult of unreason? Is a cult of the invisible, anti-intelligent? Is
it a denial of the mind?

As with all prophets, we must separate the man from his
followers. Artaud never achieved his own theatre : maybe the
power of his vision is that it is the carrot in front of our nose,
never to be reached. Certainly, he himself was always speaking of a complete way of life, of a theatre in which the activity
of the actor and the activity of the spectator were driven by
the same desperate need.

Artaud applied is Artaud betrayed : betrayed because it is
always just a portion of his thought that is exploited, betrayed
because it is easier to apply rules to the work of a handful of

dedicated actors than to the lives of the unknown spectators
who happen by chance to come through the theatre door.

None the less, from the arresting words 'Theatre of Cruelty'
comes a groping towards a theatre, more violent, less rational,
more extreme, less verbal, more dangerous. There is a joy in
violent shocks. The only trouble with violent shocks is that
they wear off. What follows a shock? Here's the snag. I fire
a pistol at the spectator – I did so once – and for a second I
have a possibility to reach him in a different way. I must
relate this possibility to a purpose, otherwise a moment later
he is back where he was: inertia is the greatest force we
know. I show a sheet of blue – nothing but the colour blue –
blueness is a direct statement that arouses an emotion, the
next second that impression fades. I hold up a brilliant flash
of scarlet – a different impression is made, but unless someone
can grab this moment, knowing why and how and what for
– it too begins to wane. The trouble is that one can easily find
oneself firing the first shots without any sense of where the
battle could lead. One look at the average audience gives us
an irresistible urge to assault it – to shoot first and ask
questions later. This is the road to the Happening.

A Happening is a powerful invention, it destroys at one
blow many deadly forms, like the dreariness of theatre buildings, and the charmless trappings of curtain, usherette, cloak-
room, programme, bar. A Happening can be anywhere, any
time, of any duration: nothing is required, nothing is taboo.
A Happening may be spontaneous, it may be formal, it may
be anarchistic, it can generate intoxicating energy. Behind
the Happening is the shout 'Wake up!' Van Gogh made
generations of travellers see Provence with new eyes, and the
theory of Happenings is that a spectator can be jolted eventually into new sight, so that he wakes to the life around him.
This sounds like sense, and in Happenings, the influence
of Zen and Pop Art combine to make a perfectly logical

E.S.—4

twentieth-century American combination. But the sadness of a bad Happening must be seen to be believed. Give a child a paintbox, and if he mixes all the colours together the result is always the same muddy browny grey. A Happening is always the brainchild of someone and unavoidably it reflects the level of its inventor : if it is the work of a group, it reflects the inner resources of the group. This free form is all too often imprisoned in the same obsessional symbols : flour, custard pies, rolls of paper, dressing, undressing, dressing-up, undressing again, changing clothes, making water, throwing water, blowing water, hugging, rolling, writhing – you feel that if a Happening became a way of life then by contrast the most humdrum life would seem a fantastic happening. Very easily a Happening can be no more than a series of mild shocks followed by let-downs which progressively combine to neutralize the further shocks before they arrive. Or else the frenzy of the shocker bludgeons the shockee into becoming still another form of the Deadly Audience – he starts willing and is assaulted into apathy.

The simple fact is that Happenings have brought into being not the easiest but the most exacting forms of all. As shocks and surprises make a dent in a spectator's reflexes, so that he is suddenly more open, more alert, more awake, the possibility and the responsibility arise for onlooker and performer alike. The instant must be used, but how, what for? Here, we are back to the root question – what are we searching for anyway? Do-it-yourself Zen hardly fits the bill. The Happening is a new broom of great efficacy : it is certainly sweeping away the rubbish, but as it clears the way the old dialogue is heard again, the debate of form against formlessness, freedom against discipline; a dialectic as old as Pythagoras, who first set in opposition the terms Limited and Unlimited. It is all very well to use crumbs of Zen to assert the principle that existence is existence, that every manifestation contains with-

in it all of everything, and that a slap on the face, a tweak of the nose or a custard pie are all equally Buddha. All religions assert that the invisible is visible all the time. But here's the crunch. Religious teaching – including Zen – asserts that this visible-invisible cannot be seen automatically – it can only be seen given certain conditions. The conditions can relate to certain states or to a certain understanding. In any event, to comprehend the visibility of the invisible is a life's work. Holy art is an aid to this, and so we arrive at a definition of a holy theatre. A holy theatre not only presents the invisible but also offers conditions that make its perception possible. The Happening could be related to all of this, but the present inadequacy of the Happening is that it refuses to examine deeply the problem of perception. Naïvely it believes that the cry 'Wake up!' is enough : that the call 'Live!' brings life. Of course, more is needed. But what?

A happening was originally intended to be a painter's creation – which instead of paint and canvas, or glue and saw-dust, or solid objects, used people to make certain relation-ships and forms. Like a painting, a happening is intended as a new object, a new construction brought into the world, to enrich the world, to add to nature, to sit alongside everyday life. To those who find happenings dreary the supporter re-torts that any one thing is as good as another. If some seem 'worse' than others, this, they say, is the result of the spec-tator's conditioning and his jaded eye. Those who take part in a happening and get a kick out of doing so can afford to regard the outsider's boredom with indifference. The very fact that they participate heightens their perception. The man who puts on a dinner jacket for the opera, saying, 'I enjoy a sense of occasion', and the hippy who puts on a flowered suit for an all-night light-show are both reaching incoherently in the same direction. Occasion, Event, Happening – the words are interchangeable. The structures are different – the opera is

constructed and repeated according to traditional principles, the light-show unfolds for the first and last time according to accident and environment; but both are deliberately constructed social gatherings that seek for an invisibility to interpenetrate and animate the ordinary. Those of us who work in theatres are implicitly challenged to go ahead to meet this hunger.

There are many people attempting in their own ways to take up the challenge. I will quote three.

There is Merce Cunningham. Stemming from Martha Graham, he has evolved a ballet company whose daily exercises are a continual preparation for the shock of freedom. A classical dancer is trained to observe and follow every detail of a movement that he is given. He has trained his body to obey, his technique is his servant, so that instead of being wrapped up in the making of the movement he can let the movement unfold in intimate company with the unfolding of the music. Merce Cunningham's dancers, who are highly trained, use their discipline to be more aware of the fine currents that flow within a movement as it unfolds for the first time – and their technique enables them to follow this fine prompting, freed from the clumsiness of the untrained man. When they improvise – as notions are born and flow between them, never repeating themselves, always in movement – the intervals have shape, so that the rhythms can be sensed as just and the proportions as true : all is spontaneous and yet there is order. In silence there are many potentialities; chaos or order, muddle or pattern, all lie fallow – the invisible-made-visible is of sacred nature, and as he dances Merce Cunningham strives for a holy art.

Perhaps the most intense and personal writing of our time comes from Samuel Beckett. Beckett's plays are symbols in an exact sense of the word. A false symbol is soft and vague : a true symbol is hard and clear. When we say 'symbolic' we

often mean something drearily obscure: a true symbol is specific, it is the only form a certain truth can take. The two men waiting by a stunted tree, the man recording himself on tape, the two men marooned in a tower, the woman buried to her waist in sand, the parents in the dustbins, the three heads in the urns: these are pure inventions, fresh images sharply defined – and they stand on the stage as objects. They are theatre machines. People smile at them, but they hold their ground: they are critic-proof. We get nowhere if we expect to be told what they mean, yet each one has a relation with us we can't deny. If we accept this, the symbol opens in us a great and wondering O.

This is how Beckett's dark plays are plays of light, where the desperate object created is witness to the ferocity of the wish to bear witness to the truth. Beckett does not say 'no' with satisfaction; he forges his merciless 'no' out of a longing for 'yes' and so his despair is the negative from which the contour of its opposite can be drawn.

There are two ways of speaking about the human condition: there is the process of inspiration – by which all the positive elements of life can be revealed, and there is the process of honest vision – by which the artist bears witness to whatever it is that he has seen. The first process depends on revelation; it can't be brought about by holy wishes. The second one depends on honesty, and it mustn't be clouded over by holy wishes.

Beckett expresses just this distinction in *Happy Days*. The optimism of the lady buried in the ground is not a virtue, it is the element that blinds her to the truth of her situation. For a few rare flashes she glimpses her condition, but at once she blots them out with her good cheer. Beckett's action on some of his audience is exactly like the action of this situation on the leading character. The audience wriggles, squirms and yawns, it walks out or else invents and prints every form of

imaginary complaint as a mechanism to ward off the uncomfortable truth. Sadly, it is the wish for optimism that many writers share that prevents them from finding hope. When we attack Beckett for pessimism it is we who are the Beckett characters trapped in a Beckett scene. When we accept Beckett's statement as it is, then suddenly all is transformed. There is after all quite another audience, Beckett's audience; those in every country who do not set up intellectual barriers, who do not try too hard to analyse the message. This audience laughs and cries out – and in the end celebrates with Beckett; this audience leaves his plays, his black plays, nourished and enriched, with a lighter heart, full of a strange irrational joy. Poetry, nobility, beauty, magic – suddenly these suspect words are back in the theatre once more.

In Poland there is a small company led by a visionary, Jerzy Grotowski, that also has a sacred aim. The theatre, he believes, cannot be an end in itself; like dancing or music in certain dervish orders, the theatre is a vehicle, a means for self-study, self-exploration, a possibility of salvation. The actor has himself as his field of work. This field is richer than that of the painter, richer than that of the musician, because to explore he needs to call on every aspect of himself. His hand, his eye, his ear, and his heart are what he is studying and what he is studying with. Seen this way, acting is a life's work – the actor is step by step extending his knowledge of himself through the painful, everchanging circumstances of rehearsal and the tremendous punctuation points of performance. In Grotowski's terminology, the actor allows a role to 'penetrate' him; at first he is all obstacle to it, but by constant work he acquires technical mastery over his physical and psychic means by which he can allow the barriers to drop. 'Auto-penetration' by the role is related to exposure: the actor does not hesitate to show himself exactly as he is, for he realizes that the secret

of the role demands his opening himself up, disclosing his own secrets. So that the act of performance is an act of sacrifice, of sacrificing what most men prefer to hide – this sacrifice is his gift to the spectator. Here there is a similar relation between actor and audience to the one between priest and worshipper. It is obvious that not everyone is called to priesthood and no traditional religion expects this of all men. There are laymen – who have necessary roles in life – and those who take on other burdens, for the laymen's sake. The priest performs the ritual for himself and on behalf of others. Grotowski's actors offer their performance as a ceremony for those who wish to assist : the actor invokes, lays bare what lies in every man – and what daily life covers up. This theatre is holy because its purpose is holy; it has a clearly defined place in the community and it responds to a need the churches can no longer fill. Grotowski's theatre is as close as anyone has got to Artaud's ideal. It is a complete way of life for all its members, and so it is in contrast with most other *avant-garde* and experimental groups whose work is scrambled and usually invalidated through lack of means. Most experimental products cannot do what they want because outside conditions are too heavily loaded against them. They have scratch casts, rehearsal time eaten into by the need to earn their living, inadequate sets, costumes, lights, etc. Poverty is their complaint and their excuse. Grotowski makes poverty an ideal; his actors have given up everything except their own bodies; they have the human instrument and limitless time – no wonder they feel the richest theatre in the world.

These three theatres, Cunningham, Grotowski, and Beckett, have several things in common : small means, intense work, rigorous discipline, absolute precision. Also, almost as a condition, they are theatres for an *élite*. Merce Cunningham usually plays to poor houses, and if his admirers are scandalized by his lack of support he himself takes it in his stride.

Beckett only rarely fills an average sized auditorium. Grotowski plays for thirty spectators – as a deliberate choice. He is
convinced that the problems facing himself and the actor are
so great that to consider a larger audience could only lead to
a dilution of the work. He said to me : 'My search is based on
the director and the actor. You base yours on the director,
actor, audience. I accept that this is possible, but for me it is
too indirect.' Is he right? Are these the only possible theatres
to touch 'reality'? They are certainly true to themselves, they
certainly face the basic question, 'Why theatre at all?' and
each one has found its answer. They each start from their
hunger, each works to lessen his own need. And yet the very
purity of their resolve, the high and serious nature of their
activity inevitably brings a colour to their choices and a limi-
tation to their field. They are unable to be both esoteric and
popular at one and the same time. There is no crowd in
Beckett, no Falstaff. For Merce Cunningham, as once for
Schoenberg, it would need a *tour de force* to re-invent Ring a
ring o' Roses or to whistle *God Save The Queen*. In life, Grotowski's leading actor avidly collects jazz records, but there
are no pop lyrics on the stage which is his life. These theatres
explore life, yet what counts as life is restricted. 'Real' life
precludes certain 'unreal' features. If we read today Artaud's
descriptions of his imaginary productions, they reflect his
own tastes and the current romantic imagery of his time, for
there is a certain preference for darkness and mystery, for
chanting, for unearthly cries, for single words rather than
sentences, for vast shapes, masks, for kings and emperors and
popes, for saints and sinners and flagellants, for black tights
and writhing naked skin.

A director dealing with elements that exist outside of himself can cheat himself into thinking his work more objective
than it is. By his choice of exercises, even by the way he en-
courages an actor to find his own freedom, a director cannot

help projecting his own state of mind on to the stage. The supreme jiujitsu would be for the director to stimulate such an outpouring of the actor's inner richness that it completely transforms the subjective nature of his original impulse. But usually the director or the choreographer's pattern shows through and it is here that the desired objective experience can turn into the expression of some individual director's private imagery. We can try to capture the invisible but we must not lose touch with common sense – if our language is too special we will lose part of the spectator's belief. The model, as always, is Shakespeare. His aim continually is holy, metaphysical, yet he never makes the mistake of staying too long on the highest plane. He knew how hard it is for us to keep company with the absolute – so he continually bumps us down to earth – and Grotowski recognizes this, speaking of the need for both 'apotheosis' and 'derision'. We have to accept that we can never see all of the invisible. So after straining towards it, we have to face defeat, drop down to earth, then start up again.

I have refrained from introducing the Living Theatre until now because this group, led by Julian Beck and Judith Malina, is special in every sense of the word. It is a nomad community. It moves across the world according to its own laws and often in contradiction to the laws of the country in which it happens to be. It provides a complete way of life for every one of its members, some thirty men and women who live and work together; they make love, produce children, act, invent plays, do physical and spiritual exercises, share and discuss everything that comes their way. Above all, they are a community; but they are only a community because they have a special function which gives their communal existence its meaning. This function is acting. Without acting the group would run dry : they perform because the act and fact of performing corresponds to a great shared need. They are in search of

meaning in their lives, and in a sense even if there were no audiences, they would still have to perform, because the theatrical event is the climax and centre of their search. Yet without an audience their performances would lose their substance – the audience is always the challenge without which a performance would be a sham. Also, it is a practical community that makes performances for a living and offers them for sale. In the Living Theatre, three needs become one: it exists for the sake of performing, it earns its living through performing and its performances contain the most intense and intimate moments of its collective life.

One day this caravan may halt. This could be in a hostile environment – like its origins in New York – in which case its function will be to provoke and divide audiences by increasing their awareness of uncomfortable contradiction between a way of life on stage and a way of life outside. Their own identity will be constantly drawn and redrawn by the natural tension and hostility between themselves and their surroundings. Alternatively, they may come to rest in some wider community that shares some of their values. Here there would be a different unity and a different tension: the tension would be shared by stage and audience – it would be the expression of the unresolved quest for a holiness eternally undefined.

In fact, the Living Theatre, exemplary in so many ways, has still not yet come to grips with its own essential dilemma. Searching for holiness without tradition, without source, it is compelled to turn to many traditions, many sources – yoga, Zen, psychoanalysis, books, hearsay, discovery, inspiration – a rich but dangerous eclecticism. For the method that leads to what they are seeking cannot be an additive one. To subtract, to strip away can only be effected in the light of some constant. They are still in search of this constant.

In the meantime, they are continually nourished by a very

American humour and joy that is surrealist, but with both feet firmly on the ground.

In Haitian voodoo, all you need to begin a ceremony is a pole and people. You begin to beat the drums and far away in Africa the gods hear your call. They decide to come to you, and as voodoo is a very practical religion, it takes into account the time that a god needs to cross the Atlantic. So you go on beating your drum, chanting and drinking rum. In this way, you prepare yourself. Then five or six hours pass and the gods fly in – they circle above your heads, but it is not worth looking up as naturally they are invisible. This is where the pole becomes so vital. Without the pole nothing can link the visible and the invisible worlds. The pole, like the cross, is the junction. Through the wood, earthed, the spirits slide, and now they are ready for the second step in their metamorphosis. Now they need a human vehicle, and they choose one of the participants. A kick, a moan or two, a short paroxysm on the ground and a man is possessed. He gets to his feet, no longer himself, but filled with the god. The god now has form. He is someone who can joke, get drunk and listen to everyone's complaints. The first thing that the priest, the Houngan, does when the god arrives is to shake him by the hand and ask him about his trip. He's a god all right, but he is no longer unreal: he is there, on our level, attainable. The ordinary man or woman now can talk to him, pump his hand, argue, curse him, go to bed with him – and so, nightly, the Haitian is in contact with the great powers and mysteries that rule his day.

In the theatre, the tendency for centuries has been to put the actor at a remote distance, on a platform, framed, decorated, lit, painted, in high shoes – so as to help to persuade the ignorant that he is holy, that his art is sacred. Did this express reverence? Or was there behind it a fear that something

would be exposed if the light were too bright, the meetings too near? Today, we have exposed the sham. But we are re-discovering that a holy theatre is still what we need. So where should we look for it? In the clouds or on the ground?

3

THE
ROUGH
THEATRE

It is always the popular theatre that saves the day. Through the ages it has taken many forms, and there is only one factor that they all have in common – a roughness. Salt, sweat, noise, smell: the theatre that's not in a theatre, the theatre on carts, on wagons, on trestles, audiences standing, drinking, sitting round tables, audiences joining in, answering back; theatre in back rooms, upstairs rooms, barns; the one-night stands, the torn sheet pinned up across the hall, the battered screen to conceal the quick changes – that one generic term, *theatre*, covers all this and the sparkling chandeliers too. I have had many abortive discussions with architects building new theatres – trying vainly to find words with which to communicate my own conviction that it is not a question of good buildings and bad: a beautiful place may never bring about explosion of life, while a haphazard hall may be a tremendous meeting place; this is the mystery of the theatre, but in the understanding of this mystery lies the only possibility of ordering it into a science. In other forms of architecture there is a relationship between conscious, articulate design and good functioning: a well-designed hospital may be more efficacious than a higgledy-piggledy one; but as for theatres, the problem of design cannot start logically. It is not a matter of saying analytically what are the requirements, how best they can be organized – this will usually bring into existence a tame, conventional, often cold hall. The science of theatre-building must come from studying what it is that

brings about the most vivid relationship between people – and is this best served by asymmetry, even by disorder? If so, what can be the rule of this disorder? An architect is better off if he works like a scene designer, moving scraps of cardboard by intuition, than if he builds his model from a plan, prepared with compass and ruler. If we find that dung is a good fertilizer, it is no good being squeamish; if the theatre seems to need a certain crude element, this must be accepted as part of its natural soil. At the beginning of electronic music, some German studios claimed that they could make every sound that a natural instrument could make – only better. They then discovered that all their sounds were marked by a certain uniform sterility. So they analysed the sounds made by clarinets, flutes, violins, and found that each note contained a remarkably high proportion of plain noise; actual scraping, or the mixture of heavy breathing with wind on wood: from a purist point of view this was just dirt, but the composers soon found themselves compelled to make synthetic dirt – to 'humanize' their compositions. Architects remain blind to this principle – and era after era the most vital theatrical experiences occur outside the legitimate places constructed for the purpose. Gordon Craig influenced Europe for half a century through a couple of performances given in Hampstead in a church hall – the signature of the Brecht theatre, the white half-curtain, originated quite practically in a cellar, when a wire had to be slung from wall to wall. The Rough Theatre is close to the people: it may be a puppet theatre, it may – as in Greek villages to this day – be a shadow show: it is usually distinguished by the absence of what is called style. Style needs leisure: putting over something in rough conditions is like a revolution, for anything that comes to hand can be turned into a weapon. The Rough Theatre doesn't pick and choose: if the audience is restive, then it is obviously more important to holler at the trouble makers – or improvise a

gag – than to try to preserve the unity of style of the scene. In the luxury of the high-class theatre, everything can be all of a piece; in a rough theatre a bucket will be banged for a battle, flour used to show faces white with fear. The arsenal is limitless: the aside, the placard, the topical reference, the local jokes, the exploiting of accidents, the songs, the dances, the tempo, the noise, the relying on contrasts, the shorthand of exaggeration, the false noses, the stock types, the stuffed bellies. The popular theatre, freed of unity of style, actually speaks a very sophisticated and stylish language: a popular audience usually has no difficulty in accepting inconsistencies of accent and dress, or in darting between mime and dialogue, realism and suggestion. They follow the line of story, unaware in fact that somewhere there is a set of standards which are being broken. Martin Esslin has written that in San Quentin prisoners seeing a play for the first time in their lives and being confronted with *Waiting for Godot* had no problem at all in following what to regular theatregoers was incomprehensible.

One of the pioneer figures in the movement towards a renewed Shakespeare was William Poel. An actress once told me that she had worked with Poel in a production of *Much Ado About Nothing* that was presented some fifty years ago for one night in some gloomy London hall. She said that at the first rehearsal Poel arrived with a case full of scraps out of which he brought odd photographs, drawings, pictures torn out of magazines. 'That's you,' he said, giving her a picture of a débutante at the Royal Garden Party. To someone else it was a knight in armour, a Gainsborough portrait or else just a hat. In all simplicity, he was expressing the way he saw the play when he read it – directly, as a child does – not as a grown-up monitoring himself with notions of history and period. My friend told me that the total pre-pop-art mixture had an extraordinary homogeneity. I am sure of it. Poel was

a great innovator and he clearly saw that consistency had no relation to real Shakespearian style. I once did a production of *Love's Labour's Lost* where I dressed the character called Constable Dull as a Victorian policeman because his name at once conjured up the typical figure of the London bobby. For other reasons the rest of the characters were dressed in Watteau-eighteenth-century clothes, but no one was conscious of an anachronism. A long time ago I saw a production of *The Taming of the Shrew* where all the actors dressed themselves exactly the way they saw the characters – I still remember a cowboy, and a fat character busting the buttons of a pageboy's uniform – and that it was far and away the most satisfying rendering of this play I have seen.

Of course, it is most of all dirt that gives the roughness its edge; filth and vulgarity are natural, obscenity is joyous: with these the spectacle takes on its socially liberating role, for by nature the popular theatre is anti-authoritarian, anti-traditional, anti-pomp, anti-pretence. This is the theatre of noise, and the theatre of noise is the theatre of applause.

Think of those two awful masks that glower at us from so many books on theatre – in ancient Greece, we are told, these masks represented two equal elements, tragedy and comedy. At least, they are always shown as equal partners. Since then, though, the 'legitimate' theatre has been considered the important one while the Rough Theatre has been thought less serious. But every attempt to revitalize the theatre has gone back to the popular source. Meyerhold had the highest aims, he sought to present all of life on the stage, his revered master was Stanislavsky, his friend was Chekhov; but in fact it was to the circus and the music hall that he turned. Brecht was rooted in the cabaret; Joan Littlewood longs for a fun-fair; Cocteau, Artaud, Vakhtangov, the most improbable bedfellows, all these highbrows return to the people; and Total Theatre is just a mix-up of these ingredients. All the time,

experimental theatre comes out of the theatre buildings and returns to the room or the ring: it is the American musical, on the rare occasion when it fulfils its promise, and not the opera, that is the real meeting place of the American arts. It is to Broadway that American poets, choreographers and composers turn. A choreographer like Jerome Robbins is an interesting example, moving from the pure and abstract theatres of Balanchine and Martha Graham towards the roughness of the popular show. But the word 'popular' doesn't quite fill the bill: 'popular' conjures up the country fair and the people in a jolly harmless way. The popular tradition is also bearbaiting, ferocious satire and grotesque caricature. This quality was present in the greatest of rough theatres, the Elizabethan one, and in the English theatre today obscenity and truculence have become the motors of revival. Surrealism is rough – Jarry is rough. Spike Milligan's theatre, in which the imagination, freed by anarchy, flies like a wild bat in and out of every possible shape and style, has it all. Milligan, Charles Wood and a few others are a pointer towards what may become a powerful English tradition.

I saw two productions of Jarry's *Ubu Roi* which illustrated the difference between a rough and an artistic tradition. There was a production of *Ubu* on French television that by electronic means pulled off a great feat of virtuosity. The director very brilliantly succeeded in capturing with live actors the impression of black and white marionettes; the screen was subdivided into narrow bands so that it looked like a comic strip. M. Ubu and Mme Ubu were Jarry's drawings animated – they were Ubu to the letter. But not to the life; the television audiences never accepted the crude reality of the story: it saw some pirouetting dolls, got baffled and bored and soon switched off. The virulent protest play had become a highbrow *jeu d'esprit*. At about the same time, on German tele-

vision there was a Czech production of *Ubu*. This version disregarded every one of Jarry's images and indications: it invented an up-to-the-minute pop-art style of its own, made out of dustbins, garbage and ancient iron bedsteads: M. Ubu was no masked Humpty-Dumpty, but a recognizable and shifty slob; Mme Ubu was a sleazy, attractive whore; the social context was clear. From the first shot of M. Ubu stumbling in his underpants out of bed while a nagging voice from the pillows asked why he wasn't King of Poland, the audience's belief was caught and it could follow the surrealist developments of the story because it accepted the primitive situation and characters on their own terms.

This all concerns the appearance of roughness, but what is this theatre's intent? First of all it is there unashamedly to make joy and laughter, what Tyrone Guthrie calls 'theatre of delight', and any theatre that can truly give delight has earned its place. Along with serious, committed and probing work, there must be irresponsibility. This is what the commercial theatre, the boulevard theatre, can give us – but all too often it is tired and threadbare. Fun continually needs a new electric charge: fun for fun's sake is not impossible, but seldom enough. Frivolity can be its charge: high spirits can make a good current, but all the time the batteries have to be replenished: new faces, new ideas have to be found. A new joke flashes and is gone; then it is the old joke that returns. The strongest comedy is rooted in archetypes, in mythology, in basic recurrent situations; and inevitably it is deeply embedded in the social tradition. Comedy does not always stem from the main flow of a social argument: it is as though different comic traditions branch away in many directions; for a certain time, although the course is out of sight, the stream continues to flow on, then one day, unexpectedly, it dries up completely.

There is no hard and fast rule to say that one must never

just cultivate effects and surfaces for their own sake. Why
not? Personally, I find staging a musical can be more
thoroughly enjoyable than any other form of theatre. Cultivating a deft sleight of hand can give one great delight. But
an impression of freshness is everything – preserved foods
lose their taste. The Holy Theatre has one energy, the Rough
has others. Lightheartedness and gaiety feed it, but so does
the same energy that produces rebellion and opposition. This
is a militant energy : it is the energy of anger, sometimes the
energy of hate. The creative energy behind the richness of
invention in the Berliner Ensemble's production of *The Days
of the Commune* is the same energy that could man the barri-
cades : the energy of *Arturo Ui* could go straight to war. The
wish to change society, to get it to confront its eternal hypo-
crisies, is a great powerhouse. Figaro or Falstaff or Tartuffe
lampoon and debunk through laughter, and the author's
purpose is to bring about a social change.

John Arden's remarkable play *Sergeant Musgrave's Dance*
can be taken amongst many other meanings as an illustration
of how true theatre comes into being. Musgrave faces a crowd
in a market place on an improvised stage and he attempts to
communicate as forcibly as possible his sense of the horror and
futility of war. The demonstration that he improvises is like a
genuine piece of popular theatre, his props are machine-guns,
flags, and a uniformed skeleton that he hauls aloft. When this
does not succeed in transmitting his complete message to the
crowd, his desperate energy drives him to find still further
means of expression and in a flash of inspiration he begins a
rhythmic stamp, out of which develops a savage dance and
chant. Sergeant Musgrave's dance is a demonstration of how
a violent need to project a meaning can suddenly call into
existence a wild unpredictable form.

Here we see the double aspect of the rough : if the holy is
the yearning for the invisible through its visible incarnations,

the rough also is a dynamic stab at a certain ideal. Both theatres feed on deep and true aspirations in their audiences, both tap infinite resources of energy, of different energies; but both end by setting up areas in which certain things just aren't admitted. If the holy makes a world in which a prayer is more real than a belch, in the rough theatre it is the other way round. The belching, then, is real and prayer would be considered comic. The Rough Theatre has apparently no style, no conventions, no limitations – in practice, it has all three. Just as in life the wearing of old clothes can start as defiance and turn into a posture, so roughness can become an end in itself. The defiant popular theatre man can be so down-to-earth that he forbids his material to fly. He can even deny flight as a possibility, or the heavens as a suitable place to wander. This brings us to the point where the Holy Theatre and the Rough Theatre show their true antagonism to one another. The Holy Theatre deals with the invisible and this invisible contains all the hidden impulses of man. The Rough Theatre deals with men's actions, and because it is down to earth and direct – because it admits wickedness and laughter – the rough and ready seems better than the hollowly holy.

It is impossible to consider this further without stopping to look at the implications of the strongest, most influential and the most radical theatre man of our time, Brecht. No one seriously concerned with the theatre can by-pass Brecht. Brecht is the key figure of our time, and all theatre work today at some point starts or returns to his statements and achievement. We can turn directly to the word that he brought into our vocabulary – *alienation*. As coiner of the term *alienation*, Brecht must be considered historically. He began working at a time when most German stages were dominated either by naturalism or by great total-theatre onslaughts of an operatic nature designed to sweep up the spectator by his emotions so

that he forgot himself completely. Whatever life there was on-stage was offset by the passivity it demanded of the audience.

For Brecht, a necessary theatre could never for one moment take its sights off the society it was serving. There was no fourth wall between actors and audience – the actor's unique aim was to create a precise response in an audience for whom he had total respect. It was out of respect for the audience that Brecht introduced the idea of alienation, for alienation is a call to halt: alienation is cutting, interrupting, holding some-thing up to the light, making us look again. Alienation is above all an appeal to the spectator to work for himself, so to become more and more responsible for accepting what he sees only if it is convincing to him in an adult way. Brecht rejects the romantic notion that in the theatre we all become children again.

The alienation effect and the happening effect are similar and opposite : the happening shock is there to smash through all the barriers set up by our reason, alienation is to shock us into bringing the best of our reason into play. Alienation works in many ways in many keys. A normal stage action will appear real to us if it is convincing and so we are apt to take it, temporarily, as objective truth. A girl, raped, walks on to a stage in tears – and if her acting touches us sufficiently, we automatically accept the implied conclusion that she is a victim and an unfortunate one. But suppose a clown were to follow her, mimicking her tears, and suppose by his talent he succeeds in making us laugh. His mockery destroys our first response. Then where do our sympathies go? The truth of her character, the validity of her position, are both put into question by the clown, and at the same time our own easy sentimentality is exposed. If carried far enough, such a series of events can suddenly make us confront our shifting views of right and wrong. All this stems from a strict sense of pur-pose. Brecht believed that, in making an audience take stock

of the elements in a situation, the theatre was serving the purpose of leading its audience to a juster understanding of the society in which it lived, and so to learning in what ways that society was capable of change.

Alienation can work through antithesis; parody, imitation, criticism, the whole range of rhetoric is open to it. It is the purely theatrical method of dialectical exchange. Alienation is the language open to us today that is as rich in potentiality as verse : it is the possible device of a dynamic theatre in a changing world, and through alienation we could reach some of those areas that Shakespeare touched by his use of dynamic devices in language. Alienation can be very simple, it can be no more than a set of physical tricks. The first alienation device I ever saw was as a child, in a Swedish church; the collection bag had a spike on the end of it to nudge those of the congregation whom the sermon had sent to sleep. Brecht used placards and visible spotlights for the same purpose; Joan Littlewood dressed her soldiers as Pierrots – alienation has endless possibilities. It aims continually at pricking the balloons of rhetorical playing – Chaplin's contrasting sentimentality and calamity is alienation. Often when an actor is carried away by his part he can get more and more exaggerated, more and more cheaply emotional, and yet sweep the audience along with him. Here the alienating device will keep us awake when part of us wishes to surrender wholly to the tug on the heartstrings. But it is very hard to interfere with a spectator's stock reactions. At the end of the first act of *Lear* when Gloucester is blinded, we brought the house lights up before the last savage action was completed – so as to make the audience take stock of the scene before being engulfed in automatic applause. In Paris, with *The Representative* we again did all in our power to inhibit applause, because appreciation of the actor's talents seemed irrelevant in a concentration camp document. None the less, both the unfortunate

Gloucester and the most nauseating character of them all, the Auschwitz doctor, always left the stage to similar rounds of applause.

Jean Genet can write the most eloquent language, but the amazing impressions in his plays are very often brought about by the visual inventions with which he juxtaposes serious, beautiful, grotesque and ridiculous elements. There are few things in the modern theatre as compact and spellbinding as the climax of the first portion of *The Screens* when the stage action is a scribbling graffiti of war on to vast white surfaces, while violent phrases, ludicrous people and outsize dummies all together form a monument of colonialism and revolution. Here the potency of the conception is inseparable from the multi-levelled series of devices that become its expression. Genet's *The Blacks* takes on its full meaning when there is a powerful shifting relationship between actors and public. In Paris, witnessed by intellectuals, the play was baroque literary entertainment; in London, where no audience could be found who cared about either French literature or Negroes, the play was meaningless; in New York, in Gene Frankel's superb production it was electric and vibrant. I am told the vibrations changed from night to night depending on the proportion of blacks to whites in the house.

The *Marat/Sade* could not have existed before Brecht: it is conceived by Peter Weiss on many alienating levels: the events of the French Revolution cannot be accepted literally because they are being played by madmen, and their actions in turn are open to further question because their director is the Marquis de Sade – and moreover the events of 1780 are being seen with the eyes both of 1808 and of 1966 – for the people watching the play represent an early nineteenth-century audience and yet are also their twentieth-century selves. All these criss-crossing planes thicken the reference at

each moment and compel an activity from each member of the public. At the end of the play the asylum goes berserk : all the actors improvise with the utmost violence and for an instant the stage image is naturalistic and compelling. Nothing, we feel, could ever stop this riot : nothing, we conclude, can ever stop the madness of the world. Yet it was at this moment, in the Royal Shakespeare Theatre version, that a stage manageress walked on to the stage, blew a whistle, and the madness immediately ended. In this action, a conundrum was presented. A second ago, the situation had been hopeless: now it is all over, the actors are pulling off their wigs : of course, it's just a play. So we begin to applaud. But unexpectedly, the actors applaud us back, ironically. We react to this by a momentary hostility against them as individuals, and we stop clapping. I quote this as a typical alienation series, of which each incident forces us to readjust our position.

There is an interesting relationship between Brecht and Craig – Craig wanted a token shadow to take the place of a complete painted forest and he only did so because he recognized that useless information absorbed our attention *at the expense of something more important*. Brecht took this rigour and applied it not only to scenery but to the work of the actor and to the attitude of the audience. If he cut out superfluous emotion, and the development of characteristics and feelings that related only to the character, it was because he saw that the clarity of his theme was threatened. An actor in other German theatres of Brecht's day – and many an English actor today – believes that his entire job is to present his character as fully as possible, in the round. This means that he spends his observation and his imagination in finding additional details for his portrait, for, like the society painter, he wants the picture to be as life-like and recognizable as possible. No one has told him there could be any other aim.

Brecht introduced the simple and devastating idea that 'fully' need not mean 'lifelike' nor 'in the round'. He pointed out that every actor has to serve the action of the play, but until the actor understands what the true action of the play is, what its true purpose is, from the author's point of view and in relation to the needs of a changing world outside (and what side is he himself on in the struggles that divide the world), he cannot possibly know what he is serving. However, when he understands precisely what is demanded of him, what he must fulfil, then he can properly understand his role. When he sees himself in relation to the wholeness of the play he will see that not only is too much characterizing often opposed to the play's needs but also that many unnecessary characteristics can actually work against him and make his own appearance less striking. He will then see the character he is playing more impartially, he will look at its sympathetic or unsympathetic features from a different viewpoint, and in the end will make different decisions from those he made when he thought 'identifying' with the character was all that mattered. Of course, this is a theory that can easily muddle an actor, because if he attempts to implement it naïvely by squashing his instincts and becoming an intellectual, he will end in disaster. It is a mistake to think that any actor can do work by theory alone. No actor can play a cipher : however stylized or schematic the writing, the actor *must* always believe to some degree in the stage life of the odd animal he represents. But none the less an actor can play in a thousand ways, and playing a portrait is not the only alternative. What Brecht introduced was the idea of the intelligent actor, capable of judging the value of his contribution. There were and still are many actors who pride themselves on knowing nothing about politics and who treat the theatre as an ivory tower. For Brecht such an actor is not worthy of his place in adult company : an actor in a community that supports a

theatre must be as much involved in the outside world as in his own craft.

When theory is put into words, the door is opened to confusion. Brecht productions outside the Berliner Ensemble that are based on Brecht's essays have had Brecht economy, but rarely his richness of thought and feeling. These are often shunned, and so the work appears dry. The liveliest of theatres turns deadly when its coarse vigour goes : and Brecht is destroyed by deadly slaves. When Brecht talks of actors understanding their function, he never imagined that all could be achieved by analysis and discussion. The theatre is not the classroom, and a director with a pedagogic understanding of Brecht can no more animate his plays than a pedant those of Shakespeare. The quality of the work done in any rehearsal comes entirely from the creativity of the working climate – and creativity cannot be brought into being by explanations. The language of rehearsals is like life itself : it uses words, but also silences, stimuli, parody, laughter, unhappiness, despair, frankness and concealment, activity and slowness, clarity and chaos. Brecht recognized this and in his last years he surprised his associates by saying that the theatre must be naïve. With this word he was not reneging his life's work; he was pointing out that the action of putting together a play is always a form of playing, that watching a play is playing; he spoke disconcertingly of elegance and of entertainment. It is not by chance that in many languages the word for a play and to play is the same.

In his theoretical writing Brecht separates the real from the unreal, and I believe that this has been the source of a giant confusion. In terms of semantics the subjective is always opposed to the objective, the illusion separated from the fact. Because of these, his theatre is forced to maintain two positions : public and private, official and unofficial, theoretical and practical. Its practical work is based on a deep feeling for

an inner life in the actor; but in public life it denies this life because in a character inner life takes on the dread label 'psychological'. This word 'psychological' is invaluable in coloured argument – like 'naturalistic' it can be used with contempt to close a subject or score a point. Unfortunately, it also leads to a simplification, contrasting the language of action – this language is hard, bright and effective – with the language of psychology – this is Freudian, mushy, shifting, dark, imprecise. Looked at this way, of course psychology must lose. But is the division a true one? Everything is illusion. The exchange of impressions through images is our basic language: at the moment when one man expresses an image at that same instant the other man meets him in belief. The shared association is the language: if the association evokes nothing in the second person, if there is no instant of shared illusion, there is no exchange. Brecht often took the case of a man describing a street accident as a narrative situation – so let us take his example and examine the process of perception that is involved. When someone describes to us a street accident the psychic process is complicated: it can best be seen as a three-dimensional collage with built-in sound, for we experience many unrelated things at once. We see the speaker, we hear his voice, we know where we are and, at one and the same time, we perceive superimposed on top of him the scene he is describing – the vividness and the fullness of this momentary illusion depends on his conviction and skill. It also depends on the speaker's type. If he is a cerebral type, I mean a man whose alertness and vitality is mainly in the head, we will receive more impressions of ideas than of sensations. If he is emotionally free, other currents will also flow so that without any effort or research on his part he will inevitably recreate a fuller image of the street accident that he is remembering, and we will receive it accordingly. Whatever it is, he sends in our direction a complex network of impres-

sions, and as we perceive them, we believe in them, thus losing ourselves in them at least momentarily.

In all communication, illusions materialize and disappear. The Brecht theatre is a rich compound of images appealing for our belief. When Brecht spoke contemptuously of illusion, this was not what he was attacking. He meant the single sustained Picture, the statement that continued after its purpose had been served – like the painted tree. But when Brecht stated there was something in the theatre called illusion, the implication was that there was something else that was not illusion. So illusion became opposed to reality. It would be better if we clearly opposed dead illusion to living illusion, glum statement to lively statement, fossilized shape to moving shadow, the frozen picture to the moving one. What we see most often is a character inside a picture frame surrounded by a three-walled interior set. This is naturally an illusion, but Brecht suggests we watch it in a state of anaesthetized uncritical belief. If, however, an actor stands on a bare stage beside a placard reminding us that this is a theatre, then in basic Brecht we do not fall into illusion, we watch as adults – and judge. This diversion is neater in theory than in practice.

It is not possible that anyone watching either a naturalistic production of a play by Chekhov or a formalized Greek tragedy should surrender to the belief that he is in Russia or Ancient Thebes. Yet it is sufficient in either case for an actor of power to speak a powerful text for the spectator to be caught up in an illusion, although, of course, he will still know that he is at every instant in a theatre. The aim is not how to avoid illusion: everything is illusion, only some things seem more illusory than others. It is the heavyhanded Illusion that does not begin to convince us. On the other hand, the illusion that is composed by the flash of quick and changing impressions keeps the dart of the imagination at play. This

illusion is like the single dot in the moving television picture: it only lasts for the instant its function demands.

It is an easy mistake to consider Chekhov as a naturalistic writer, and in fact many of the sloppiest and thinnest plays of recent years called 'slice of life' fondly think themselves Chekhovian. Chekhov never just made a slice of life – he was a doctor who with infinite gentleness and care took thousands and thousands of fine layers off life. These he cultured, and then arranged them in an exquisitely cunning, completely artificial and meaningful order in which part of the cunning lay in so disguising the artifice that the result looked like the keyhole view it never had been. Any page of *The Three Sisters* gives the impression of life unfolding as though a tape-recorder had been left running. If examined carefully it will be seen to be built of coincidences as great as in Feydeau – the vase of flowers that overturns, the fire-engine that passes at just the right moment; the word, the interruption, the distant music, the sound in the wings, the entrance, the farewell – touch by touch, they create through the language of illusions an overall illusion of a slice of life. This series of impressions is equally a series of alienations: each rupture is a subtle provocation and a call to thought.

I have already quoted performances in Germany after the war. In a Hamburg garret I once saw a production of *Crime and Punishment*, and that evening became, before its four-hour stretch was over, one of the most striking theatre experiences I have ever had. By sheer necessity, all problems of theatre style vanished: here was the real main stream, the essence of an art that stems from the storyteller looking round his audience and beginning to speak. All the theatres in the town had been destroyed, but here, in this attic, when an actor in a chair touching our knees began quietly to say, 'It was in the year of 18— that a young student, Roman

Rodianovitch Raskolnikov ...' we were gripped by living theatre.

Gripped. What does that mean? I cannot tell. I only know that these words and a soft serious tone of voice conjured something up, somewhere, for us all. We were listeners, children hearing a bedside story yet at the same time adults, fully aware of all that was going on. A moment later, a few inches away, an attic door creaked open and an actor impersonating Raskolnikov appeared, and already we were deep in the drama. The door at one instant seemed a total evocation of a street lamp; an instant later it became the door of the money-lender's apartment, and still a second later the passage to her inner room. Yet, as these were only fragmentary impressions that only came into being at the instant they were required, and at once vanished again, we never lost sight of being crammed together in a crowded room, following a story. The narrator could add details, he could explain and philosophize, the characters themselves could slip from naturalistic acting into monologue, one actor could, by hunching his back, slip from one characterization to another, and point for point, dot for dot, stroke for stroke, the whole complex world of Dostoevsky's novel was recreated.

How free is the convention of a novel, how effortless the relationship of writer to reader : backgrounds can be evoked and dismissed, the transition from the outer to the inner world is natural and continuous. The success of the Hamburg experiment reminded me again of how grotesquely clumsy, how inadequate and pitiful the theatre becomes, not only when a gang of men and creaking machines are needed to move us only from one place to the next, but even when the transition from the world of action to the world of thought has to be explained by any device – by music, changing lights or clambering on to platforms.

In the cinema Godard has, singlehanded, brought about a

revolution by showing how relative the reality of a photo-graphed scene can be. Where generations of film-makers had evolved laws of continuity and canons of consistency so as not to break the reality of a continuous action, Godard showed that this reality was yet another false and rhetorical conven-tion. By photographing a scene and at once smashing its apparent truth, he has cracked into dead Illusion and enabled a stream of opposing impressions to stream forth. He is deeply influenced by Brecht.

The Berliner Ensemble's recent production of *Coriolanus* underlies the whole question of where illusion begins and ends. In most respects, this version was a triumph. Many aspects of the play were revealed as though for the first time; much of it can seldom have been so well staged. The company approached the play socially and politically and this meant that the stock mechanical ways of staging Shakespearian crowds were no longer possible. It would have been impossible to get any one of those intelligent actors playing an anony-mous citizen merely to make cheers, mutters and jeers on cue like bit players through the ages. The energy that fed the months of work that eventually illuminated all the structure of sub-plot came from the actor's interest in the social themes. The small parts were not boring to the actors – they never became background because they obviously carried issues fascinating to study and provocative to discuss. The people, the tribunes, the battle, the assemblies, were rich in texture: all forms of theatre were pressed into service – the costumes had the feel of everyday life but the stage positions had the formality of tragedy. The speech was sometimes heightened, sometimes colloquial, the battles used ancient Chinese tech-niques to carry modern meanings. There was not a moment of stock theatricality nor any noble emotion used for its own sake. Coriolanus was not idealized nor even likeable: he was explosive, violent – not admirable but convincing.

Everything served the action which itself was crystal clear.
And then appeared a tiny defect that became for me a deep,
interesting flaw. The major confrontation scene between
Coriolanus and Volumnia at the gates of Rome was rewritten.
I do not for one moment question the principle of rewriting
Shakespeare – after all, the texts do not get burned – each
person can do what he thinks necessary with a text and still
no one suffers. What is interesting is the result. Brecht and
his colleagues did not wish to allow the lynch-pin of the entire
action to be the relation between Coriolanus and his mother.
They felt that this did not make an interesting contemporary
point: in its place they wished to illustrate the theme that no
leader is indispensable. They invented an additional piece of
narrative. Coriolanus commanded the citizens of Rome to give
a smoke signal if they were prepared to surrender. At the end
of his discussion with his mother he sees a column of smoke
rising from the ramparts and is jubilant. His mother points
out that the smoke is not a sign of surrender, but the smoke
from the forges of the people arming themselves to defend
their homes. Coriolanus realizes that Rome can carry on without him and senses the inevitability of his own defeat. He
yields.

In theory, this new plot is as interesting and works as well
as the old one. But any play of Shakespeare's has an organic
sense. On paper it would look as though the episode can
reasonably be substituted for another, and certainly in many
plays there are scenes and passages that can easily be cut or
transposed. But if one has a knife in one hand, one needs a
stethoscope in the other. The scene between Coriolanus and
his mother is close to the heart of the play: like the storm in
Lear or a Hamlet monologue, its emotional content engenders
the heat by which strands of cool thought and patterns of
dialectical argument are eventually fused. Without the clash
of the two protagonists in its most intense form, the story

remains castrated. When we leave the theatre we carry a less insistent memory with us. The force of the scene between Coriolanus and his mother depends on just those elements that do not necessarily make apparent sense. Psychological language, also, gets us nowhere, for labels don't count; it is the deeper ring of truth that can command our respect – the dramatic fact of a mystery we can't completely fathom.

The Berliner Ensemble's choice implied that their social attitude would be weakened by accepting the unfathomable nature of the man-within-the-social-scene. Historically it is clear how a theatre loathing the self-indulgent individualism of bourgeois art should have turned to actions instead.

In Peking today it seems to make good sense to show giant Wall Street caricature figures plotting war and destruction and getting their just deserts. In relation to countless other factors of today's militant China, this is lively, meaningful popular art. In many South American countries, where the only theatre activity has been poor copies of foreign successes put on by flybynight impresarios, a theatre only begins to find its meaning and its necessity in relation to the revolutionary struggle on the one hand and the glimmers of a popular tradition suggested by workers' songs and village legends on the other. In fact, an expression of today's militant themes through traditional Catholic morality-play structures may well be the only possibility in certain regions of finding a lively contact with popular audiences. In England, on the other hand, in a changing society, where nothing is truly defined, least of all in the realm of politics and political ideas, but where there is a constant re-examination in process that varies from the most intensely honest to the most frivolously evasive – when the natural common-sense and the natural idealism, the natural debunking and the natural romanticism, the

natural democracy, the natural kindness, the natural sadism and the natural snobbery all make a mish-mash of intellectual confusion – it would be no use expecting a committed theatre to follow a party line, even supposing that such a line could be found.

The accumulation of events of the last few years, the assassinations, schisms, downfalls, uprisings and the local wars have had an increasingly demystifying effect. When the theatre comes closest to reflecting a truth in society, it now reflects more the wish for change than the conviction that this change can be brought about in a certain way. Certainly the role of the individual in the society, his duties and his needs, the issues of what belongs to him and what belongs to the state, are in question again. Again, as in Elizabethan times, man is asking why he has a life and against what he can measure it. It is not by chance that the new metaphysical theatre of Grotowski arises in a country drenched in both Communism and Catholicism. Peter Weiss, combining Jewish family, Czech upbringing, German language, Swedish home, Marxist sympathies, emerges just at the moment when his Brechtianism is related to obsessive individualism to a degree unthinkable in Brecht himself. Jean Genet relates colonialism and racialism to homosexuality, and explores the French consciousness through his own degradation. His images are private yet national, and he comes close to discovering myths.

The problem is different for each centre of population. On the whole, though, the stifling effects of a nineteenth-century obsessive interest in middle-class sentiment cloud much twentieth-century work in all languages. The individual and the couple have long been explored in a vacuum or in a social context so insulated as to be the equivalent of a vacuum. The relationship between a man and the evolving society around him is always the one that brings new life, depth and truth to

his personal theme. In New York and London play after play presents serious leading characters within a softened, diluted or unexplored context – so that heroism, self-torture or martyrdom become romantic agonies, in the void.

Whether the emphasis falls on the individual or on the analysis of society has become almost completely a division between Marxists and non-Marxists. It is the Marxist and the Marxist alone who approaches a given situation dialectically and scientifically, attempting to explore the social and economic factors that determine the action. There are non-Marxist economists and non-Marxist sociologists, but any writer who begins to set a historical character fully in his context is almost certain to be working from a Marxist point of view. This is because Marxism provides the writer with a structure, a tool and an aim – bereft of these three elements the non-Marxist turns to Man. This can easily make the writer vague and woolly. But the very best non-political writer may be another sort of expert, who can discriminate very precisely in the treacherous world of individual shades of experience. The epic writer of Marxist plays seldom brings to his work this same fine sense of human individuality – perhaps because he is unwilling to regard a man's strength and a man's weakness with equal impartiality. It is perhaps for this reason that strangely the pop tradition in England has such wide appeal: non-political, unaligned, it is none the less tuned in on a fragmented world in which bombs, drugs, God, parents, sex, and private anxieties are inseparable – and all illuminated by a wish – not a very strong wish, but a wish all the same – for some sort of change or transformation.

There is a challenge to all the theatres in the world who have not yet begun to face the movements of our time, to saturate themselves in Brecht, to study the Ensemble and see all those facets of society that have found no place in their shut-off stages. There is a challenge to revolutionary theatres

in countries with a clear-cut revolutionary situation as in
Latin America to harness their theatres boldly to unmistak-
ably clear-cut themes. Equally, there is a challenge now to the
Berliner Ensemble and its followers to reconsider their attitude
to the darkness of the individual man. This is our only possibility: to look at the affirmations of Artaud, Meyerhold,
Stanislavsky, Grotowski, Brecht, then compare them with the
life of the particular place in which we work. What is our
purpose, now, in relation to the people we meet every day?
Do we need liberation? From what? In what way?

Shakespeare is a model of a theatre that contains Brecht and
Beckett, but goes beyond both. Our need in the post-Brecht
theatre is to find a way forwards, back to Shakespeare. In
Shakespeare the introspection and the metaphysics soften
nothing. Quite the reverse. It is through the unreconciled
opposition of Rough and Holy, through an atonal screech of
absolutely unsympathetic keys that we get the disturbing and
the unforgettable impressions of his plays. It is because the
contradictions are so strong that they burn on us so deeply.
    Obviously, we can't whistle up a second Shakespeare. But
the more clearly we see in what the power of Shakespearian
theatre lies, the more we prepare the way. For example, we
have at last become aware that the absence of scenery in the
Elizabethan theatre was one of its greatest freedoms. In
England at least, all productions for quite some time have
been influenced by the discovery that Shakespeare's plays
were written to be performed continuously, that their cine-
matic structure of alternating short scenes, plot intercut with
subplot, were all part of a total shape. This shape is only revealed dynamically, that is, in the uninterrupted sequence of
these scenes, and without this their effect and power are
lessened as much as would be a film that was projected with

breaks and musical interludes between each reel. The Elizabethan stage was like the attic I was describing in Hamburg:
it was a neutral open platform – just a place with some doors
– and so it enabled the dramatist effortlessly to whip the
spectator through an unlimited succession of illusions, cover-
ing, if he chose, the entire physical world. It has also been
pointed out that the nature of the permanent structure of the
Elizabethan playhouse, with its flat open arena and its large
balcony and its second smaller gallery, was a diagram of the
universe as seen by the sixteenth-century audience and playwright – the gods, the court and the people – three levels,
separate and yet often intermingling – a stage that was a
perfect philosopher's machine.

What has not been appreciated sufficiently is that the freedom of movement of the Elizabethan theatre was not only a
matter of scenery. It is too easy to think that so long as a
modern production moves fast from scene to scene, it has
learnt the essential lesson from the old playhouse. The
primary fact is that this theatre not only allowed the playwright to roam the world, it also allowed him free passage
from the world of action to the world of inner impressions. I
think it is here that we find what is most important to us
today. In Shakespeare's time, the voyage of discovery in the
real world, the adventure of the traveller setting out into the
unknown, had an excitement that we cannot hope to re-
capture in an age when our planet has no secrets and when
the prospect of interplanetary travel seems a pretty considerable bore. However, Shakespeare was not satisfied with the
mysteries of the unknown continents: through his imagery
– pictures drawn from the world of fabulous discoveries – he
penetrates a psychic existence whose geography and movements remain just as vital for us to understand today.

In an ideal relation with a true actor on a bare stage we
would continually be passing from long shot to close, track-

ing or jumping in and out – and the planes often overlap. Compared with the cinema's mobility, the theatre once seemed ponderous and creaky, but the closer we move towards the true nakedness of theatre, the closer we approach a stage that has a lightness and range far beyond film or television. The power of Shakespeare's plays is that they present man simultaneously in all his aspects : touch for touch, we can identify and withdraw. A primitive situation disturbs us in our subconscious; our intelligence watches, comments, philosophizes. Brecht and Beckett are both contained in Shakespeare unreconciled. We identify emotionally, subjectively – and yet at one and the same time we evaluate politically, objectively in relation to society. Because the profound reaches past the everyday, a heightened language and a ritualistic use of rhythm bring us to those very aspects of life which the surface hides; and yet because the poet and the visionary do not seem like ordinary people, because the epic state is not one on which we normally dwell, it is equally possible for Shakespeare, with a break in his rhythm, a twist into prose, a shift into slangy conversation or else a direct word from the audience to remind us – in plain common sense – of where we are, and to return us to the familiar rough world of spades as spades. So it is that Shakespeare succeeded where no one has succeeded before or since in writing plays that pass through many stages of consciousness. What enabled him technically to do so, the essence, in fact, of his style, is a roughness of texture and a conscious mingling of opposites which in other terms could be called an absence of style. Voltaire could not bring himself to understand it, and could only label it 'barbaric'.

We could take *Measure for Measure* as a test case. As long as scholars could not decide whether this play was a comedy or not, it never got played. In fact, this ambiguity makes it one of the most revealing of Shakespeare's works – and one

that shows these two elements, Holy and Rough, almost schematically, side by side. They are opposed and they coexist. In *Measure for Measure* we have a base world, a very real world in which the action is firmly rooted. This is the disgusting, stinking world of medieval Vienna. The darkness of this world is absolutely necessary to the meaning of the play: Isabella's plea for grace has far more meaning in this Dostoevskian setting than it would in lyrical comedy's never-never land. When this play is prettily staged, it is meaningless – it demands an absolutely convincing roughness and dirt. Also, when so much of the play is religious in thought, the loud humour of the brothel is important as a device, because it is alienating and humanizing. From the fanatical chastity of Isabella and the mystery of the Duke we are plunged back to Pompey and Barnadine for douches of normality. To execute Shakespeare's intentions we must animate all this stretch of the play, not as fantasy, but as the roughest comedy we can make. We need complete freedom, rich improvisation, no holding back, no false respect – and at the same time we must take great care, for all round the popular scenes are great areas of the play that clumsiness could destroy. As we enter this holier land, we will find that Shakespeare gives us a clear signal: the rough is in prose, the rest in verse. In the prose scenes, very broadly speaking, the work can be enriched by our own invention – the scenes need added external details to assure them of their fullest life. In the passages in verse we are already on our guard: Shakespeare needs verse because he is trying to say more, to compact together more meaning. We are watchful: behind each visible mark on paper lurks an invisible one that is hard to seize. Technically we now need less abandon, more focus – less breadth, more intensity.

Quite simply we need a different approach, a different style. There is nothing to be ashamed of in changing style – look at

a page of a Folio with half-closed eyes and you see a chaos of irregularly spaced symbols. If we iron Shakespeare into any one typography of theatre we lose the real meaning of the play – if we follow his ever-shifting devices, he will lead us through many different keys. If we follow the movement in *Measure for Measure* between the Rough and the Holy we will discover a play about justice, mercy, honesty, forgiveness, virtue, virginity, sex and death : kaleidoscopically one section of the play mirrors the other; it is in accepting the prism as a whole that its meanings emerge. When I once staged the play I asked Isabella, before kneeling for Angelo's life, to pause each night until she felt the audience could take it no longer – and this used to lead to a two-minute stopping of the play. The device became a voodoo pole – a silence in which all the invisible elements of the evening came together, a silence in which the abstract notion of mercy became concrete for that moment to those present.

This Rough/Holy structure also shows clearly in the two parts of *Henry IV* – Falstaff and the prose realism of the inn scenes on the one hand and the poetic levels of so much else – both elements contained within one complex whole.

In *The Winter's Tale* a very subtle construction hinges on the key moment when a statue comes to life. This is often criticized as a clumsy device, an implausible way of winding up the plot, and it is usually justified only in terms of romantic fiction : an awkward convention of the times that Shakespeare was forced to use. In fact, the statue that comes to life is the truth of the play. In *The Winter's Tale* we find a natural division into three sections. Leontes accuses his wife of infidelity. He condemns her to death. The child is put to sea. In the second part the child grows up, and now in a different pastoral key the very same action is repeated. The man falsely accused by Leontes now in turn behaves just as unreasonably. The consequence is the same – the child again takes flight.

Her journey takes her back to Leontes' palace and the third
part is now in the same place as the first, but twenty years
later. Again, Leontes finds himself in similar conditions, in
which he could be as violently unreasonable as before. Thus
the main action is presented first ferociously, then a second
time by charming parody but in a bold major key, for the
pastoral of the play is a mirror as well as a straight device.
The third movement is in another contrasting key – a key of
remorse. When the young lovers enter Leontes' palace the
first and second sections overlap: both put into question the
action that Leontes now can take. If the dramatist's sense of
truth forces him to make Leontes vindictive with the children,
then the play cannot move out of its particular world, and its
end would have to be bitter and tragic: if he can truthfully
allow a new equality to enter Leontes' actions, then the whole
time-pattern of the play is transformed: the past and the
future are no longer the same. The level changes, and even if
we call it a miracle, the statue has none the less come to life.
When working on *The Winter's Tale* I discovered that the
way to understand this scene is not to discuss it but to play
it. In performance this action is strangely satisfying – and
so it makes us wonder deeply.

Here we have an example of the 'happening' effect – the
moment when the illogical breaks through our everyday
understanding to make us open our eyes more widely. The
whole play has established questions and references: the
moment of surprise is a jolt to the kaleidoscope, and what
we see in the playhouse we can retain and relate to the play's
questions when they recur transposed, diluted and disguised,
in life.

If we imagine for a moment *Measure for Measure* and *The
Winter's Tale* written by Sartre, it would be reasonable to
guess that in the one case Isabella would not kneel for Angelo
– so that the play would end with the hollow crackle of the

firing squad – and in the other the statue would not come to life, so that Leontes would be faced with the bleak consequences of his actions. Both Shakespeare and Sartre would be fashioning plays according to their sense of truth: one author's inner material contains different intimations from the other's. The mistake would be to take events or episodes from a play and question them in the light of some third outside standard of plausibility – like 'reality' or 'truth'. The sort of play that Shakespeare offers us is never just a series of events: it is far easier to understand if we consider the plays as objects – as many-faceted complexes of form and meaning in which the line of narrative is only one amongst many aspects and cannot profitably be played or studied on its own.

Experimentally, we can approach Lear not as a linear narrative, but as a cluster of relationships. First, we try to rid ourselves of the notion that because the play is called King Lear it is primarily the story of one individual. So we pick an arbitrary point in the vast structure – the death of Cordelia, say – and now instead of looking towards the King we turn instead towards the man who is responsible for her death. We focus on this character, Edmund, and now we begin to pick our way to and fro across the play, sifting the evidence, trying to discover who this Edmund is. He is clearly a villain, whatever our standards, for in killing Cordelia he is responsible for the most gratuitous act of cruelty in the play – yet if we look at our first impression of him in the early scenes, we find he is by far the most attractive character we meet. In the opening scenes there is a denial of life in Lear's rusty ironclad power; Gloucester is tetchy, fussy and foolish, a man blind to everything except his inflated image of his own importance; and in dramatic contrast we see the relaxed freedom of his bastard son. Even if in theory we observe that the way he leads Gloucester by the nose is hardly moral, instinctively we

cannot but side with his natural anarchy. Not only do we sympathize with Goneril and Regan for falling in love with him, but we tend to side with them in finding Edmund so admirably wicked, because he affirms a life that the sclerosis of the older people seems to deny. Can we keep this same attitude of admiration towards Edmund when he has Cordelia killed? If not, why not? What has changed? Is it Edmund who has changed, through outside events? Or is it just the context that is different? Is a scale of value implied? What are Shakespeare's values? What is the value of a life? We flick through the play again and find an incident importantly situated, unrelated to the main plot, often quoted as an example of Shakespeare's slovenly construction. This is the fight between Edmund and Edgar. If we look closely, we are struck by one fact : it is not the powerful Edmund, but his younger brother who wins. In the first scenes of the play, Edmund had no trouble at all in outwitting Edgar – now five acts later in single combat it is Edgar who dominates. Accepting this as dramatic truth rather than romantic convention, we are forced to ask how it has come about. Can we explain it all quite simply in terms of moral growth – Edgar has grown up, Edmund has decayed – or is the whole question of Edgar's undoubted development from *naïveté* to understanding – and Edmund's visible change from freedom to entanglement – far more complex than a cut-and-dried question of the triumph of the good? Aren't we compelled in fact to relate this to all the evidence connected with the question of growth and decline, i.e. youth and age, i.e. strength and weakness? If for a moment we assume this point of view, then suddenly the whole play seems concerned with sclerosis opposing the flow of existence, of cataracts that dissolve, of rigid attitudes that yield, while at the same time obsessions form and positions harden. Of course the whole play is about sight and blindness, what sight amounts to, what blindness means –

how the two eyes of Lear ignore what the instinct of the Fool apprehends, how the two eyes of Gloucester miss what his blindness knows. But the object has many facets; many themes criss-cross its prismatic form. Let us stay with the strands of age and youth, and in pursuit of them move on to the very last lines of the play. When we read or hear them first our reaction is, 'How obvious. What a trite end', for Edgar says:

> 'We that are young
> Shall never see so much, nor live so long.'

The more we look at them the more troubling they become, because their apparent precision vanishes, making way for a strange ambiguity hidden in the naïve jangle. The last line is, at its face value, plain nonsense. Are we to understand that the young will never grow up, or are we to understand that the world will never again know old men? Both of these seem a pretty feeble winding up by Shakespeare of a consciously written masterpiece. However, if we look back through Edgar's own line of action, we see that although Edgar's experience in the storm parallels Lear's, it certainly has not wrought in him the intense inner change that has taken place in Lear. Yet Edgar acquired the strength for two killings – first Oswald, then his brother. What has this done to him – how deeply has he experienced this loss of innocence? Is he still wide-eyed? Is he saying in his closing words that youth and age are limited by their own definitions – that the only way to see as much as Lear is to go through Lear's mill, and then *ipso facto* one is young no longer. Lear lives longer than Gloucester – in time and in depth – and as a result he undoubtedly 'sees' more than Gloucester before he dies. Does Edgar wish to say that it is experience of this order and intensity that really means 'living long'. If so, the 'being

young' is a state with its own blindness, like that of the early Edgar, and its own freedom like that of the early Edmund. Age in turn has its blindness and decay. However, true sight comes from an acuteness of living that can transform the old. Indeed, it is clearly shown to use in the unfolding of the play that Lear suffers most and 'gets farthest'. Undoubtedly, his brief moment of captivity with Cordelia is as a moment of bliss, peace and reconciliation, and Christian commentators often write as though this were the end of the story – a clear tale of the ascent from the inferno through purgation to paradise. Unfortunately for this neat view the play continues, pitilessly, away from reconciliation.

> 'We that are young
> Shall never see so much, nor live so long.'

The power of Edgar's disturbing statement – a statement that rings like a half-open question – is that it carries no moral overtones at all. He does not suggest for one moment that youth or age, seeing or not seeing, are in any way superior, inferior, more desirable or less desirable one than the other. In fact we are compelled to face a play which refuses all moralizing – a play which we begin to see not as a narrative any longer, but as a vast, complex, coherent poem designed to study the power and the emptiness of nothing – the positive and negative aspects latent in the zero. So what does Shakespeare mean? What is he trying to teach us? Does he mean that suffering has a necessary place in life and is worth cultivating for the knowledge and inner development it brings? Or does he mean us to understand that the age of titanic suffering is now over and our role is that of the eternally young? Wisely, Shakespeare refuses to answer. But he has given us his play, and its whole field of experience is both question and answer. In this light, the play is directly

related to the most burning themes of our time, the old and the new in relation to our society, our arts, our notions of progress, our way of living our lives. If the actors are interested, this is what they will bring out. If we are interested, that is what we shall find. Fancy dress, then, will be left far behind. The meaning will be for the moment of performance.

Of all the plays, none is so baffling and elusive as *The Tempest*. Again, we discover that the only way to find a rewarding meaning in it is to take it as a whole. As a straightforward plot it is uninteresting; as a pretext for costumes, stage effects and music it is hardly worth reviving; as a pot-pourri of knockabout and pretty writing it can at best please a few matinée-goers – but usually it only serves to put generations of school children off theatre for life. But when we see how nothing in the play is what it seems, how it takes place on an island and not on an island, during a day and not during a day, with a tempest that sets off a series of events that are still within a tempest even when the storm is done, that the charming pastoral for children naturally encompasses rape, murder, conspiracy and violence; when we begin to unearth the themes that Shakespeare so carefully buried, we see that it is his complete final statement, and that it deals with the whole condition of man. In a similar way, Shakespeare's first play *Titus Andronicus* begins to yield its secrets the moment one ceases to regard it as a string of gratuitous strokes of melodrama and begins to look for its completeness. Everything in *Titus* is linked to a dark, flowing current out of which surge the horrors, rhythmically and logically related. If one searches in this way one can find the expression of a powerful and eventually beautiful barbaric ritual. But in *Titus* this unearthing is comparatively simple – today we can always find our way to the violent sub-conscious. *The Tempest* is another matter. From first play to last, Shakespeare moved through many limbos. Maybe the conditions cannot be found today for

the play's nature to be revealed fully. Until, however, a way
of presenting can be found, we can at least be wary of confusing unsuccessful attempts at wrestling with the text with
the thing itself. Even if unplayable today, it remains an
example of how a metaphysical play can find a natural idiom
that is holy, comic and rough.

So it is that in the second half of the twentieth century in
England where I am writing these words, we are faced with
the infuriating fact that Shakespeare is still our model. In this
respect, our work on Shakespeare production is always to
make the plays 'modern', because it is only when the audience
comes into direct contact with the plays' themes that time and
conventions vanish. Equally, when we approach the modern
theatre, in whatever form, whether the play with a few
characters, the happening, or the play with hordes of characters and scenes, the problem is always the same: where are
the equivalents of the Elizabethan strengths, in the sense of
range and stretch. What form, in modern terms, could that
rich theatre take? Grotowski, like a monk who finds a universe in a grain of sand, calls his holy theatre a theatre of
poverty. The Elizabethan theatre that encompassed all of life
including the dirt and the wretchedness of poverty is a rough
theatre of great richness. The two are not nearly as far apart
as they might seem.

I have talked a lot about inner and outer worlds, but like
all oppositions it is a relative one, a convenience of notation.
I have talked about beauty, magic, love, knocking these words
with one hand, seeming to reach towards them with the
other. And yet the paradox is a simple one. All that we see
connected with these words seems deadly: what they imply
corresponds to what we need. If we do not understand
catharsis, that is because it has become identified with an

emotional steam-bath. If we do not understand tragedy, it is because it has become confused with Acting the King. We may want magic, but we confuse it with hocus-pocus, and we have hopelessly mixed up love with sex, beauty with aestheticism. But it is only by searching for a new discrimination that we shall extend the horizons of the real. Only then could the theatre be useful, for we need a beauty which could convince us : we need desperately to experience magic in so direct a way that our very notion of what is substantial could be changed.

It is not as though the period of necessary debunking were now over. On the contrary, all through the world in order to save the theatre almost everything of the theatre still has to be swept away. The process has hardly begun, and perhaps can never end. The theatre needs its perpetual revolution. Yet wanton destruction is criminal; it produces violent reaction and still greater confusion. If we demolish a pseudo-holy theatre, we must endeavour not to bamboozle ourselves into thinking that the need for the sacred is old-fashioned and that cosmonauts have proved once and for all that angels do not exist. Also, if we get dissatisfied with the hollowness of so much of the theatre of revolutionaries and propagandists, we must not for this reason assume that the need to talk of people, of power, of money and of the structure of society is a passing fashion.

But if our language must correspond to our age, then we must also accept that today roughness is livelier and holiness deadlier than at other times. Once, the theatre could begin as magic : magic at the sacred festival, or magic as the footlights came up. Today, it is the other way round. The theatre is hardly wanted and its workers are hardly trusted. So we cannot assume that the audience will assemble devoutly and attentively. It is up to us to capture its attention and compel its belief.

To do so we must prove that there will be no trickery, nothing hidden. We must open our empty hands and show that really there is nothing up our sleeves. Only then can we begin.

4

THE
IMMEDIATE
THEATRE

There is no doubt that a theatre can be a very special place. It is like a magnifying glass, and also like a reducing lens. It is a small world, so it can easily be a pretty one. It is different from everyday life so it can easily be divorced from life. On the other hand, while we live less and less in villages or neighbourhoods, and more and more in open-ended global communities, the theatre community stays the same: the cast of a play is still the size that it has always been. The theatre narrows life down. It narrows it down in many ways. It is always hard for anyone to have one single aim in life. In the theatre, however, the goal is clear. From the first rehearsal, the aim is always visible, not too far away, and it involves everyone. We can see many model social patterns at work: the pressures of a first night, with its unmistakable demands, produce that working-together, that dedication, that energy and that consideration of each other's needs that governments despair of ever evoking outside wars.

Furthermore, in society in general the role of art is nebulous. Most people could live perfectly well without any art at all, and even if they regretted its absence it would not hamper their functioning in any way. But in the theatre there is no such separation: at every instant the practical question is an artistic one; the most incoherent, uncouth player is as much involved in matters of pitch and pace, intonation and rhythm, position, distance, colour and shape as the most sophisticated. In rehearsal, the height of the chair, the texture of the

costume, the brightness of the light, the quality of emotion, matter all the time: the aesthetics are practical. One would be wrong to say that this is because the theatre is an art. The stage is a reflection of life, but this life cannot be re-lived for a moment without a working system based on observing certain values and making value-judgements. A chair is moved up or down stage, because it's 'better so'. Two columns are wrong – but adding a third makes them 'right' – the words 'better', 'worse', 'not so good', 'bad' are used day after day, but these words which rule decisions carry no moral sense whatsoever.

Anyone interested in processes in the natural world would be greatly rewarded by a study of theatre conditions. His discoveries would be far more applicable to general society than the study of bees or ants. Under the magnifying glass he would see a group of people living all the time according to precise, shared, but unnamed standards. He would see that in any community a theatre has either no particular function – or a unique one. The uniqueness of the function is that it offers something that cannot be found in the street, at home, in the pub, with friends, or on a psychiatrist's couch, in a church or at the movies. There is only one interesting difference between the cinema and the theatre. The cinema flashes on to a screen images from the past. As this is what the mind does to itself all through life, the cinema seems intimately real. Of course, it is nothing of the sort – it is a satisfying and enjoyable extension of the unreality of everyday perception. The theatre, on the other hand, always asserts itself in the present. This is what can make it more real than the normal stream of consciousness. This also is what can make it so disturbing.

No tribute to the latent power of the theatre is as telling as that paid to it by censorship. In most régimes, even when the written word is free, the image free, it is still the stage

designer evolves step by step with the director, going back, changing, scrapping, as a conception of the whole gradually takes form. A director who does his own designs naturally never believes that the completion of the designs can be an end in itself. He knows that he is just at the beginning of a long cycle of growth, because his own work lies before him. Many designers, however, tend to feel that with the delivery of the sets and costume sketches a major portion of their own creative work is genuinely complete. This particularly applies to good painters working in the theatre. For them, a completed design is complete. Art lovers can never understand why all stage designing isn't done by 'great' painters and sculptors. What is necessary, however, is an incomplete design; a design that has clarity without rigidity; one that could be called 'open' as against 'shut'. This is the essence of theatrical thinking : a true theatre designer will think of his designs as being all the time in motion, in action, in relation to what the actor brings to a scene as it unfolds. In other words, unlike the easel painter, in two dimensions, or the sculptor in three, the designer thinks in terms of the fourth dimension, the passage of time – not the stage picture, but the stage moving picture. A film editor shapes his material after the event : the stage designer is often like the editor of an Alice-Through-the-Looking-Glass film, cutting dynamic material in shapes, before this material has yet come into being. The later he makes his decisions, the better.

It is very easy – and it happens quite often – to spoil an actor's performance with the wrong costume. The actor who is asked his views about a costume design before rehearsals start is in a similar position to the director who is asked for a decision before he is ready. He has not yet had a physical experience of his role – so his views are theoretical. If the designer sketches with panache – and if the costume is beautiful in its own right – the actor will often accept it with en-

thusiasm, only to discover weeks later that it is out of tune with all that he is trying to express. Fundamental to the work of designing is the problem – what should an actor wear? A costume doesn't just come out of the designer's head: it springs from a background. Take the situation of a white European actor playing a Japanese. Even if every contrivance is used, his costume will never have the allure of a Samurai in a Japanese film. In the authentic setting, the details are right and related to one another: in the copy based on a study of documents, there is almost inevitably a steady series of compromises; the material is only more or less the same, the detail of the cut adapted and approximate, eventually the actor himself is unable to inhabit the costume with the instinctive rightness of the men close to the source.

If we cannot present a Japanese or an African satisfactorily by processes of imitation, the same holds good for what we call 'period'. An actor whose work seems real in rehearsal clothes easily loses this integrity when dressed in a toga copied from a vase in the British Museum. Yet wearing everyday clothes is seldom the answer, they are usually inadequate as a uniform for performance. The Noh theatre, for instance, has preserved ritual performing clothes that are of great beauty, and so has the Church. In baroque periods, a contemporary 'finery' existed – and so could be the base of clothing for play or opera. The romantic ball was still recently a valid source for remarkable designers like Oliver Messel or Christian Bérard. In the USSR after the Revolution, the white tie and tails, dropped from social life, still supplied the formal basis for clothing musicians aptly and elegantly in a manner that separated the performance from the rehearsal.

For us, every time we start a new production we are compelled to reopen this question as though for the first time. What can the actors wear? Is there a period implied in the action? What is a 'period'? What is its reality? Are the

aspects given to us by documents real? Or is some flight of fancy and inspiration more real? What is the dramatic purpose? What needs clothing? What needs stating? What, physically, does the actor require? What does the eye of the spectator demand? Should this demand of the spectator be met harmoniously or opposed, dramatically? What can colour and texture heighten? What might they blur?

Casting creates a new set of problems. If rehearsals are short, type casting is inevitable – but everyone deplores it, naturally. In re-action, every actor wants to play everything. In fact, he can't: each actor is eventually blocked by his own true limits, which outline his real type. All one can say is that most attempts to decide in advance what an actor can *not* do are usually abortive. The interest in actors is their capacity for producing unsuspected traits in rehearsal: the disappointment in an actor is when he is true to form. To try to cast 'knowingly' is usually a vanity; it is better to have the time and conditions in which it is possible to take risks. One may often be wrong – but in exchange these will be quite unexpected revelations and developments. No actor stands completely still in his career. It is easy to imagine that he has got stuck at a certain level when in fact a considerable unseen change is under way inside him. The actor who seems very good at an audition may be very talented, but on the whole this is unlikely – he is more probably just efficient and his effectiveness is only skin-deep. The actor who seems very bad at an audition is most likely the worst actor present, but this is not necessarily the case, and it is just possible he is the best. There is no scientific way round this: if the system dictates the employing of actors one doesn't know, one is forced to work largely by guesswork.

At the beginning of rehearsals the actors are the opposite of the ideally relaxed creatures they would like to be. They bring with them a heavy baggage of tensions. So varied are

these tensions that we can find some very unexpected phenomena. For instance, a young actor playing with a group of inexperienced friends may reveal a talent and a technique that put professionals to shame. Yet take the very same actor who has, as it were, proved his worth and surround him with the older actors he most respects, and often he becomes not only awkward and stiff, but even his talent goes. Put him then amongst actors he despises and he will come into his own again. For talent is not static, it ebbs and flows according to many circumstances. Not all actors of the same age are at the same stage of their professional work. Some have a blend of enthusiasm and knowledge that is supported by a confidence based on previous small successes and is not undermined by fear of imminent total failure. They start rehearsals from a different position from the perhaps equally young actor who has made a slightly greater name and who is already beginning to wonder how much farther he can go : has he really got anywhere yet, what is his status, is he recognized, what does the future hold? The actor who believes he may one day play Hamlet has endless energy; the one who sees that the outside world is not convinced he will ever play a lead is already tying himself into painful knots of introspection with a consequent need for self-assertion.

In the group that gathers for a first rehearsal, whether a scratch cast or a permanent company, an infinite number of personal questions and worries hang unspoken in the air. Of course, these are all enhanced by the presence of the director: if he were in a God-sent state of total relaxation he could greatly help, but much of the time he too is tense and involved with the problems of his production, and here too the need publicly to deliver the goods is fuel to his own vanity and his self-absorption. In fact, a director can never afford to begin with his first production. I remember hearing that a budding hypnotist never confesses to a subject that he is

hypnotizing for the first time. He has 'done it successfully many times'. I began with my second production, because when at seventeen I faced my first group of sharp and critical amateurs, I was forced to invent a non-existent, just-completed triumph to give them and myself the confidence we all required.

The first rehearsal is always to a degree the blind leading the blind. On the first day a director may sometimes make a formal speech explaining the basic ideas behind the coming work. Or else he may show models or costume sketches, or books or photographs, or he may make jokes, or else get the actors to read the play. Having drinks or playing a game together or marching round the theatre or building a wall all work in the same way : no one is in a state to abolish what is said – the purpose of anything you do on the first day is to get you through the second one. The second day is already different : a process is now at work, and after twenty-four hours every single factor and relationship has subtly changed. Everything you do in rehearsal affects this process : playing games together is a process that has certain results, like a greater feeling of confidence, friendliness and informality. One can play games at auditions just to bring about an easier atmosphere. The goal is never in the game alone – in the short time available for rehearsing a play, social ease is not enough. A harrowing collective experience – like the improvisations on madness we had to do for the *Marat/Sade* – brings about another result : the actors having shared difficulties are open to one another and to the play in a different way.

A director learns that the growth of rehearsals is a developing process; he sees that there is a right time for everything, and his art is the art of recognizing these moments. He learns that he has no power to transmit certain ideas in the early days. He will come to recognize the look on the face of an apparently relaxed but inwardly anxious actor who cannot

follow what he is being told. He will then discover that all he needs is to wait, not push too hard. In the third week all will have changed, and a word or a nod will make instant communication. And the director will see that he too does not stay still. However much home-work he does, he cannot fully understand a play by himself. Whatever ideas he brings on the first day must evolve continually, thanks to the process he is going through with the actors, so that in the third week he will find that he is understanding everything differently. The actors' sensibilities turn searchlights on to his own, and he will either know more, or at least see more vividly that he has so far discovered nothing valid.

In fact, the director who comes to the first rehearsal with his script prepared with the moves and business, etc. noted down, is a real deadly theatre man.

When Sir Barry Jackson asked me to direct *Love's Labour's Lost* in Stratford in 1945, it was my first big production and I had already done enough work in smaller theatres to know that actors, and above all stage managers, had the greatest contempt for anyone who, as they always put it, 'did not know what he wanted'. So the night before the first rehearsal I sat agonized in front of a model of the set, aware that further hesitation would soon be fatal, fingering folded pieces of cardboard – forty pieces representing the forty actors to whom the following morning I would have to give orders, definite and clear. Again and again, I staged the very first entry of the Court, recognizing that this was when all would be lost or won, numbering the figures, drawing charts, manoeuvring the scraps of cardboard to and fro, on and off the set, trying them in big batches, then in small, from the side, from the back, over grass mounds, down steps, knocking them all over with my sleeve, cursing and starting again. As I did so, I noted the moves, and with no one to notice my indecision, crossed them out, then made fresh notes. The next morning

I arrived at rehearsal, a fat prompt-book under my arm, and the stage management brought me a table, reacting to my volume, I observed, with respect.

I divided the cast into groups, gave them numbers and sent them to their starting places, then, reading out my orders in a loud confident way, I let loose the first stage of the mass entrance. As the actors began to move I knew it was no good. These were not remotely like my cardboard figures, these large human beings thrusting themselves forward, some too fast with lively steps I had not foreseen, bringing them suddenly on top of me – not stopping, but wanting to go on, staring me in the face, or else lingering, pausing, even turning back with elegant affectations that took me by surprise. We had only done the first stage of the movement, letter A on my chart, but already everyone was wrongly placed and movement B could not follow. My heart sank and, despite all my preparation, I felt quite lost. Was I to start again, drilling these actors so that they conformed to my notes? One inner voice prompted me to do so, but another pointed out that my pattern was much less interesting than this new pattern that was unfolding in front of me – rich in energy, full of personal variations, shaped by individual enthusiasms and lazinesses, promising such different rhythms, opening so many unexpected possibilities. It was a moment of panic. I think, looking back, that my whole future work hung in the balance. I stopped, and walked away from my book, in amongst the actors, and I have never looked at a written plan since. I recognized once and for all the presumption and the folly of thinking that an inanimate model can stand for a man.

Of course, all work involves thinking : this means comparing, brooding, making mistakes, going back, hesitating, starting again. The painter naturally does this, so does the writer, but in secret. The theatre director has to expose his uncertainties to his cast, but in reward he has a medium

which evolves as it responds: a sculptor says that the choice of material continually amends his creation; the living material of actors is talking, feeling and exploring all the time – rehearsing is a visible thinking-aloud.

Let me quote a strange paradox. There is only one person as effective as a very good director – and that is a rotten one. It sometimes happens that a director is so bad, so completely without direction, so incapable of imposing his will, that his lack of ability becomes a positive virtue. It drives the actors to despair. Gradually his incompetence makes a gulf that yawns in front of the cast, and as the first night approaches insecurity gives way to terror, which becomes a force. It has happened that in the last moments a company found a strength and a unity as though by magic – and they gave a first-night performance for which the director got high praise. Equally, when a director is fired, the new man taking over often has an easy job: I once entirely re-staged someone else's production in the course of one night – and got unfair credit for the result. Despair had so prepared the ground that a touch from one finger was all that was required.

However, when the director is plausible enough, stern enough, articulate enough to get the actors' partial trust, then the result can misfire most easily of all. Even if the actor ends by disagreeing with some of what he is told, he still passes some of the load on to the director, feeling that 'he may be right', or at least that the director is vaguely 'responsible' and will somehow 'save the day'. This spares the actor the final personal responsibility and prevents the conditions for the spontaneous combustion of a company coming into being. It is the modest director, the honourable unassuming one, often the nicest man, who should be trusted least.

What I am saying can very easily be misunderstood – and directors who do not wish to be despots are sometimes tempted to the fatal course of doing nothing, cultivating non-

intervention in the belief that this is the only way of respecting the actor. This is a wretched fallacy – without leadership a group cannot reach a coherent result within a given time. A director is not free of responsibility – he is totally responsible – but he is not free of the process either, he is part of it. Every now and then an actor turns up who proclaims that directors are unnecessary: actors could do it by themselves. This may be true. But what actors? For actors to develop something alone, they would need to be creatures so highly developed that they would hardly need rehearsal either; they would read the script and in a wink the invisible substance of the play would appear fully articulated amongst them. This is unreal: a director is there to help a group evolve towards this ideal situation. The director is there to attack and yield, provoke and withdraw until the indefinable stuff begins to flow. The anti-director wants the director out of the way from the first rehearsal: any director disappears, a little later, on the first night. Sooner or later the actor must appear and the ensemble take command. The director must sense where the actor wants to go and what it is he avoids, what blocks he raises to his own intentions. No director injects a performance. At best a director enables an actor to reveal his own performance, that he might otherwise have clouded for himself.

Acting begins with a tiny inner movement so slight that it is almost completely invisible. We see this when we compare film and stage acting: a good stage actor can act in films, not necessarily vice versa. What happens? I make a proposition to an actor's imagination such as, 'She is leaving you.' At this moment deep in him a subtle movement occurs. Not only in actors. The movement occurs in anyone, but in most non-actors the movement is too slight to manifest itself in any way: the actor is a more sensitive instrument and in him the tremor is detected. In the cinema the great magnifier, the lens, describes this to the film that notes it down, so for the cinema

the first flicker is all. In early theatre rehearsals, the impulse may get no further than a flicker – even if the actor wishes to amplify it, all sorts of extraneous psychic psychological tensions can intervene – then the current is short-circuited, earthed. For this flicker to pass into the whole organism, a total relaxation must be there, either god-given or brought about by work. This, in short, is what rehearsals are all about. In this way actors are mediumistic: the idea suddenly envelops the whole in an act of possession: in Grotowski's terminology the actors are 'penetrated' – penetrated by themselves. In very young actors, the obstacles are sometimes very elastic, penetration can happen with surprising ease and they can give subtle and complex incarnations that are the despair of those who have evolved their skill over years. Yet later, with success and experience, the same young actors build up their barriers to themselves. Children can often act with extraordinary natural technique. People from real life are marvellous on screen. But with adult professionals there has to be a two-way process, and the stirring from within has to be aided by the stimulus from outside. Sometimes study and thought can help an actor to eliminate the preconceptions that blind him to deeper meanings, but sometimes it is the reverse. To reach an understanding of a difficult role, an actor must go to the limits of his personality and intelligence – but sometimes great actors go farther still if they rehearse the words and at the same time listen acutely to the echoes that arise in them.

John Gielgud is a magician – his form of theatre is one that is known to reach above the ordinary, the common, the banal. His tongue, his vocal chords, his feeling for rhythm compose an instrument that he has consciously developed all through his career in a running analogy with his life. His natural inner aristocracy, his outer social and personal beliefs, have given him a hierarchy of values, an intense discrimination

between base and precious, and a conviction that the sifting, the weeding, the selecting, the dividing, the refining and the transmuting are activities that never end. His art has always been more vocal than physical: at some early stage in his career he decided that for himself the body was a less supple instrument than the head. He thus jettisoned part of an actor's possible equipment but made true alchemy with the rest. It is not just speech, not melodies, but the continual movement between the word-forming mechanism and his understanding that has made his art so rare, so touching and especially so aware. With Gielgud, we are conscious both of what is expressed and of the skill of the creator: that a craft can be so deft adds to our admiration. The experience of working with him has been amongst my most special and my greatest joys.

Paul Scofield talks to his audience in another way. While in Gielgud the instrument stands halfway between the music and the hearer, and so demands a player, trained and skilled – in Scofield, instrument and player are one – an instrument of flesh and blood that opens itself to the unknown. Scofield, when I first knew him as a very young actor, had a strange characteristic: verse hampered him, but he would make un-forgettable verse out of lines of prose. It was as though the act of speaking a word sent through him vibrations that echoed back meanings far more complex than his rational thinking could find: he would pronounce a word like 'night' and then he would be compelled to pause: listening with all his being to the amazing impulses stirring in some mysterious inner chamber, he would experience the wonder of discovery at the moment when it happened. Those breaks, those sallies in depth, give his acting its absolutely personal structure of rhythms, its own instinctive meanings: to rehearse a part, he lets his whole nature – a milliard of super-sensitive scanners – pass to and fro across the words. In performance the same

process makes everything that he has apparently fixed come back again each night the same and absolutely different.

I use two well-known names as illustrations, but the phenomenon is there all the time in rehearsal, and continually reopens the problem of innocence and experience, of spontaneity and knowledge. There are also things young actors and unknown actors can do that have passed beyond the reach of fine actors with experience and skill.

There have been times in theatre history when the actor's work has been based on certain accepted gestures and expressions: there have been frozen systems of attitudes which we reject today. It is perhaps less obvious that the opposite pole, the Method Actor's freedom in choosing anything whatsoever from the gestures of everyday life is equally restricted, for in basing his gestures on his observation or on his own spontaneity the actor is not drawing on any deep creativity. He is reaching inside himself for an alphabet that is also fossilized, for the language of signs from life that he knows is the language not of invention but of his conditioning. His observations of behaviour are often observations of projections of himself. What he thinks to be spontaneous is filtered and monitored many times over. Were Pavlov's dog improvising, he would still salivate when the bell rang, but he would feel sure it was all his own doing. 'I'm dribbling,' he would say, proud of his daring.

Those who work in improvisation have the chance to see with frightening clarity how rapidly the boundaries of so-called freedom are reached. Our exercises in public with the Theatre of Cruelty quickly led the actors to the point where they were nightly ringing variations on their own clichés – like Marcel Marceau's character who breaks out of one prison to find himself within another. We experimented for instance with an actor opening a door and finding something unexpected. He had to react to the unexpected sometimes in

gesture, sometimes in sound, sometimes with paint. He was encouraged to express the first gesture, cry or splash that came to him. At first, all this showed was the actor's stock of similes. The open mouth of surprise, the step back in horror: where did these so-called spontaneities come from? Clearly the true and instantaneous inner reaction was checked and like lightning the memory substituted some imitation of a form once seen. Dabbing the paint was even more revealing: the hair's-breadth of terror before the blankness, and then the reassuring ready-made idea coming to the rescue. This Deadly Theatre lurks inside us all.

The aim of improvisation in training actors in rehearsal, and the aim of exercises, is always the same: it is to get away from Deadly Theatre. It is not just a matter of splashing about in self-indulgent euphoria as outsiders often suspect; for it aims at bringing the actor again and again to his own barriers, to the points where in place of new-found truth he normally substitutes a lie. An actor playing a big scene falsely appears false to the audience because, instant by instant, in his progression from one attitude of the character to another, he is substituting false details for real ones: tiny transitional phoney emotions through imitation attitudes. But this cannot be grappled with while rehearsing big scenes – too much is going on, it is far too complicated. The purpose of an exercise is to reduce and return: to narrow the area down and down until the birth of a lie is revealed and caught. If the actor can find and see this moment he can perhaps open himself to a deeper, more creative impulse.

Similarly, when two actors play together. What we know most is external ensemble playing: much of the teamwork of which the English theatre is so proud is based on politeness, courtesy, reasonableness, give-and-take, your turn, after you, and so on – a facsimile which works whenever the actors are in the same range of style – i.e. older actors play beautifully

together, and so do very young ones; but when they are mixed up, for all their care and mutual respect, the result is often a mess. For a production I did of Genet's *The Balcony* in Paris it was necessary to mix actors of very different backgrounds – classically trained, film trained, ballet trained and simple amateur. Here, long evenings of very obscene brothel improvisations served only one purpose – they enabled this hybrid group of people to come together and begin to find a way of responding directly to one another.

Some exercises open the actors to one another in a quite different way : for example, several actors may play completely different scenes side by side, but never speaking at the same moment, so that each has to pay close attention to the whole, in order to know just what moments depend on him. Or else developing a collective sense of responsibility for the quality of an improvisation, and switching to new situations as soon as the shared invention flags. Many exercises set out first to free the actor, so that he may be allowed to discover by himself what only exists in himself; next, to force him to accept blindly external directions, so that by cocking a sensitive enough ear he could hear in himself movements he would never have detected any other way. For instance a valuable exercise is dividing a Shakespeare soliloquy into three voices, like a canon, and then having the three actors recite at break-neck speed over and over again. At first, the technical difficulty absorbs all the actors' attention, and gradually as they master the difficulties they are asked to bring out the meaning of the words, without varying the inflexible form. Because of the speed and the mechanical rhythm this seems impossible: the actor is prevented from using any of his normal expressive equipment. Then suddenly he bursts a barrier and experiences how much freedom there can be within the tightest discipline.

Another variant is to take the two lines 'To be or not to be, That is the question' and give them to ten actors, one word

each. The actors stand in a closed circle, and endeavour to play the words one after the other, trying to produce a living phrase. This is so difficult that it instantly reveals even to the most unconvinced actor how closed and insensitive he is to his neighbour. When after long work the sentence suddenly flows, a thrilling freedom is experienced by everyone. They see in a flash the possibility of group playing, and the obstacles to it. This exercise can be developed by substituting other verbs for 'be', with the same effect of affirmation and denial – and eventually it is possible to put sounds or gestures in place of one or all of the words and still maintain a living dramatic flow between the ten participants.

The purpose of such exercises is to lead actors to the point where if one actor does something unexpected but true, the others can take this up and respond on the same level. This is ensemble playing : in acting terms it means ensemble creation, an awesome thought. It is no use thinking that exercises belong to school and only apply to a certain period of the actor's development. An actor, like any artist, is like a garden and it is no help to pull out the weeds just once, for all time. The weeds always grow, this is quite natural, and they must be cleaned away, which is natural and necessary too.

Actors must study by varying means : an actor has mainly an act of elimination to make. Stanislavsky's title 'Building a Character' is misleading – a character isn't a static thing and it can't be built like a wall. Rehearsals don't lead progressively to a first night. This is something very hard for some actors to understand – especially those who pride themselves most on their skill. For mediocre actors the process of character-building is as follows : they have an acute moment of artistic anguish, at the very start – 'What will happen this time?' – 'I know I've played many successful parts before but, this time, will inspiration come?' This actor comes in terror to the first rehearsal, but gradually his standard practices fill the

vacuum of his fear: as he 'discovers' a way of doing each section, he battens it down, relieved that once again he has been spared the final catastrophe. So on the first night, although he is nervous, his nerves are those of the marksman who knows he can hit the target but is afraid he won't get a bull's-eye again when his friends are watching.

The really creative actor reaches a different and far worse terror on the first night. All through rehearsals he has been exploring aspects of a character which he senses always to be partial, to be less than the truth – so he is compelled, by the honesty of his search, endlessly to shed and start again. A creative actor will be most ready to discard the hardened shells of his work at the last rehearsal because here, with the first night approaching, a brilliant searchlight is cast on his creation, and he sees its pitiful inadequacy. The creative actor also longs to cling on to all he's found, he too wants at all costs to avoid the trauma of appearing in front of an audience naked and unprepared. But still this is exactly what he must do. He must destroy and abandon his results even if what he picks up seems almost the same. This is easier for French actors than for English ones, because temperamentally they are more open to the idea that nothing is any good. And this is the only way that a part, instead of being built, can be born. The role that has been *built* is the same every night – except that it slowly erodes. For the part that is born to be the same it must always be reborn, which makes it always difficult. Of course, particularly in a long run, the effort of daily re-creation becomes unbearable and unthinkable, and this is where the experienced creative artist is compelled to fall back on a second level called technique to carry him through.

I did a play with that perfectionist Alfred Lunt. In the first act, he had a scene sitting on a bench. In rehearsal, he suggested, as a piece of natural business, taking off his shoe and rubbing his foot. Then he added shaking the shoe to empty

it before putting it back on again. One day when we were on tour in Boston, I walked past his dressing-room. The door was ajar. He was preparing for the performance, but I could see that he was looking out for me. He beckoned excitedly. I went into the dressing-room, he closed the door, asked me to sit down. 'There's something I want to try tonight,' he said. 'But only if you agree. I went for a walk on Boston Common this afternoon and found these.' He held out his palm. It contained two tiny pebbles. 'That scene where I shake out my shoe,' he continued: 'It's always worried me that nothing falls out. So I thought I'd try putting the pebbles in. Then when I shake it, you'd see them drop – and you'd hear the sound. What do you think?' I said it was an excellent idea and his face lit up. He looked delightedly at the two little stones, back at me, then suddenly his expression changed. He studied the stones again for a long anxious moment. 'You don't think it would be better with one?'

The hardest task of all for an actor is to be sincere yet detached – it is drummed into an actor that sincerity is all he needs. With its moral overtones, the word causes great confusion. In a way, the most powerful feature of the Brecht actors is the degree of their *insincerity*. It is only through detachment that an actor will see his own clichés. There is a dangerous trap in the word sincerity. First of all, a young actor discovers that his job is so exacting that it demands of him certain skills. For instance, he has to be heard: his body has to obey his wishes: he must be a master of his timing, not the slave of haphazard rhythms. So he searches for technique, and soon he acquires a know-how. Easily, know-how can become a pride and an end in itself. It becomes dexterity without any other aim than the display of expertise – in other words, the art becomes insincere. The young actor observes the insincerity of the old-timer and is disgusted. He searches for sincerity. Sincerity is a loaded word: like cleanliness it carries

childhood associations of goodness, truth-telling and decency. It seems a good ideal, a better aim than acquiring more and more technique, and as sincerity is a feeling, one can always tell when one's being sincere. So there is a path one can follow: one can find one's way to sincerity by emotional 'giving', by being dedicated, by honesty, by taking a no-holds-barred approach and by, as the French say, 'plunging into the bath'. Unfortunately, the result can easily be the worst kind of acting. With any of the other arts, however deep one plunges into the act of creating, it is always possible to step away and look at the result. As the painter steps back from his canvas other faculties can spring into play and warn him at once of his excesses. The trained pianist's head is physically less involved than his fingers and so however 'carried away' he is by the music, his ear carries its own degree of detachment and objective control. Acting is in many ways unique in its difficulties because the artist has to use the treacherous, changeable and mysterious material of himself as his medium. He is called upon to be completely involved while distanced – detached without detachment. He must be sincere, he must be insincere: he must practise how to be insincere with sincerity and how to lie truthfully. This is almost impossible, but it is essential and easily ignored. All too often, actors – and this is not their fault, but that of the deadly schools with which the world is littered – build their work on fag-ends of doctrine. The great system of Stanislavsky, which for the first time approached the whole art of acting from the point of view of science and knowledge, has done as much harm as good to many young actors, who misread it in detail and only take away a good hatred of the shoddy. After Stanislavsky, Artaud's equally significant writings, half-read and a tenth digested, have led to a naïve belief that emotional commitment and unhesitating self-exposure are all that really count. This is now fed further by ill-digested, misunderstood bits of

Grotowski. There is now a new form of sincere acting which consists of living everything through the body. It is a kind of naturalism. In naturalism, the actor tries sincerely to imitate the emotions and actions of the everyday world and to live his role. In this other naturalism the actor gives himself over just as completely to living his unrealistic behaviour, through and through. This is where he fools himself. Just because the type of theatre he's connected with seems poles removed from old-fashioned naturalism, he believes that he, too, is far from this despised style. In fact, he approaches the landscape of his own emotions with the same belief that every detail must be photographically reproduced. So he is always at full flood. The result is often soft, flabby, excessive and unconvincing.

There are groups of actors, particularly in the United States, nourished in Genet and Artaud, who despise all forms of naturalism. They would be very indignant if they were called naturalistic actors, but this is precisely what limits their art. To commit every fibre of one's being into an action may seem a form of total involvement – but the true artistic demand may be even more stringent than total involvement – and need fewer manifestations or quite different ones. To understand this, we must see that along with the emotion there is always a role for a special intelligence, that is not there at the start, but which has to be developed as a selecting instrument. There is a need for detachment, in particular, there is a need for certain forms: all of which is hard to define, but impossible to ignore. For instance, actors can pretend to fight with total abandon and genuine violence. Every actor is prepared for death scenes – and he throws himself into them with such abandon that he does not realize he knows nothing at all about death.

In France an actor comes to an audition, asks to be shown the most violent scene in the play and without a qualm plunges into it to demonstrate his paces. The French actor

playing a classical part pumps himself up in the wings then plunges into the scene : he judges the success or failure of the evening by the degree he can surrender to his emotions, whether his inner charge is at its maximum pitch, and from this comes a belief in the Muse, in inspiration and so on. The weakness of his work is that this way he tends to play generalizations. By this I mean that in an angry scene he gets on to his note of anger – or rather he plugs into his anger-point and this force drives him through the scene. This may give him a certain force and even at times a certain hypnotic power over the audience, and this power is falsely considered to be 'lyrical' and 'transcendental'. In fact, such an actor in his passion becomes its slave and is unable to drop out of the passion if a subtle change of text demands something new. In a speech that contains both natural and lyrical elements he declaims everything as though all the words were equally pregnant. It is this clumsiness that makes actors appear stupid and grand acting seem unreal.

Jean Genet wishes the theatre to come out of the banal, and he wrote a series of letters to Roger Blin when Blin was directing *The Screens*, urging him to push the actors towards 'lyricism'. This sounds well enough in theory but what is lyricism? What is 'out of the ordinary' acting? Does it dictate a special voice, a high-blown manner? Old classical actors seem to sing their lines, is this the relic of some valid old tradition? At what point is a search for form an acceptance of artificiality? This is one of the greatest problems we face today, and so long as we retain any sneaking belief that grotesque masks, heightened make-ups, hieratic costumes, declamation, balletic movement are somehow 'ritualistic' in their own right and consequently lyrical and profound, we will never get out of a traditional art-theatre rut.

At least one can see that everything is a language for something and nothing is a language for everything. Every action

happens in its own right and every action is an analogy of something else. I crumple a piece of paper: this gesture is complete in itself: I can stand on a stage and what I do need be no more than what appears at the moment of happening. It can also be a metaphor. Anyone who saw Patrick Magee slowly tearing strips of newspaper precisely as in life and yet utterly ritualistically in Pinter's *The Birthday Party* will know what this means. A metaphor is a sign and is an illustration – so it is a fragment of language. Every tone of speech, every rhythmic pattern is a fragment of language and corresponds to a different experience. Often, nothing is so deadly as a well-schooled actor speaking verse: there are of course academic laws of prosody and they can help to clarify certain things for an actor at a certain stage of his development, but he must eventually discover that the rhythms of each character are as distinctive as thumb-prints: then he must learn that every note in the musical scale corresponds – what to? That also he must find.

Music is a language related to the invisible by which nothingness suddenly is there in a form that cannot be seen but can certainly be perceived. Declamation is not music, yet it corresponds to something different to ordinary speech. *Sprechgesang* also: Carl Orff has set Greek tragedy on to a heightened level of rhythmic speech supported and punctuated by percussion and the result is not only striking, it is essentially different from tragedy spoken and tragedy sung: it speaks of a different thing. We can separate neither the structure nor the sound of Lear's 'Never never never never never' from its complex of meanings, and we cannot isolate Lear's 'Monster Ingratitude' without seeing how the shortness of the line of verse brings a tremendous thick emphasis on to the syllables. There is a moving beyond words in 'Monster Ingratitude'. The texture of language is reaching towards the experiences that Beethoven imitated in patterns of sound –

yet it is not music, it cannot be abstracted from its sense. Verse is deceptive.

An exercise we once developed involved taking a scene of Shakespeare's, such as Romeo's farewell to Juliet, and trying (artificially of course) to disentangle the different intertwining styles of writing. The scene reads:

Juliet: Wilt thou be gone? It is not yet near day.
It was the nightingale, and not the lark,
That pierced the fearful hollow of thine ear.
Nightly she sings on yond pomegranate tree.
Believe me, love, it was the nightingale.

Romeo: It was the lark, the herald of the morn;
No nightingale. Look, love, what envious streaks
Do lace the severing clouds in yonder East.
Night's candles are burnt out, and jocund day
Stands tiptoe on the misty mountain tops.
I must be gone and live, or stay and die.

Juliet: Yond light is not daylight; I know it, I.
It is some meteor that the sun exhales
To be to thee this night a torchbearer
And light thee on thy way to Mantua.
Therefore stay yet. Thou needest not to be gone.

Romeo: Let me be ta'en, let me be put to death.
I am content, so thou wilt have it so.
I'll say yon grey is not the morning's eye;
'Tis but the pale reflex of Cynthia's brow.
Nor that is not the lark whose notes do beat
The vaulty heaven so high above our heads.
I have more care to stay than will to go.
Come, death, and welcome! Juliet wills it so.
How is't, my soul? Let's talk. It is not day.

The actors then were asked to select only those words that they could play in a realistic situation, the words that

they could use unselfconsciously in a film. This produced :

Juliet: Wilt thou be gone? It is not yet near day.
It was the nightingale [pause] not the lark [pause]

Romeo: It was the lark [pause] no nightingale. Look,
love [pause] I must be gone and live, or stay and die.

Juliet: Yond light is no daylight; [pause] therefore
stay yet. Thou needest not to be gone.

Romeo: Let me be ta'en, let me be put to death. I
am content, so thou wilt have it so. [pause]
Come, death and welcome! Juliet wills it so.
How is't, my soul? Let's talk. It is not day.

Then the actors played this as a genuine scene from a
modern play full of living pauses – speaking the selected
words out loud, but repeating the missing words silently to
themselves to find the uneven lengths of the silences. The
fragment of scene that emerged would have made good
cinema, for the moments of dialogue linked by a rhythm of
silences of unequal duration in a film would be sustained by
close shots and other silent, related images.

Once this crude separation had been made, it was then
possible to do the reverse : to play the erased passages with
full recognition that they had nothing whatsoever to do with
normal speech. Then it was possible to explore them in many
different ways – turning them into sounds or movements –
until the actor saw more and more vividly how a single line of
speech can have certain pegs of natural speech round which
twist unspoken thoughts and feelings rendered apparent by
words of another order. This change of style from the
apparently colloquial to the evidently stylized is so subtle
that it cannot be observed by any crude attitudes. If the actor
approaches a speech looking for its form, he must beware not
to decide too easily what is musical, what is rhythmic. It is

not enough for an actor playing Lear in the storm to take a running jump at the speeches, thinking of them as splendid slabs of storm music. Nor is it any use speaking them quietly for their meaning on the grounds that they are actually taking place inside his head. A passage of verse can be understood more like a formula carrying many characteristics – a code in which each letter has a different function. In the storm speeches, the explosive consonants are there to suggest by imitation the explosive pattern of thunder, wind and rain. But the consonants are not everything : within these crackling letters writhes a meaning, a meaning that's ever on the change, a meaning that's carried by meaning's bearer, images. Thus, 'you cataracts and hurricanes spout' is one thing 'All germens spill at once That make Ingrateful man', is quite another. With writing as compact as this, the last degree of skill is needed : any loud actor can roar both lines with the same noise, but the artist must not only present us with absolute clarity the Hieronymus Bosch–Max Ernst-like image in the second line of the heavens spilling their spermatozoa, he must present this within the context of Lear's own rage. He will observe again that the verse gives great weight to 'That make Ingrateful man', this will reach him as a very precise stage direction from Shakespeare himself, and he will sense and grope for a rhythmic structure that enables him to give to these four words the strength and weight of a longer line and in so doing hurl on to the longshot of man in storm a tremendous close-up of his absolute belief in human ingratitude. Unlike a close-up in the cinema, this sort of close-up, close-up with an idea, frees us from an exclusive preoccupation with the man himself. Our complex faculties engage more fully and in our minds we place Ingrateful man over Lear and over the world, his world, our world, at one and the same time.

Yet this is the point where we most need to keep in touch

with commonsense, where the right artifice turns stilted or bombastic. 'Have a whisky' – the content of this phrase clearly is better rendered by a conversational tone of voice than by song. 'Have a whisky'. This phrase we would agree has only one dimension, one weight, one function. Yet in *Madame Butterfly* these words are sung and indirectly Puccini's one phrase has brought the whole form of opera into ridicule. 'Dinner, ho!' in Lear's scene with his knights is similar to 'Have a whisky'. Lears often declaim this phrase, bringing the play into artificialities, yet when Lear says the words, he is not acting in a poetic tragedy, he is simply a man calling for his dinner. 'Ingrateful man' and 'Dinner, ho!' are both lines by Shakespeare in a verse tragedy, but in fact they belong to quite different worlds of acting.

In rehearsal, form and content have to be examined sometimes together, sometimes separately. Sometimes an exploration of the form can suddenly open us up to the meaning that dictated the form – sometimes a close study of content gives us a fresh sound of rhythm. The director must look for where the actor is messing up his own right urges – and here he must help the actor to see and overcome his own obstacles. All this is a dialogue and a dance between director and player. A dance is an accurate metaphor, a waltz between director, player and text. Progression is circular, and deciding who's the leader depends on where you stand. The director will find that all the time new means are needed: he will discover that any rehearsal technique has its use, that no technique is all-embracing. He will follow the natural principle of rotation of crops: he will see that explanation, logic, improvisation, inspiration, are methods that rapidly run dry and he will move from one to the other. He will know that thought, emotion and body can't be separated – but he will see that a pretended separation must often take place. Some actors do not respond to explanation, while others do. This differs in

each situation, and one day it is unexpectedly the non-intellectual actor who responds to a word from the director, while the intellectual understands all from a gesture.

In early rehearsals, improvisation, exchange of associations and memories, reading of written material, reading of period documents, looking at films and at paintings can all serve to stimulate the material relevant to the theme of a play inside each individual. None of these methods means much in itself – each is a stimulus. In the *Marat/Sade*, as kinetic images of insanity rose up and possessed the actor and as he yielded to them in improvisation, the others observed and criticized. So a true form was gradually detached from the standardized clichés that are part of an actor's equipment for mad scenes. Then as he produced an imitation of madness that convinced his fellows by its seeming reality, he had to come up against a new problem. He may have used an image from observation, from life, but the play is about madness as it was in 1808 – before drugs, before treatment, when a different social attitude to the insane made them behave differently, and so on. For this, the actor had no outside model – he looked at faces in Goya not as models to imitate but as prods to encourage his confidence in following the stronger and more worrying of his inner impulses. He had to allow himself to serve these voices completely; and in parting from outside models, he was taking greater risks. He had to cultivate an act of possession. As he did so, he faced a new difficulty, his responsibility to the play. All the shaking, juddering and roaring, all the sincerity in the world can still get the play nowhere. He has lines to speak – if he invents a character incapable of speaking them he will be doing his job badly. So the actor has to face two opposite requirements. The temptation is to compromise – to tone down the impulses of the character to suit the stage needs. But his real task lies in the opposite direction. Make the character vivid – and

functional. How? It is just there that the need for intelligence arises.

There is a place for discussion, for research, for the study of history and documents as there is a place for roaring and howling and rolling on the floor. Also, there is a place for relaxation, informality, chumminess, but also there is a time for silence and discipline and intense concentration. Before his first rehearsal with our actors, Grotowski asked for the floor to be swept and for all clothes and personal belongings to be taken out of the room. Then he sat behind a desk, speaking to the actors from a distance, allowing neither smoking nor conversation. This tense climate made certain experiences possible. If one reads Stanislavsky's books, one sees that some of the things said are purely to evoke a seriousness from an actor at a time when the majority of theatres were slipshod. Yet at times, nothing is more liberating than informality and the chucking away of all holy, high-minded ways. Sometimes all the attention must be given to one actor; at other times the collective process demands a halt to the individual's work. Not every facet can be explored. To discuss every possible way with everyone can be just too slow and so it can be destructive to the whole. Here the director has to have a sense of time: it is for him to feel the rhythm of the process and observe its divisions. There is a time for discussing the broad lines of a play, there is a time for forgetting them, for discovering what can only be found through joy, extravagance, irresponsibility. There is a time when no one must worry himself about the results of his efforts. I hate letting people watch rehearsals because I believe that the work is privileged, thus private: there must be no concern about whether one is being foolish or making mistakes. Also a rehearsal may be incomprehensible – often excesses can be left or encouraged even to the amazement and dismay of the company until the moment is ripe to call a halt. But even in

rehearsal there is a time when one needs outside people watching, when what always seem to be hostile faces can create a good new tension and the tension a new focus : the work must all the time set new demands. There is another point the director must sense. He must sense the time when a group of actors intoxicated by their own talent and the excitement of the work loses sight of the play. Suddenly one morning the work must change : the result must become all-important. Jokes and embroideries are then ruthlessly pared away and all the attention put on to the function of the evening, on the narrating, the presenting, the technique, the audibility, the communicating to the audience. So it is foolish for a director to take a doctrinaire view, either talking technical language about pace, volume, etc. – or avoiding one because it is inartistic. It is woefully easy for a director to get stuck in a method. There comes a moment when talk about speed, precision, diction is all that counts. 'Speed up', 'get on with it', 'it's boring', 'vary the pace', 'for Christ's sake' is then the patter, yet a week before such old-timer talk could have stultified all creativity.

The closer the actor approaches the task of performing, the more requirements he is asked to separate, understand and fulfil simultaneously. He must bring into being an unconscious state of which he is completely in charge. The result is a whole, indivisible – but emotion is continually illuminated by intuitive intelligence so that the spectator, though wooed, assaulted, alienated and forced to reassess, ends by experiencing something equally indivisible. Catharsis can never have been simply an emotional purge : it must have been an appeal to the whole man.

Now the moment of performance, when it comes, is reached through two passageways – the foyer and the stage door. Are these, in symbolic terms, links or are they to be seen as symbols of separation? If the stage is related to life, if the

auditorium is related to life, then the openings must be free and open passageways must allow an easy transition from outside life to meeting place. But if the theatre is essentially artificial, then the stage door reminds the actor that he is now entering a special place that demands costume, make-up, disguise, change of identity – and the audience also dresses up, so as to come out of the everyday world along a red carpet into a place of privilege. Both of these are true and both must be carefully compared, because they carry quite different possibilities with them and relate to quite different social circumstances. The only thing that all forms of theatre have in common is the need for an audience. This is more than a truism : in the theatre the audience completes the steps of creation. In the other arts, it is possible for the artist to use as his principle the idea that he works for himself. However great his sense of social responsibility, he will say that his best guide is his own instinct – and if he is satisfied when standing alone with his completed work, the chances are that other people will be satisfied too. In the theatre this is modified by the fact that the last lonely look at the completed object is not possible – until an audience is present the object is not complete. No author, no director, even in a megalomaniac dream, would want a private performance, just for himself. No megalomaniac actor would want to play for himself, for his mirror. So for the author or the director to work for his own taste and his own judgement, he must work approximately for himself in rehearsal and only truly for himself when he is hemmed in by a dense bank of audience. I think any director will agree that his own view of his own work changes completely when he is sitting surrounded by people.

Seeing a first public performance of a play one has directed is a strange experience. Only a day before, one sat at a run-through and was completely convinced that a certain actor was playing well, that a certain scene was interesting, a

movement graceful, a passage full of clear and necessary meaning. Now surrounded by audience part of oneself is responding like this audience, so it is oneself who is saying 'I'm bored', 'he's said that already', 'if she moves once more in that affected way I'll go mad' and even 'I don't understand what they're trying to say'. Apart from the over-sensibility brought about by nerves, what actually is happening to make such a startling change in the director's view of his own work? I think that it is above all a question of the order in which the events now occur. Let me explain this by a single example. In the first scene of a play a girl meets her lover. She has rehearsed with great tenderness and truth and invests a simple greeting with an intimacy that touches everyone – out of context. In front of an audience, it suddenly becomes clear that the preceding lines and actions have in no way prepared for this: in fact, the audience may be busy trying to pick up quite different trails relating to other characters and themes – then suddenly it is faced with a young actress murmuring half inaudibly to a young man. In a later scene, the sequence of events could have led to a hush in which this murmuring would be exactly right – here it seems half-hearted, the intention unclear and even incomprehensible.

The director tries to preserve a vision of the whole, but he rehearses in fragments and even when he sees a run-through it is unavoidably with foreknowledge of all the play's intentions. When an audience is present, compelling him to react as an audience, this foreknowledge is filtered away and for the first time he finds himself receiving the impressions given by the play in their proper time-sequence, one after another. Not surprisingly he finds that everything appears different.

For this reason any experimenter is concerned with all aspects of his relationships with an audience. He tries by placing the audience in different positions to bring about new

possibilities. An apron stage, an arena, a fully lit house, a
cramped barn or room – already these condition different
events. But the difference may be superficial: a more profound difference can arise when the actor can play on a
changing inner relationship with the spectator. If the actor
can catch the spectator's interest, thus lower his defences and
then coax the spectator to an unexpected position or an awareness of a clash of opposing beliefs, of absolute contradictions,
then the audience becomes more active. This activity does not
demand manifestations – the audience that answers back may
seem active, but this may be quite superficial – true activity
can be invisible, but also indivisible.

The one thing that distinguishes the theatre from all the
other arts is that it has no permanence. Yet it is very easy to
apply – almost from force of critical habit – permanent standards and general rules to this ephemeral phenomenon. One
night in an English provincial town, Stoke-on-Trent, I saw
a production of *Pygmalion*, staged in a theatre-in-the-round.
The combination of lively actors, lively building, lively
audience, brought out the most sparkling elements of the
play. It 'went' marvellously. The audience participated fully.
The performance was triumphantly complete. The cast were
all too young for their parts: they had unconvincing grey
lines painted on their hair and very obvious make-ups. If by
magic they had been transported that very instant to the
West End of London and found themselves surrounded by a
London audience in a conventional London building they
would have seemed unconvincing and the audience would
have been unconvinced. However, this does not mean that
the London standard is better or higher than the provincial
one. It is more likely to be the reverse, because it is unlikely
that anywhere in London that evening the theatrical temperature was nearly so high as in Stoke. But the comparison
can never been made. The hypothetical 'if' can never be put

to the test, when it's not just the actors or the script, but the whole of the performance that one is assessing.

At the Theatre of Cruelty part of our study was the audience, and our very first public performance was an interesting experience. The audience that came to see an 'experimental' evening arrived with the usual mixture of condescension, playfulness and faint disapproval that the notion of the *avant-garde* arouses. We presented to them a number of fragments. Our own purpose was uniquely selfish – we wanted to see some of our experiments in performance conditions. We did not give the audience a programme, list of authors, of names, of items, nor any commentary or explanation of our own intentions.

The programme began with Artaud's three-minute play, *The Spurt of Blood*, made more Artaud than Artaud because his dialogue was entirely replaced by screams. Part of the audience was immediately fascinated, part giggled. We meant it seriously, but next we played a little interlude that we ourselves considered a joke. Now the audience was lost: the laughers did not know whether to laugh any more, the serious-minded who had disapproved of their neighbours' laughter no longer knew what attitude to take. As the performance continued, the tension grew: when Glenda Jackson, because a situation demanded it, took off all her clothes a new tension came into the evening because the unexpected now might have no bounds. We could observe how an audience is in no way prepared to make its own instant judgements second for second. At the second performance the tension was no longer the same. There were no reviews, and I do not believe that many people on the second night had been primed by friends who had come the night before. Yet the audience was less tense. Rather I think that other factors were at work – they *knew* we had already performed once before and the fact that there was *nothing* in the papers in itself

telegraphed a reassurance. The ultimate horrors could not have taken place: if one of the audience had been injured, if we had set fire to the building, then it would have been on the front page. No news was good news. Then as the run wore on, word of mouth got around that there were improvisations, some dull bits, a chunk of Genet, a shake-up of Shakespeare, some loud sounds, and so the audience arrived, selected, because of course some now preferred to stay at home, and gradually only the enthusiasts or the determined scoffers filtered through. Whenever one has a real critical flop, for the remainder of the run there is always a small audience of great enthusiasm – and on the last night of a 'failure' there are always cheers. Everything helps to condition an audience. Those who go to a theatre despite bad notices go with a certain wish, a certain expectation; they are prepared, if only for the worst. Almost always we take our places in a theatre with an elaborate set of references conditioning us before the performance begins: when the play ends, we are automatized into getting up and leaving straight away. When at the end of 'US' we offered the audience the possibility of silence, of sitting still for a while if it wanted – it was interesting to see how this possibility offended some and gratified others. In fact, there is no reason why one should be hustled from a theatre the moment the action is done, and after 'US' many people sat still for ten minutes or more, then began spontaneously to speak to one another. This seems to me to be more natural and more healthy an end to a shared experience than rushing away – unless the rushing away is also an act of choice, not of social habit.

Today, the question of the audience seems to be the most important and difficult one to face. We find that the usual theatre audience is usually not a very lively one, certainly not a particularly loyal one, so we set off in search of a 'new' audience. This is surely understandable – and yet at the same

time rather artificial. On the whole it is true that the younger an audience, the more swift and free its reactions. It is true that on the whole what alienates young people from the theatre is what is bad in theatre anyway, so in changing our forms to woo the young we would seem to be killing two birds with one stone. An observation that can easily be checked at football matches and dog races is that a popular audience is far more vivid in its responses than a middle-class one. So again it would seem to make sense to woo the popular audience through a popular idiom.

But this logic easily breaks down. The popular audience exists and yet it is something of a will-o'-the-wisp. When Brecht was alive, it was the intellectuals of West Berlin who flocked to his theatre in the East. Joan Littlewood's support came from the West End, and she never found a working-class audience from her own district large enough to carry her through difficult times. The Royal Shakespeare Theatre sends groups out to factories and youth clubs – following Conti-nental patterns – to sell the notion of theatre to those sections of society who have perhaps never set foot in a theatre and are perhaps convinced that theatre is not for them. These commandos aim at evoking interest, breaking down barriers, making friends. This is splendid, stimulating work. But behind it lurks an issue perhaps too dangerous to touch – what truly are they selling? We are implying to a working man that theatre is part of Culture – that is to say, part of the big new hamper of goods now available to everyone. Behind all attempts to reach new audiences there is a secret patronage – 'you too can come to the party' – and like all patronage, it conceals a lie. The lie is the implication that the gift is worth receiving. Do we truly believe in its worth? When people, whose age or class has kept them away from theatres, are lured into them, is it enough to give them 'the best'? The Soviet Theatre attempts to give 'the best'. National

Theatres offer 'the best'. At the Metropolitan Opera in New York in a brand-new building the best of Europe's singers under the baton of the best Mozart conductor, and organized by the best producer, play a *Magic Flute*. Apart from the music and the acting, on a recent occasion the cup of culture was really filled to the brim because a splendid series of paintings by Chagall were also displayed scene by scene at the same time. According to the addictive view of culture, it would be impossible to go further – the young man privileged to take his girl to the *Magic Flute* reaches the pinnacle of what his community can offer in terms of the civilized life. The ticket is 'hot' – but what is the evening worth? In a sense, all forms of audience-wooing flirt dangerously with this same proposition – come and share in the good life which is good, because it has to be good, because it contains the best.

This can never really change so long as culture or any art is simply an appendage on living, separable from it and, once separated, obviously unnecessary. Such art then is only fought for by the artist to whom, temperamentally, it is necessary, for it is his life. In the theatre we always return to the same point: it is not enough for writers and actors to experience this compulsive necessity, audiences must share it, too. So in this sense it is not just a question of wooing an audience. It is an even harder matter of creating works that evoke in audiences an undeniable hunger and thirst.

A true image of necessary theatre-going I know is a psycho-drama session in an asylum. Let us examine for a moment the conditions that prevail there. There is a small community, which leads a regular, monotonous life. On certain days, for some of the inmates, there is an event, something unusual, something to look forward to, a session of drama. When they come into the room where the session is to take place, they know that whatever is going to happen is different from what happens in the wards, the garden, the television room. They

all sit in a circle. At the start, they are often suspicious, hostile, withdrawn. The doctor in charge takes the initiative and asks the patients to propose themes. Suggestions are made, they are discussed and slowly there emerge points that interest more than one patient, points that literally become points of contact. Conversation develops painfully around these subjects and the doctor will at once pass to dramatizing them. In the circle, soon, everyone will have this role – but this does not mean that everyone is performing. Some will naturally step forward as protagonists, while others will prefer to sit and watch, either identifying with the protagonist, or following his actions, detached and critical.

A conflict will develop: this is true drama because the people on their feet will be speaking about true issues shared by all present in the only manner that can make these issues really come to life. They may laugh. They may cry. They may not react at all. But behind all that goes on, amongst the so-called insane, lurks a very simple, very sane basis. They all share a wish to be helped to emerge from their anguish, even if they don't know what this help may be, or what form it could take. At this point, let me make it clear that I have no views at all on the value of psychodrama as a treatment. Perhaps it has no lasting medical result at all. But in the immediate event there is an unmistakable result. Two hours after any session begins all the relations between the people present are slightly modified, because of the experience in which they have been plunged together. As a result, something is more animated, something flows more freely, some embryonic contacts are being made between previously sealed-off souls. When they leave the room, they are not quite the same as when they entered. If what has happened has been shatteringly uncomfortable, they are invigorated to the same degree as if there have been great outbursts of laughter. Neither pessimism nor optimism apply: simply, some par-

ticipants are temporarily, slightly, more alive. If, as they go out of the door, this all evaporates, it does not matter either. Having had this taste, they will wish to come back for more. The drama session will seem an oasis in their lives.

This is how I understand a necessary theatre, one in which there is only a practical difference between actor and audience, not a fundamental one.

As I write, I do not know whether it is only on a tiny scale, in tiny communities, that drama can be renewed. Or whether it is possible on a large scale, in a big playhouse in a capital city. Can we find, in terms of present need, what Glyndebourne and Bayreuth achieved in quite other circumstances, with quite different ideals? That is to say, can we produce homogeneous work that shapes its audience before it has even passed through its doors? Glyndebourne and Bayreuth were in tune with their society and the classes for whom they catered. Today, it is hard to see how a vital theatre and a necessary one can be other than out of tune with society – not seeking to celebrate the accepted values, but to challenge them. Yet the artist is not there to indict, nor to lecture, nor to harangue, and least of all to teach. He is a part of 'them'. He challenges the audience truly when he is the spike in the side of an audience that is determined to challenge itself. He celebrates with an audience most truly when he is the mouthpiece of an audience that has a ground of joy.

Were new phenomena to come into being in front of an audience, and were the audience open to them, a powerful confrontation would occur. Were this to occur, the scattered nature of social thinking would gather round certain bass notes; certain deep aims would be refelt, renewed, reasserted. In this way the divisions between positive and negative experience, between optimism and pessimism, would become meaningless.

At a time when all sands are shifting, the search is auto-

matically a search for form. The destruction of old forms, the experimenting with new ones: new words, new relationships, new places, new buildings: they all belong to the same process, and any individual production is just a separate shot at an unseen target. It is foolish today to expect any single production, group, style or line of work to reveal what we're looking for. The theatre can only advance crabwise in a world whose moving forward is as often sideways as backwards. This is why for a very long time there cannot possibly be a world style for a world theatre – as there was in the theatres and opera houses of the nineteenth century.

But all is not movement, all is not destruction, all is not restlessness, all is not fashion. There are pillars of affirmation. Those are the moments of achievement which do occur, suddenly, anywhere: the performances, the occasions when collectively a total experience, a total theatre of play and spectator makes nonsense of any divisions like Deadly, Rough and Holy. At these rare moments, the theatre of joy, of catharsis, of celebration, the theatre of exploration, the theatre of shared meaning, the living theatre are one. But once gone, the moment is gone and it cannot be recaptured slavishly by imitation – the deadly creeps back, the search begins again.

Every cue to action has a call back to inertia within it. Take that holiest of experiences – music. Music is the one thing that makes life tolerable for a great number of people. So many hours of music a week remind people that life could be worth living – but these instants of solace blunt the edge of their dissatisfaction and so make them more ready to accept an otherwise intolerable way of life. Take the shocking atrocity stories, or the photo of the napalmed child, these shocks are the roughest of experiences – but they open the spectators' eyes to the need for an action which in the event they somehow sap. It is as though the fact of experiencing a

need vividly quickens this need and quenches it in the same breath. What then can be done?

I know of one acid test in the theatre. It is literally an acid test. When a performance is over, what remains? Fun can be forgotten, but powerful emotion also disappears and good arguments lose their thread. When emotion and argument are harnessed to a wish from the audience to see more clearly into itself – them something in the mind burns. The event scorches on to the memory an outline, a taste, a trace, a smell – a picture. It is the play's central image that remains, its silhouette, and if the elements are highly blended this silhouette will be its meaning, this shape will be the essence of what it has to say. When years later I think of a striking theatrical experience I find a kernel engraved on my memory : two tramps under a tree, an old woman dragging a cart, a sergeant dancing, three people on a sofa in hell – or occasionally a trace deeper than any imagery. I haven't a hope of remembering the meanings precisely, but from the kernel I can reconstruct a set of meanings. Then a purpose will have been served. A few hours could amend my thinking for life. This is almost but not quite impossible to achieve.

The actor himself is hardly ever scarred by his efforts. Any actor in his dressing-room after playing a tremendous, horrifying role is relaxed and glowing. It is as though the passage of strong feelings through someone engaged in strong physical activity is very healthy. I believe it is good for a man to be an orchestral conductor, good for him to be a tragedian : as a race, they seem consistently to reach a ripe old age. But I also think that there is a price. The material you use to create these imaginary people who you can pick up and discard like a glove is your own flesh and blood. The actor is giving of himself all the time. It is his possible growth, his possible understanding that he is exploiting, using this material to weave these personalities which drop away when the play is

done. Our question here is whether anything at all can prevent the same thing happening to the audience. Can the audience retain a mark of its catharsis – or is a glow of well-being the very best it can ever reach?

Even here there are many contradictions. The act of theatre is a release. Both laughter and intense feelings clear some débris from the system – in this way they are the opposite of tracemakers, for like all purgations they make all clean and new. Yet are the experiences that free and the experiences that remain so completely different? Isn't it a verbal naïvety to believe that one is opposed to the other? Isn't it truer to say that in a renewal all things are possible again?

There are many pink old men and women. There are those who have astonishing vigour, but who are great babies; unlined in face and nature, jolly, but not grown-up. There are also other old people, not crabbed, not decrepit: lined, marked, used – who are glowing, renewed. Even youth and age can superimpose. The real question for the old actor is whether in an art that so renews him he could also, if he actively wished, find another growth. The question for the audience, happy and refreshed by a joyous evening at the theatre, is also the same one. Is there a further possibility? We know a fleeting liberation can happen; can something also stay?

Here the question comes back to the spectator. Does he want any change in his circumstances? Does he want anything different in himself, his life, his society? If he doesn't, then he doesn't need the theatre to be an aid, a magnifying glass, a searchlight or a place of confrontation.

On the other hand, he may need one or all of these things. In this case, he not only needs the theatre, he needs everything he can get there. He desperately needs that trace that scorches, he desperately needs it to stay.

We are on the verge of a formula, an equation that reads

Theatre=R r a. To arrive at these letters we are forced to draw from an unexpected source. The French language does not contain the words adequate for the translation of Shakespeare, yet strangely it is just in this language that we find three words used every day which reflect the problems and the possibilities of the theatre event.

Repetition, representation, assistance. The words work just as well in English. But we normally speak of a rehearsal: *répétition* say the French, and their word conjures up the mechanical side of the process. Week after week, day after day, hour after hour, practice makes perfect. It is a drudge, a grind, a discipline; it is a dull action that leads to a good result. As every athlete knows, repetition eventually brings about change : harnessed to an aim, driven by a will, repetition is creative. There are cabaret singers who practise a new song again and again for a year or more before venturing to perform it in public: then they may repeat this song to audiences for a further fifty years. Laurence Olivier repeats lines of dialogue to himself again and again until he conditions his tongue muscles to a point of absolute obedience – and so gains total freedom. No clown, no acrobat, no dancer would question that repetition is the only way certain actions become possible, and anyone who refuses the challenge of repetition knows that certain regions of expression are automatically barred to him. At the same time, repetition is a word with no glamour; it is a concept without warmth; the immediate association is a deadly one. Repetition is the piano lessons we remember from childhood, the repeated scales; repetition is the touring musical comedy repeating automatically, with its fifteenth cast, actions that have lost their meaning and lost their savour. Repetition is what leads to all that is meaningless in tradition : the soul-destroying long run, the understudy rehearsals, all that sensitive actors dread. These carbon-copy imitations are lifeless. Repetition denies the living. It is

as though in one word we see the essential contradiction in the theatre form. To evolve, something needs to be prepared and the preparation often involves going over the same ground again and again. Once completed, this needs to be seen and may evoke a legitimate demand to be repeated again and again. In this repetition, lie the seeds of decay.

What can reconcile this contradiction? Here, the French word for performance – *représentation* – contains an answer. A representation is the occasion when something is re-presented, when something from the past is shown again – something that once was, now is. For representation is not an imitation or description of a past event, a representation denies time. It abolishes that difference between yesterday and today. It takes yesterday's action and makes it live again in every one of its aspects – including its immediacy. In other words, a representation is what it claims to be – a making present. We can see how this is the renewal of the life that repetition denies and it applies as much to rehearsal as to performance.

The study of what exactly this means opens a rich field. It compels us to see what living action means, what constitutes a real gesture in the immediate present, what forms the fakes assume, what is partially alive, what is completely artificial – until slowly we can begin to define the actual factors that make the act of representation so difficult. And the more we study this the more we see that for a repetition to evolve into a representation, something further is called for. The making present will not happen by itself, help is needed. This help is not always there: yet without this true aid, the true making present will not take place. We wonder what this necessary ingredient could be, and we look at a rehearsal, watching the actors toiling away at their painful repetitions. We realize that in a vacuum their work would be meaningless. Here we find a clue. It leads us naturally to the idea of an audience; we

see that without an audience there is no goal, no sense. What is an audience? In the French language amongst the different terms for those who watch, for public, for spectator, one word stands out, is different in quality from the rest. *Assistance* – I watch a play: *j'assiste à une pièce.* To assist – the word is simple: it is the key. An actor prepares, he enters into a process that can turn lifeless at any point. He sets out to capture something, to make it incarnate. In rehearsal, the vital element of assistance comes from the director, who is there to aid by watching. When the actor goes in front of an audience, he finds that the magic transformation does not work by magic. The spectators may just stare at the spectacle, expecting the actor to do all the work and before a passive gaze he may find that all he can offer is a repetition of rehearsals. This may disturb him deeply, he may put all his goodwill, integrity, ardour into working up liveliness and yet he senses all the time a lack. He talks about a 'bad' house. Occasionally, on what he calls a 'good night', he encounters an audience that by chance brings an active interest and life to its watching role – this audience assists. With this assistance, the assistance of eyes and focus and desires and enjoyment and concentration, repetition turns into representation. Then the word representation no longer separates actor and audience, show and public: it envelops them: what is present for one is present for the other. The audience too has undergone a change. It has come from a life outside the theatre that is essentially repetitive to a special arena in which each moment is lived more clearly and more tensely. The audience assists the actor, and at the same time for the audience itself assistance comes back from the stage.

Repetition, representation, assistance. These words sum up the three elements, each of which is needed for the event to come to life. But the essence is still lacking, because any three words are static, any formula is inevitably an attempt to

capture a truth for all time. Truth in the theatre is always on the move.

As you read this book, it is already moving out of date. It is for me an exercise, now frozen on the page. But unlike a book, the theatre has one special characteristic. It is always possible to start again. In life this is a myth; we ourselves can never go back on anything. New leaves never turn, clocks never go back, we can never have a second chance. In the theatre the slate is wiped clean all the time.

In everyday life, 'if' is a fiction, in the theatre 'if' is an experiment.

In everyday life, 'if' is an evasion, in the theatre 'if' is the truth.

When we are persuaded to believe in this truth, then the theatre and life are one.

This is a high aim. It sounds like hard work.

To play needs much work. But when we experience the work as play, then it is not work any more.

A play is play.

PENGUIN MODERN CLASSICS

RHINOCEROS, THE CHAIRS, THE LESSON
EUGÈNE IONESCO

'It's not a certain society that seems ridiculous to me, it's mankind'

These three great plays by one of the founding fathers of the Theatre of the Absurd are alive and kicking with tragedy and humour, bleakness and farce. In *Rhinoceros* we are shown the innate brutality of people when everyone, except for Berenger, turns into clumsy, unthinking rhinoceroses. *The Chairs* depicts the futile struggle of two old people to convey the meaning of life to the rest of humanity, while *The Lesson* is a chilling, but anarchically funny drama of verbal domination. In these three 'antiplays', dream, nonsense and fantasy combine to create an unsettling, bizarre view of society.

'Ionesco's verbal rhythms are subtle and brilliant, creating their own kind of hypnotic tension' Raymond Williams

Rhinoceros Translated by Derek Prouse
The Chairs/The Lesson Translated by Donald Watson

PENGUIN MODERN CLASSICS

OUR TOWN AND OTHER PLAYS

OUR TOWN/ THE SKIN OF OUR TEETH/THE MATCHMAKER

THORNTON WILDER

'A wizard, a magus, a waver of wands who summons up shapes from chaos and conjures worlds out of clouds, all in an instant' *Washington Post*

Finding the theatre in the 1920s lacking in bite and conviction, Thornton Wilder set out to bring back realism and to celebrate the innocent, simple and religious. Yet he also tried to endow the individual experience with cosmic significance, and *Our Town* is both an affectionate portrait of American life and 'an attempt to find a value above all price for the smallest events in our daily life'. *The Skin of Our Teeth* deals with human survival in a 'comic strip' way, and *The Matchmaker* is a hilarious farce which urges rebellion against all the constraints that deny a rich, full life.

CPSIA information can be obtained
at www.ICGtesting.com
Printed in the USA
LVHW07s0134070518
576202LV00028B/366/P